MONOGRAPH 45

Pathways to Prismatic Blades

A Study in Mesoamerican
Obsidian Core-Blade Technology

EDITED BY
KENNETH HIRTH AND BRADFORD ANDREWS

The Cotsen Institute of Archaeology
University of California, Los Angeles

2002

Edited by Rita Demsetz, Marilyn Gatto, Brenda Johnson-Grau, and Kathy Talley-Jones
Designed by Brenda Johnson-Grau
Production by Erin Carter, Merlin Ramsey, and Alice Wang

Library of Congress Cataloging-in-Publication Data

Pathways to prismatic blades : a study in Mesoamerican obsidian
core-blade technology / edited by Kenneth Hirth and Bradford Andrews.
p. cm.
ISBN 0-917956-99-0
1. Indians of Mexico--Implements. 2. Indians of Central
America--Implements. 3. Obsidian--Mexico. 4. Obsidian--Central
America. 5. Mexico--Antiquities. 6. Central America--Antiquities. I.
Hirth, Kenn. II. Andrews, Bradford.
F1219.3.I4 P36 2002
621.9'3--dc21

2002000652

Cover illustration: Intact blade core, with ground platform, from a Late Aztec or Early Colonial midden associated with a blade workshop at Otumba (TA-80, Op. 2, feature 1, level 3, item 3.
Illustration prepared by William J. Parry and Bradford Andrews

Contents

CHAPTER ONE

Pathways to Prismatic Blades

Sources of Variation in Mesoamerican Lithic Technology

KENNETH HIRTH AND BRADFORD ANDREWS

INCE PAYSON SHEET'S PIONEERING ARTICLE IN 1975, researchers working in Mesoamerica have employed a lithic technology approach for analyzing flaked stone collections. The results have been good: Researchers have avoided classifications based solely on functional considerations or artifact morphology in favor of technological categories derived from processual sequences of artifact production. Technology is viewed not as a monolithic and unchanging aspect of the manufacturing process but as a variable of production adapted to a variety of distinct social and environmental conditions. The result has been an emerging research paradigm that does not focus on the functional or temporal questions that lithic analysis can address but strives to examine behavioral and processual issues that relate to flaked-stone tool production and use. This paradigm is one of many theoretical and methodological contributions that have occurred in archaeology since the 1960s as a result of the conscious efforts by many researchers to make the discipline more scientific.

The lithic technology approach has two fundamental strengths. First, it provides a useful heuristic framework for classifying lithic artifacts encountered in archaeological investigation. Like it or not, archaeological research requires some form of artifact classification to handle the volume of material recovered in normal investigations. Since archaeology needs to maintain a comparative base, these classifications need to both capture the variation and be intuitively understood by the archaeologists that use them (Adams and Adams 1991). From this perspective, the lithic technology approach, while requiring some specialized understanding of manufacturing techniques, has been particularly useful for classifying a standardized lithic assemblage like that produced by Mesoamerican core-blade technology.

The second and more important strength of the lithic technology approach is that it provides a means of discerning a variety of behavioral decisions made by artisans during the production process. It provides a means of reconstructing the structure of lithic tool production and identifying the variables that shaped it with a precision rarely available in archaeological analysis. The lithic technology approach has reaped the benefits of experimental replication and has developed into an accurate and precise means of interpreting prehistoric remains.

Numerous researchers have contributed to the development and application of conceptual tools for technological analysis, and that has been the strength of Mesoamerican obsidian studies (Clark 1982, 1985, 1986, 1988, 1989a, 1989b, 1990b, 1997; Clark and Bryant 1997; Hay 1978; Santley 1984, 1989; Sheets 1975, 1978b, 1983a; Sheets and Muto 1972; Sollberger and Patterson 1976). One weakness in research over the past twenty-five years has been the delayed application of these conceptual tools to the analysis of lithic assemblages from multiple sites throughout Mesoamerica. As a result, much of our understanding of prismatic blade technology is based on material from only a few key places in Mesoamerica (for example, Teotihuacan, Ojo de Agua) and we lack a comprehensive understanding of how obsidian core-blade technology varied over time and space.

The purpose of this volume is twofold. First and fundamentally, it attempts to broaden our understanding of the variability in Mesoamerican core-blade technology. Unfortunately, researchers have tended to view prismatic blade production as a relatively homogenous technology exhibiting little modification throughout Mesoamerica. This certainly was not the case and the contributions presented here demonstrate some of the spatial and temporal variability present in Mesoamerican core-blade production. The chapters in this volume seek to identify *some* of the parameters contributing to this broad array of technological variation. They do not, however, comprehensively define the entire range of production variation since this will only be accomplished when systematic technological analyses are available from all areas of Mesoamerica. Instead, the chapters point the way to a productive path of research that can be pursued by future problem-oriented investigation. Second and most important, this volume seeks to identify the causes that produced variation in obsidian blade technology in particular times and places throughout Mesoamerica. This objective is more difficult to achieve because of the multiple variables contributing to productive variation. We will only be able to identify the variables that structure prismatic blade production by increasing our understanding of the settings and conditions affecting core-blade production and employing an approach that compares lithic assemblages from many different areas of Mesoamerica. Technology is the means to solving problems posed by the physical and social environments, and the study of ancient technology provides a framework for assessing the causes of variability within and among lithic assemblages (Carr 1994:1).

It is this second dimension of lithic research that holds the most potential for interpreting cultural process in prehistoric Mesoamerica. Once we demonstrate how variation in lithic assemblages is linked to the socioeconomic variables structuring production (Nelson 1991:57), the lithic technology approach should gain a more prominent role in studying the structure and organization of regional economic systems. Our ability to use lithic technology to study prehistoric economic systems depends upon discovering the parameters along which technological variation was produced. Once identified, we can use technological analysis of the material remains recovered in archaeological investigation to more fully understand the structure of pre-Hispanic production and distribution systems.

Structure of Mesoamerican Prismatic Blade Technology

Throughout this volume we adhere to a common set of conventions in the presentation. First, we discuss the technology in different areas of Mesoamerica using a common terminology. For convenience we follow much of the terminology for core-blade production in the recent work of Clark (1988, 1997) and Clark and Bryant (1997). Adopting a common terminology is difficult given the number, backgrounds, and diverse objectives of the volume participants. Nevertheless, where authors use slightly different analytical categories, they define or relate their usage to the general terminology. The result we believe makes it possible for the reader to navigate a straight course through the shoals of technical terminology and discussion.

Second, we also use the Clark and Bryant (1997)

sequence of core production (macrocore, polyhedral core, prismatic core) as a heuristic device for describing core morphology. This is done without assuming that the same stages of production were replicated everywhere in Mesoamerica. For example, we hold that it is possible to have a percussion core with the same characteristics as Clark and Bryant's polyhedral core, although it may have been fabricated in such a way that prevented it from passing through the macrocore stage as they describe it. We do not contest the suitability of their models for their archaeological materials, just that they are not universally applicable to all production sequences in Mesoamerica.

Because we use the Clark and Bryant (1997) reduction sequence as a starting point for discussing Mesoamerican core-blade industries, we'll describe it briefly for readers unfamiliar with obsidian pressure-blade production. This process involved forming polyhedral cores using percussion techniques (figure 1.1) and producing prismatic blades using pressure techniques (figure 1.2). This sequence is usually described as linear, although percussion procedures occasionally were employed during pressure-blade reduction for core maintenance and rejuvenation. To our knowledge, the entire core-blade sequence has yet to be identified at a single site in Mesoamerica and has been reconstructed by linking production activities that occurred in different points across the landscape.

Obsidian occurs naturally in both block and nodular form, and its initial reduction can vary because of the shape and condition of the raw material. Nevertheless, the first step in percussion shaping is to establish a suitable platform surface (figure 1.1). This was usually accomplished by removing a large *platform preparation* flake, which prepared the proximal end of the new core. Successful removal of this flake created a smooth concave platform surface, which is usually referred to as a *single-facet platform*. Occasionally, several platform preparation flakes had to be detached, resulting in a *multifacet platform surface*. Platform preparation flakes often have a cortex on at least part of their dorsal surface. The larger portion of the obsidian mass, which will eventually become the core, is referred to as the *core preform* (Clark and Bryant 1997) or *hemisphere* (Sheets 1975:375).

The next step involves the removal of relatively large *decortication flakes* and *macroflakes* from the lateral sides of the core preform (figure 1.1). This step leads to the formation of a *primary macrocore*, which has irregular ridges on its lateral sides and may have some intact cortical surface. *Crested blades* may be produced during this shaping process. These distinctive blades involve the removal of an alternating series of small flakes down one lateral ridge. This process creates an irregular crested ridge that guides the

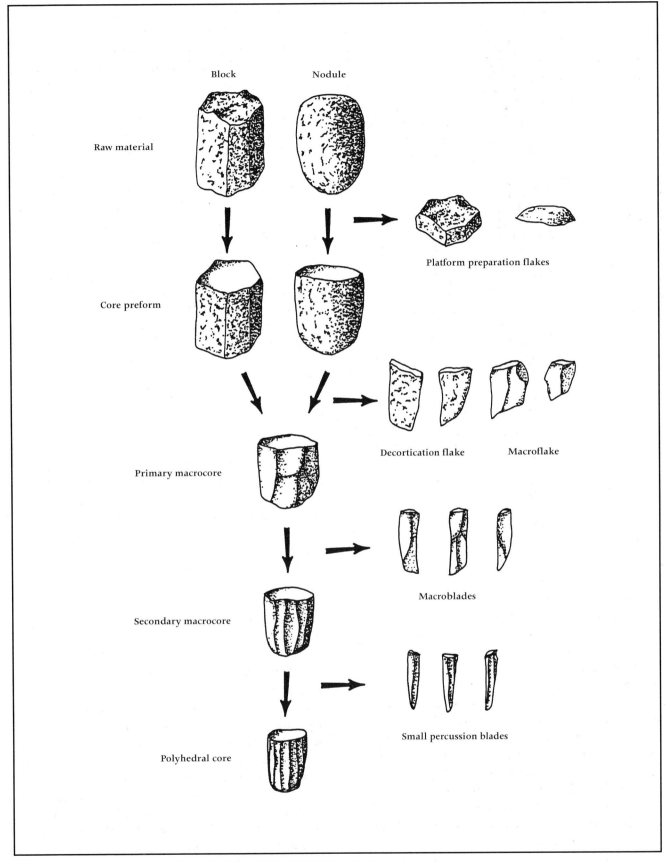

Block   Nodule

Raw material

Platform preparation flakes

Core preform

Decortication flake   Macroflake

Primary macrocore

Macroblades

Secondary macrocore

Small percussion blades

Polyhedral core

1.1 Core reduction using percussion techniques. *Illustration by Bradford Andrews*

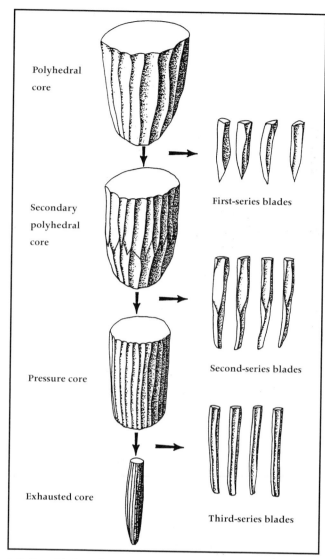

1.2 Core-blade reduction using pressure techniques.
Illustration by Bradford Andrews

percussion-derived force applied to detach the crested blade.

A primary macrocore is subsequently transformed into a *secondary macrocore* by the removal of *macroblades*. Typological distinction of macroflakes from macroblades is often subjective. Flakes have been defined as artifacts whose length is less than twice their width (Clark and Bryant 1997:117), whereas blades are "specialized flakes twice as long as they are wide, usually having parallel sides and at least one dorsal ridge" (Kerley 1989:165). In general, macroblades are distinguished from macroflakes by their more regular shape; they are much longer than they are wide, have roughly parallel sides, and are often more than 2.5 cm wide. The detachment of macroblades removes additional cortex and forms irregular parallel ridges down the length of the secondary macrocore.

After removing macroblades, *small percussion blades* are detached to produce a *polyhedral core*. Small percussion

blades are thinner than macroblades, and generally less than 2.5 cm wide. The objective of removing small percussion blades is to regularize the lateral parallel ridges of the core. The polyhedral core produced by these procedures signifies the end of the reduction sequence dominated by the percussion techniques.

The pressure sequence begins with the removal of *first-series blades* from the *polyhedral core* (figure 1.2). The objective of these blades is to remove the percussion scars from the core and create regular ridges, or *arrises*, that will be used to guide the removal of subsequent prismatic blades. First-series blades are readily identifiable by their irregular shape, the presence of percussion scars on their dorsal surfaces, and pressure attributes on their ventral surfaces.

Some production assemblages contain *second-series blades* depending on the shape of the polyhedral core formed during initial core reduction (Clark and Bryant 1997:115). If the polyhedral core was cone-shaped, the first-series blades only extended about halfway down the sloping lateral core surface resulting in the production of a *secondary polyhedral core*. Second-series blades would in turn extend blade arrises down the entire lateral surface of the polyhedral core. Second-series blades are distinct from first-series blades because they only have dorsal percussion scars on the distal portions of their length (figure 1.2).

The product of first- and second-series blade removal is a final *pressure core*. The blades removed from a pressure core are called *third-series blades* (figure 1.2). These blades are generally regular and consistent in shape with two parallel arrises on their dorsal surface. The dorsal arrises have a very important mechanical function in that they act to guide the force applied at the platform down the length of the core allowing for the successful removal of third-series blades.

Third-series blades were the basic product of the pressure sequence and were further modified for specific uses in a number of different ways. Most blades were initially snapped into sections and used in this form for various cutting activities. Sometimes they were hafted in wood or other materials such as bone for easier use. In addition, blade sections were modified into more specialized forms such as projectile points, needles, notched tools, and eccentrics. The end by-product of the core-blade sequence was the exhausted pressure core.

Flaked stone tool production is no longer practiced by ethnographic groups around the world and as a result, reconstruction of a production technology like that of Mesoamerican prismatic blades must be based largely on controlled archaeological experimentation and comparison to archaeological assemblages (Ascher 1961; Crabtree 1966). This approach is called *replicative systems analysis* by Flenniken (1981, 1989) and is the fundamental means for reconstructing the steps and techniques of production. Identifying the causes behind the variation in production technology for prismatic blades requires us to take two inferential steps beyond simply reconstructing the techniques of production. First, it requires identifying the normal range of technological variation over time and space through fundamental descriptive and analytic investigation. This variation represents the range of solutions that prehistoric artisans employed in producing prismatic blades. Second, it requires taking the range of technological variation and inferring from it the problems or causes that various techniques sought to resolve. These inferences are based on comparing the technological solutions employed by ancient artisans to differences in the natural and social environments in which they arose. How technological solutions are repeated or vary under the same or different conditions provides insight for assigning causes to the technological variation found in the archaeological record.

Understanding the causes of variation in lithic technology can be enhanced by understanding the problems and adaptations that societies employ in provisioning themselves with other types of raw materials and finished craft goods. Figure 1.3 summarizes some of the conditions that we believe may have led to variation in prismatic blade technology in Mesoamerica. This variation is grouped into three broad categories representing the technological, provisioning, and production factors affecting production. These three conditions combine in different ways to produce variation in the techniques used in prismatic blade production, the reduction strategies, debitage classes, the morphological attributes of artifacts found in lithic assemblages, and the level of specialization and form of production found in different areas of Mesoamerica. The range of variation for any single factor represented in figure 1.3 increases as the spatial scale and diachronic scope becomes amplified.

Technological Factors Affecting Production

The technological factors affecting production are those where the tool kits used in making prismatic blades or the factors affecting the working ability of the artisan have a direct bearing on the type, quantity, or quality of prismatic blades produced. Three common technological constraints (figure 1.3) include

- variation in manufacturing tools and tool kits,
- conditions of artisan training and apprenticeship, and
- idiosyncratic artisan practices and skill.

Differences in the composition of *manufacturing tool kits*

Technological Constraints
Variation in manufacturing tools and tool kits
Conditions of training and apprenticeship
Idiosyncratic artisan practices and skill

Provisioning Constraints
Type and form of raw material
Availability and distance from source
Sociopolitical conditions governing distribution

Production Constraints
Structure of demand
Organization of production
Level of specialization
Production linkage relationships
Sociopolitical conditions governing production

1.3 Sources of variation in prismatic blade technology.
Illustration by the authors

is a source of variation directly affecting the morphology of flaked stone tools. Archaeologists have discussed the differing effects of direct and indirect percussion and the use of hard or soft percussors on flake morphology during flaked stone reduction (Crabtree 1972; Sollberger and Patterson 1976; Whittaker 1994). Clearly the material type and availability of hammerstones will shape whether artisans employ them or turn to such alternative materials as wood, bone, or antler billets to work obsidian.

Archaeologists have followed one of two paths when considering whether variation in tool-kit composition produced variation in prismatic blades in Mesoamerica; either they have ignored the problem completely or they have discussed the issue using information from experimental replication. Unfortunately, there are few cases where these concerns have been directly applied to the analysis of an archaeological assemblage. John Clark's excellent ethnohistoric study (1982, 1989a) established that pressure blades were produced by artisans from a seated position holding the blade core with their feet, and this production technique has been accepted by most investigators as standard across Mesoamerica. Ethnographic research among the Lacandon, however, shows that the only group still producing stone tools in Mesoamerica employs punches for indirect percussion (Clark 1991). This research is significant because despite the ability of investigators to replicate prismatic pressure blades by securing cores with their feet, they have not yet been able to duplicate the complete range of Mesoamerican blades found in archaeological assemblages with this technique. There are prismatic blades in some assemblages that seem to lie outside the normal length, width, and thickness of blades capable of being produced by foot-held pressure techniques alone. Whether indirect percussion was employed remains a debatable issue that only experimental analysis and comparison to archaeological assemblages will resolve.

John Clark (1985) has examined how different materials including wood, bone, shell, chert, and copper worked as pressure bits in prismatic blade removal. Following a similar line of investigation Peter Kelterborn (ND) has explored how these alternative materials affect the morphology of the prismatic blades they were used to produce. Investigators have discussed how the *shape* of pressure bits and punches used for indirect percussion affected the morphology of the blades removed (Clark 1985:1; Titmus and Kelterborn 2000). The composition and characteristics of the pressure tool were also important factors in blade removal because the use of a flexible as opposed to a rigid wooden instrument would produce slightly different attributes on long prismatic blades using the foot-held technique.

Much of the variation in tools and tool kits relates to the natural availability of certain knapping tools (for example, soft hammerstones) as well as various cultural features. For example, the use of abrasives in local woodworking or lapidary activities may predispose obsidian craftsmen to prepare platforms on, or remove errors from, the face of obsidian cores using pecking and grinding rather than percussion techniques. Particularly important here are historic conditions or contexts when new technologies are introduced. The production of Dyuktai prismatic blades on a modified bifacial core appears to be an example of how historical circumstances can govern the development of a new technology. The fact that Dyuktai blades were produced on a bifacial core rather than a conical core like those we find in Mesoamerica reflects the development of the blade-making technology within the context of, and drawing upon the technological knowledge of, a long-standing bifacial tradition in Old World Siberia (Flenniken 1988).

Different knapping tools and techniques will produce artifacts with distinct morphological characteristics. Our ability to recognize this variation is wholly dependent on the breadth and quality of experimental lithic research. To gain a more comprehensive understanding of how such variables affect artifact morphology, we need more replication studies addressing this issue.

Variation in the *training and apprenticeship of artisans* is another variable that can lead to morphological variation in the artifacts resulting from prismatic blade production. In ancient Mesoamerica technical training was largely passed on from father to son and mother to daughter with craft specializations following patterns of familial inheritance and residence (Hirth 2000). Legislation during the Colonial period limiting the number of practicing craftsmen from

one generation to the next (Katz 1966:51) suggests considerable flexibility in the number of apprentices that craftsmen could have employed during pre-Hispanic periods. Certainly there was variation in the way training was enacted, and as several investigators have noted, the artifacts produced by apprentice knappers will look considerably different from those of skilled and experienced artisans (Andrews 1999; Clark ND; Torrence 1986).

One especially pertinent aspect of apprenticeship for obsidian craft producers is that training inevitably involves learning from one's mistakes. This means that apprentices make inefficient use and waste a large volume of obsidian when they are on the early side of the learning curve. The net result would be an assemblage with greater artifact variation and higher frequencies of errors. Apprenticeship could have been a very expensive activity if located long distances from source locales since obsidian is only available in a few areas of Mesoamerica and often moved hundreds of kilometers from quarry to workshop. Because of this, apprenticeship may have involved the relocation of novices close to obsidian sources where raw material could be readily accessed and learning was less costly in terms of the quantity of material wasted while perfecting manual skills. In this scenario, apprenticeships would have been arranged through trading partner relationships rather than solely through training along familial lines. Mary Helms (1979, 1993) documents a pattern of long-distance apprenticeship for shaman-curers among chiefdom societies in lower Central America that parallels what might have taken place for some obsidian specialists. The effect of training apprentices near quarry areas would result in greater standardization in production techniques than would be the case if all obsidian workers were trained in local workshops by family members.

A third factor affecting technological variation is *idiosyncratic artisan practices and skill*. Archaeologists have long noted the presence in archaeological settings of evidence pointing to some individuals with exceptional technical ability who must have been particularly respected artisans. In lithic studies these are the individuals who produced the exotic and well-made products such as the bifacial caches at Anzig, Montana (Wilke, Flenniken, and Ozbun 1991) and Mound 72 at Cahokia (Fowler 1991; Milner 1998), the obsidian eccentrics throughout the Maya region (Pendergast 1990; Schmidt, de la Garza, and Nalda 1998:606–607; Spence 1996), and the elaborate obsidian artifacts included in offerings at Teotihuacan (Millon, Drewitt, and Bennyhoff 1965:Figs. 93–94; Sugiyama 1991:Figs. 5–7) and Tenochtitlan (Garcia Cook and Arana 1978:Figs. 32–33, 35–37; Hasbach 1982:Fig. 1). We can add to this the variation produced in both percussion and pressure flake patterns by left- or right-handed knappers or the subtle variation in platform preparation, error recovery techniques, or the sequential combination of different but related techniques to produce prismatic blades.

One aspect of a reductive technology such as flaked stone tool production that makes it different from many other ancient crafts is that levels of artisan skill are measurable using archaeological techniques. We believe that skill can be measured by examining the proportion of errors in an archaeological assemblage, assuming that you can define an error. When a standardized product like a prismatic blade is the object of production, all attempts that fail to produce a complete prismatic blade can be classified as errors. To make accurate comparisons of skill, however, requires that the techniques used to produce different lithic assemblages be indentified. This information is reflected by the attributes on the lithic artifacts themselves and is important because viable comparisons of skill level are only meaningful if the same skills or techniques are being measured. For this reason, we must be able to determine or reasonably infer that the same basic techniques were being practiced with the same relative frequencies at the production areas being examined. A study of prismatic blade production by Bradford Andrews (1999) comparing craftsmen skill at Teotihuacan and Xochicalco indicates that archaeologists can now begin to successfully approach this dimension of craft production at least at the level of individual workshop locales.

Provisioning Factors Affecting Production

The provisioning factors affecting production technology are those where the movement and distribution of raw material and finished goods have a direct bearing on the type, quantity, or quality of prismatic blades produced. Three provisioning constraints (figure 1.3) that are particularly important include

- the type and form of raw material,
- availability and distance from source, and
- the sociopolitical conditions governing distribution.

Investigators have long recognized that the *type and form of raw material* available for flint knapping was a major factor affecting the lithic technology craftsmen employed (Ericson 1984; Crabtree 1972:4–6). The physical properties of raw material directly determine flaking properties of the stone making different types of material appropriate or inappropriate for different types of production. Bipolar technology, for example, is especially well-suited for producing flakes from small, round cobbles that cannot be flaked in other ways (Flenniken 1981; Shott 1989). Similarly, heat treatment can be used to change the physical properties of silicates with crystalline and microcrystalline structures (Crabtree and Butler 1964; Domanski et al. 1993; Flenniken and Garrison 1975; Flenniken and White 1983; Luedtke 1992).

In Mesoamerica two physical properties determined how obsidian was used: workability and the size/form of its procurement. The presence of phenocrysts and other impurities make some obsidian less desirable for the manufacture of prismatic blades because inclusions increase the frequency of hinge fracturing along the face of the core. When they are small and diffuse, impurities can also increase the difficulty of blade removal, thereby reducing the size and length of the blades being produced. Undesirable internal properties in some obsidian varieties make reduction with pressure techniques difficult. For example, Michael Spence has suggested that a secondary fracture pattern found in Otumba obsidian is a major reason why few pressure blades from Classic-period Teotihuacan were made of this nearby material (Spence et al. 1984:97). Instead, pressure blade production was predominantly carried out using superior obsidian from the Pachuca source.

Size of the raw material also affected whether obsidian was used for prismatic blade production in Mesoamerica. While pressure blade cores can be manufactured from small material (Anderson 1970), the preference in Mesoamerica was for large cores manufactured from blocky flow deposits or large cobbles. Small cobble material found at sources such as Altotongo, Veracruz; San Juan del Rio, Queretaro (Pastrana 1991:86); San Luis, Honduras (Aoyama et al. 1999), and Guinope, Honduras (Hirth 1988:Table 4) was used most frequently for percussion reduction instead of making small pressure cores. The impact of size can be seen at different points in Mesoamerican prehistory when new sources with large blocky material from deeply buried flow deposits begin to be exploited.

The *availability of obsidian and the distance from source* are other variables affecting regional variation in prismatic blade technology. Obsidian occurs in a number of localized zones across Mesoamerica (figure 1.4). The natural distribution of obsidian deposits meant that some areas of Morelos, Puebla, Oaxaca, and the Yucatan peninsula were anywhere from 200 to 700 km from source locales. Obsidian was more readily available near source locales, which, in turn, made possible greater amounts of biface reduction since it often uses more raw material than prismatic blade production.

Obsidian availability is a function of the distance to a source, which, together with other factors, determined the transportation costs. Transportation costs were the highest when obsidian had to be moved by *tlameme* (human porters) along overland routes rather than by canoe along

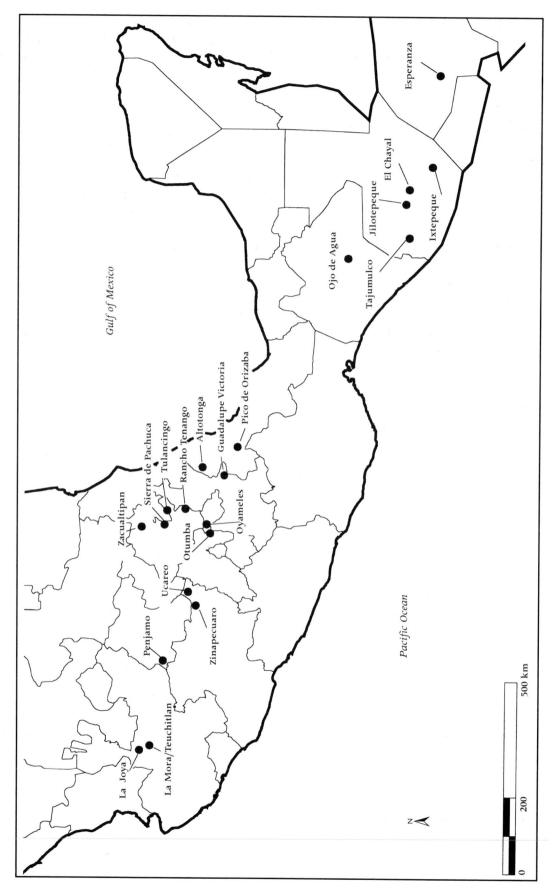

1.4 Location of obsidian sources in Mesoamerica. *Illustration by the authors*

Gulf of Mexico

Pacific Ocean

Esperanza

El Chayal

Jilotepeque

Ixtepeque

Ojo de Agua

Tajumulco

Sierra de Pachuca

Tulancingo

Rancho Tenango

Altotonga

Guadalupe Victoria

Pico de Orizaba

Zacualtipan

Otumba

Oyameles

Ucareo

Penjamo

Zinapecuaro

La Joya

La Mora/Teuchitlan

N

500 km

0 200

coastal routes or navigable rivers in areas such as the Gulf Coast lowlands (Hassig 1985:Table 10.4; Santley 1989:144). Numerous authors have discussed the effects of transportation costs on the structure of regional Mesoamerican political economies (Drennan 1984a, 1984b; Hassig 1985; Sanders and Santley 1983; Sanders and Webster 1988) and we do not repeat them here. What is important for our discussion is to recognize that transportation costs affected how obsidian was worked in different regions and that a considerable amount of technological variation may be a response to economizing scarce resources in areas of high demand. The higher the transportation costs, the more economizing behavior in production and use is likely. High transportation costs for obsidian will likely favor: 1) the movement of core preforms (macrocores) or completely processed prismatic blade cores instead of unworked raw material; 2) a conservative reduction technology emphasizing the maximization of all possible cutting edge from prismatic blade cores through more extensive core rejuvenations and/or improved efficiency in core maintenance and error recovery strategies; and 3) where possible, the efficient use and recycling of production and rejuvenation debitage into usable tools and an emphasis on tool resharpening and extended tool use.

The last provisioning constraint is *sociopolitical conditions governing the distribution* across the landscape. While we often calculate transportation costs in terms of actual distance or energetic estimates, the real-world cost of much precapitalist exchange was a combination of these factors together with social and political conditions. The form of exchange and how a resource such as obsidian moved over space are important in this regard (Renfrew 1975). If obsidian moved through individual trading partners and/or gift exchange as it probably did during the Formative period (Hirth 1984; Dalton 1977), then the costs of transporting the stone would be considerably higher than they would be under conditions of state-supported mercantilism (Pollard 2000; Santley 1983) or exchange through professional merchant groups like the *pochteca* (Berdan 1982).

We know, for instance, that at different times and places political frontiers were reinforced as formal boundaries to the movement of resources. At the time of the Conquest, the Aztecs sought to isolate Tlaxcala economically from interregional trade throughout Mesoamerica. Similarly, trade was discouraged across the Aztec-Tarascan boundary as the latter sought to control the flow of key resources including metal into the Aztec empire. The effectiveness of these policies depends on the form in which exchange was carried out. Under conditions of state-supported mercantilism, political isolation could be very effective; under merchant-*pochteca* exchange, these boundaries could be permeable, depending

upon the motivations of individual entrepreneurs.

Similarly, discussions of obsidian production at Teotihuacan have proposed that the state participated directly in the procurement or control of such key obsidian sources throughout Mesoamerica as Pachuca, Hidalgo (Charlton 1978; Spence 1981, 1984; Spence Kimberlin and Harbottle 1984) and El Chayal, Guatemala (Sanders 1977; Santley 1983). Clearly the establishment of monopolistic control over source locales would have had a direct effect on the form in which obsidian moved and the variation displayed by production technology. Monopolistic control over procurement, production, and distribution would have reduced the variability in the form in which obsidian moved throughout Mesoamerica (as macrocores, polyhedral cores, and so forth) and the technological attributes that they manifest.

Production Factors Affecting Technology

Production and organizational factors affecting lithic technology are those where the manufacturing and the consumption of finished goods have a direct bearing on the type, quantity, or quality of prismatic blades produced. Five production constraints (figure 1.3) include

- the structure of demand,
- organization of production,
- level of specialization,
- production linkage relationships, and
- sociopolitical conditions governing production.

A fundamental feature of economic systems, the *structure of demand* directly affects the structure and organization of production and distribution systems and the technology that supports them. In prehistoric societies the structure of demand for a category of resources like obsidian prismatic blades is linked to four variables: 1) the size of the consuming population, 2) the rate of consumption, 3) consumer preferences, and 4) the range of alternative resources that can be substituted for obsidian.

Whether regional demand for obsidian prismatic blades is low or high can directly affect the development of economic structures designed to meet provisioning needs. For example, low levels of demand may be met through interregional exchange of finished goods, part-time production at the household level, and/or itinerant craftsmen who produce on a periodic basis. These solutions can lead to either substantial or insubstantial variation in the technology employed to produce prismatic blades, depending on which of these alternative provisioning mechanisms were used to meet resource needs.

High regional demand, on the other hand, can support a

greater variety of provisioning mechanisms. In addition to the variables mentioned above, high demand may require both a higher volume and a more continuous and predictable level of production. It is here that we may see an increase in the number of craft specialists producing finished goods in local workshops. When this occurs, variation in prismatic blades may be a function of the greater range of technological and provisioning constraints that affect the form and type of raw material they have access to, and the training and technological solutions that craftsmen bring to production (figure 1.3).

Two topics that archaeologists have been especially interested in are the *organization of production* and the *level of specialization* associated with craft production (Brumfiel and Earl 1987; Clark and Parry 1990; Costin 1991; Rice 1987; Santley 1989; Sinopoli 1988; Torrence 1986; Tosi 1984). Although archaeologists have often combined them, they should be examined separately in terms of their effects on technological variation.

The *organization of production* should be thought of in terms of type, size, location, and structure of the production units. In the Marxian sense it involves reconstructing the mode or modes of production in the society by which obsidian goods were produced. In Mesoamerica much discussion and emphasis have been placed on determining whether obsidian tools were produced in domestic contexts, specialized nondomestic workshops (Spence 1981, 1987; Santley, Kerley and Kneebone 1986; Clark 1986), or higher guild-level economic structures organized at the level of the *calpulli* (residential barrio) (Berdan 1982:29; Charlton, Nichols and Otis Charlton 1993; Healan 1986:148). Most recent research suggests that production for most types of craft goods including obsidian prismatic blades took place within domestic settings rather than larger, more complex workshop contexts (Feinman 1999; Balkansky, Feinman, and Nicholas 1997; Santley, Arnold, and Pool 1989; Healan, Kerley and Bey 1983; Hirth 1995b).

High levels of demand can stimulate the emergence of more efficient forms of organization and/or the development of labor-saving procedures to increase production output and efficiency. The structure of demand can also affect the location of production units. Urban centers represent, by their very nature, loci of concentrated demand that may make cities the natural places for craft specialists to be located. Where demand is low, transportation costs are high. Where raw material sources are dispersed, it may be more common to find producers spread throughout communities of different size in a region (Brumfiel 1987; Feinman, Blanton, and Kowalewski 1984).

Level of specialization is often viewed as a function of two distinct aspects of production (Costin 1991). First, it is

conceptualized as the intensity or amount of time invested by artisans in craft production; in this sense specialization is often dichotomized in terms of full- or part-time involvement in manufacturing activities. Second, specialization is defined as production intended for use outside the social unit in which production takes place. This second aspect of specialization is intended to distinguish production for consumption from that intended for export and exchange. Unfortunately, the evidence for either full- or part-time specialization is used as a measure of cultural complexity and economic interdependence without understanding how any particular craft industry is organized or how this is measured using archaeological data. Although high demand may support a number of full-time craftsmen, it is the continuity and predictability of demand and the ability to delay purchases by the broader consuming population that will dictate whether full-time specialization will be found. Where purchases are discontinuous or can be delayed, craftsmen or members of their families will need to engage in staple food production to protect themselves from downturns in consumption coincident with famine or cyclical purchasing patterns. For this reason, Brumfiel (1987) argued that much craft production—including obsidian working among the Aztecs—was a part-time activity (Smith and Hodge 1994:21).

The production of any standardized flake stone tool like an obsidian prismatic blade depends, at least in part, upon the artisan maintaining his skill level at a high degree of proficiency. In this regard the more frequent use of individual skills will allow an artisan to maintain a higher level of efficiency than would be the case if they are infrequently practiced. It is reasonable to assume, therefore, that infrequent blade production by nonspecialists for their own consumption will produce more variation within the lithic assemblage than if only a few specialists produced all of the obsidian blades in the society.

Production linkage relationships refer to the incorporation of two or more commodities as part of a single production sequence. This type of production may be called sequential or linked production, and in flaked stone tools production occurs when by-products of one reduction strategy become tool blanks for another. All production steps are linked, and the steps proceed as a series of compromises between alternative ends rather than decisions oriented toward optimal or single usage intents. For example, when a craftsman only considers the manufacture of a single type of item, raw material will be procured in a form that is optimal for producing that commodity. In sequential production, however, such will not be the case. Instead, raw material will be procured in a form optimal for the production of the entire set of sequentially linked production events. Technology, raw material, and the production sequence will be intertwined and dependent upon a combination of potentially competing production goals that can shape archaeological remains in very different ways. In flaked stone tool manufacture, sequential production promotes a single efficient procurement system and can lead to subspecialization within a single workshop locale or to interdependencies between two or more workshop locales.

Lastly, variation in lithic technology can also be produced by the *sociopolitical conditions governing production* in a society. Control of production by the elite through patron-client relations or formal state-sponsored craft activity can have the effect of reducing technological variation within a region as the number of artisans producing prismatic blades is kept small. Conversely, uncontrolled production of craft goods under a system of marketplace exchange can have the reverse effect by significantly increasing the number of artisans producing goods for sale. It is this condition that best accounts for the large number of craftsmen reported in Huexotzingo where 20% of the population were engaged in some form of craft activity of which only 5% were full-time specialists (Brumfiel 1987:Fig. 8.2; Carrasco 1974; Prem 1974).

The conditions that we believe contributed to variation in core-blade technology in Mesoamerica were grouped in the foregoing discussion into the three broad categories of technological, provisioning, and production constraints. These categories should not be thought of as either all-inclusive, fixed, or of equal weight. Instead, they serve as a beginning point for the investigation into the causes behind technological variation in prismatic blade production. The chapters that follow serve to highlight the form that this technological variation takes and what the social and economic conditions were that brought it about.

Discussing Variability in Prismatic Blade Technology: Contents of this Volume

The chapters in this volume discuss prismatic blade technology in different regions of Mesoamerica (figure 1.5). They describe the technology and production sequence(s) found in their regions and compare them to those found in other areas. In so doing they identify and discuss the key variables that structured obsidian craft production in their region. Outlining how different technological, provisioning, and production constraints shaped the structure of obsidian craft activity is the goal of the chapters and the volume as a whole.

Chapters are not, however, grouped by regional or chronological period but in terms of distance from the source, which is a potentially important provisioning constraint affecting variation in prismatic blade technology. Distance is

an important variable with regard to the energy costs of moving heavy tool stone material such as obsidian (Sanders and Santley 1983). This is especially the case in Mesoamerica where all obsidian deposits are located in inland areas away from navigable rivers or waterways where raw material could be moved in bulk (Torrence 1986). Moving away from the source, there was some point in the pre-Hispanic landscape where energetic constraints affected acquisition and provisioning patterns. With an increase in distance from the source, direct obsidian procurement by individual households would change from frequent to sporadic. In addition, as distance increased, individual household acquisition would have given way to organized procurement expeditions by groups or communities as we find among the Tungei, Jimi, and Sikeing of Papua New Guinea, where lineages and communities organize to mine, preform, and transport axes from quarry sources (Burton 1989). With proprietary ownership of—or greater distance from—specific sources, access to raw material became more difficult and would have fallen increasingly into the arena of specialized commerce by merchants.

The contributions are separated into three broad categories that group regions and their production activities in terms of the distance from the obsidian source deposits they exploited. *At-source* production activities deal with quarrying, shaping, and manufacturing behavior at the actual obsidian source locale. Although the subject has received limited attention, quarries can be expected to reflect changes in the form, organization, and intensity of exploitation over time. *Proximate source* areas are those that lie within a 10 to 100 km radius of source locations. This distance, although selected somewhat arbitrarily, precluded round-trip obsidian collection in a single day and required some degree of planning in the procurement of raw material. Groups up to 75 to 100 km from sources could make round-trip collection forays to the source in a one- to three-week time frame depending on whether they mined the obsidian themselves or procured it in partially processed form from groups at the quarry. *Distant source* areas are those that lie beyond a 100 km radius of sources and include regions where knowledge of source locales and the groups that control them would have been limited. Although distances beyond 100 km did not preclude direct procurement, we believe that procurement mechanisms changed with increased distance from the source. Procurement became more indirect, and exchange mechanisms became more important in provisioning household and craft workshops.

The contribution by Alejandro Pastrana examines variation in at-source production activities at the important obsidian source of Sierra de las Navajas in central Mexico. This locale was exploited as early as 700 BC and was the

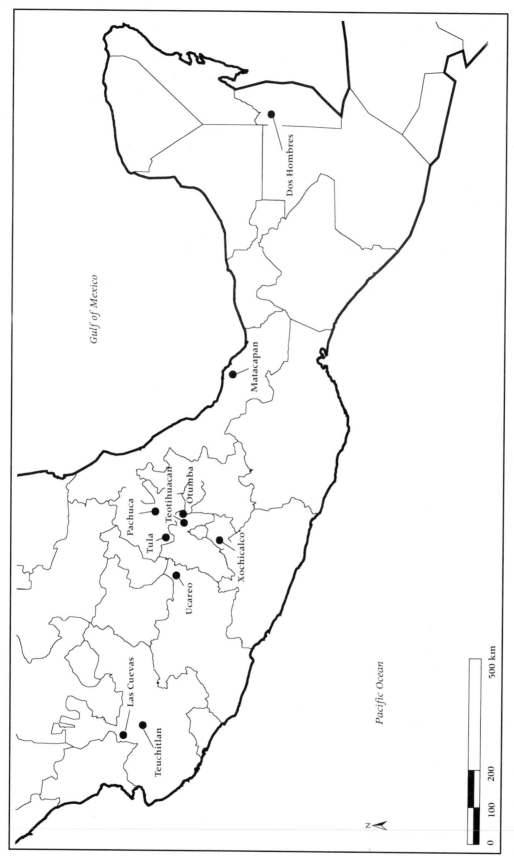

1.5 Location of sites and regions discussed in this volume. *Illustration by the authors*

Gulf of Mexico

Pacific Ocean

Dos Hombres

Matacapan

Pachuca
Teotihuacan
Otumba
Tula
Xochicalco
Ucareo

Las Cuevas
Teuchitlan

N

0   100   200   500 km

primary source of obsidian for the Teotihuacan, Toltec, and Aztec societies. While Pastrana's discussion is predominantly oriented toward the Aztec-period exploitation, he documents the changes in the intensity and form of exploitation over time. He dates quarrying areas within the source and compares them in terms of the form and scale of mining activity as well as the type and level of on-site craft production. He demonstrates that source locations are not homogenous areas of uniform deposits. Instead they reflect considerable variability in the type and level of pre-Hispanic exploitation both spatially and over time. At Sierra de las Navajas, the highest levels of exploitation correspond to the Aztec period when the source appears to have been controlled by the state, and obsidian mining and production were highly organized and specialized activities.

Dan M. Healan's contribution is unique because it compares quarrying and production activities at the source of Ucareo, Michoacan (an at-source analysis) with production activities at a workshop site at Tula, Hidalgo, where Ucareo obsidian was used in the manufacture of obsidian blades. He attempts to understand the spatial structure of obsidian production in what we would classify as a *distant source* relationship to the Ucareo quarry, which was a major supplier for Tula's obsidian craft industry during the Epiclassic and Early Postclassic periods. The Tula situation is interesting because the site is situated in a *proximate source* relationship to several major obsidian sources in the Basin of Mexico (Pachuca, Tulancingo, Zacualtipan). The more distant Ucareo source, is most heavily utilized during the Epiclassic period and is gradually replaced during the Early Postclassic by obsidian from the closer Pachuca source. In the discussion Healan examines activities at two opposite ends of the production spectrum and shows how distance influenced the technology employed by knappers at the Ucareo source and the Tula workshops where it was used.

Three chapters examine variation in *proximate source* sites and regions. Recent research at the Aztec center of Otumba has provided new and exciting information about pre-Hispanic craft production in a regional city-state capital in the Valley of Mexico just prior to the Spanish conquest (Charlton et al. 1993). William J. Parry explores the nature of obsidian prismatic blade production found at this site and feels that production constraints and the specialized nature of demand within the Aztec economy were more important than the energetic constraints of procuring raw material. Most interestingly is the preferred use of more distant Pachuca obsidian over local Otumba obsidian in the manufacture of prismatic blades. The technology found is different in several respects to that used in other contemporary sites and earlier time periods in the Valley of Mexico, which he relates to the demand for specific types of pris

matic blades by Aztec consumers.

The obsidian craft industries at Teotihuacan are without question one of the most widely cited (Spence 1981, 1984, 1987, 1996; Santley 1983, 1984; Sanders and Santley 1983) but poorly understood (Clark 1986) examples of specialized prismatic blade production in Mesoamerica. A lack of systematic subsurface data from any of Teotihuacan's workshop contexts is a reason. Nevertheless, Bradford Andrews addresses the nature of production linkage relationships in the San Martin workshop in the northeast portion of the city, which is believed to have engaged in large-scale production for regional export. His sample of material for this study is derived from a combination of intensive and extensive surface collections. Using this material he explores the form in which obsidian from the Pachuca and Otumba sources was brought into the workshop and used for core-blade and biface reduction. Recognizing the limitations of this data, he shows that it is perhaps incorrect to think of the core-blade industry as a simple or unitary process. Instead, the process of prismatic blade reduction appears to have been partially linked to the production of bifacial and unifacial tools from percussion blades removed from obsidian macrocores after they entered workshop locales. The extent of this linkage, in contrast to manufacturing all bifaces and pressure blades from specially prepared and imported preforms, is a subject that will only be resolved by future stratigraphic research.

The last contribution dealing with obsidian production in areas close to obsidian sources is that by Michael W. Spence, Phil C. Weigand, and Maria Soto de Arechavaleta. They examine obsidian production systems over time in west Mexico where many individual households and communities were within very short round-trip distances to a number of obsidian sources. What they find is that specialized production is generally limited, and where it occurs there is little ability or desire by local craftsmen to control production at the regional level. Equally interesting is the technological variation found in platform preparation and other aspects of production at the regional level. Elites do not appear to have developed exclusionary control of source locales. Obsidian production appears to have been carried out in all sites with elites perhaps supporting specialized prismatic blade production in the largest sites.

Three chapters examine variation in prismatic blade technology found in *distant source* sites and regions. A common theme shared by these contributions is the limitation that distant source locations face with regard to acquiring obsidian and provisioning local populations with large quantities of finished prismatic blades. The contribution by Kenneth Hirth examines the nature of prismatic blade production at the Epiclassic site of Xochicalco, Morelos, located

200 km from its primary sources of obsidian supply. Excavations in five workshop areas reveal that the technology employed in obsidian production was sharply structured by the form and availability of obsidian entering the site. Distance to obsidian sources and sociopolitical conditions governing procurement prevented direct access to raw material. Instead, workshops at Xochicalco were provisioned with obsidian by procuring already used prismatic obsidian cores through exchange with intermediary merchants or itinerant craftsmen. The result was a technology characterized by the extensive use of small rejuvenated cores and the probable use of a hand-held reduction technique to exploit them efficiently (Flenniken and Hirth ND).

Recent research in the southern Gulf Coast is beginning to provide insight into the production and demand for obsidian prismatic blades and other implements in this region. The chapter by Robert S. Santley and Thomas P. Barrett explores patterns in the acquisition of obsidian source material, reduction technology, and trade commodities in the Tuxtla and Hueyapan regions of southern Veracruz. Unlike most of the other chapters in the volume, which rely primarily on excavation data, these authors demonstrate how lithic information collected from primarily surface contexts can be used to examine variation at the regional level. They note increased reliance on a single high-quality source over time, with obsidian increasingly entering the region as shaped macrocores. Nevertheless, specialized production remains low, with prismatic blades being produced by specialists in both large and small communities.

The Maya region remains largely understudied with regard to technological analyses of obsidian craft production, and in this regard the chapter by Rissa M. Trachman is a refreshing contribution. Recovery of a large cache of obsidian cores and production debris from an Early Classic tomb at Dos Hombres, Belize, provides a unique insight into techniques of prismatic blade core rejuvenation in the southern Maya lowlands. Obsidian was a precious and scarce resource in the southern lowlands, with the site of Dos Hombres located over 300 km from the closest highland source. The result was the development of a unique rejuvenation strategy that attempted to control the segmentation of cores by combining pecked and scored lines with the initiation of a bending break that is significantly different from bipolar percussion. This previously unreported technology was apparently designed to minimize and control the loss of usable mass during platform creation and core rejuvenation. Trachman's analysis also demonstrates the valuable contribution that material from even secondary contexts can have for the study of prehistoric technology.

Presentations throughout the volume vary from author to author depending upon whether the data supporting their interpretations were derived from surface or excavated contexts. Chapters 5, 6, and 8 base their interpretations of core-blade technology on data derived primarily from surface collections. As a result, the datasets are smaller and somewhat less comprehensive in the kinds of artifacts they contain than those of contributors who have used excavated data. Nevertheless, these studies underscore the value and role that surface collections can have in technological studies and accent the way in which they can be used to define the broad patterns structuring the procurement, production, and use of flaked stone tools.

Concluding remarks by Kenneth Hirth and J. Jeffrey Flenniken summarize and comment on the technological variation presented by the volume contributors and what this means for studying the Mesoamerican blade-core production systems. Their comments show that blade-core technology employed a diverse array of production techniques and cannot be characterized by a single production model. On the whole, researchers should expect to find variation in lithic production systems and instead of trying to subsume the observed variation within a single analytical framework, they should seek to identify and interpret what technological variation can tell us about the structure and dynamics of pre-Hispanic lithic production systems.

This concluding discussion also examines three cultural historical issues that affect our broader understanding of prehistoric craft production and the production of obsidian prismatic blades in ancient Mesoamerica. The first is the origin of core-blade technology and what the role of political elites was in the implementation and spread of prismatic blade production throughout Mesoamerica. Although there is little concise data on this topic, it appears that elite sponsorship may explain some but not all of the blade-core production found in chiefdom societies during the Formative period. A second issue examined is the separation of production activities and specialization between quarry and workshop areas and how this affected changing obsidian exploitation patterns at the end of the Classic period. Changes in the frequency of obsidian moving throughout central Mexico during the Epiclassic may have more to do with disruptions in quarry-based obsidian processing than they do with a change in trade routes. This chapter ends with a discussion of variation in obsidian production technology and how archaeologists should exploit this information for investigating pre-Hispanic society. In assembling this volume we found that an important first step in identifying the range of variation in obsidian core-blade technology was reconstructing the environmental, social, political, and economic conditions that shaped it.

CHAPTER TWO

Variation at the Source

Obsidian Exploitation at Sierra de Las Navajas, Mexico

ALEJANDRO PASTRANA

IN ANCIENT MEXICO OBSIDIAN WAS AN IMPORTANT AND critical resource in the development of pre-Hispanic society in the central highlands. Obsidian tools were the foundation of domestic, agricultural, and craft production as well as being manufactured into valued ornamental goods, ritual items, and military arms. Because obsidian is not evenly distributed throughout the central highlands, goods were often manufactured in specialized locales and were distributed through complex systems of trade and exchange. The location of obsidian source areas in relation to regions of high population density and demand strongly influenced both the level of extraction at quarry areas and the quantity and type of material moving out into distribution networks.

This study examines obsidian exploitation at the Sierra de las Navajas obsidian source in the state of Hidalgo, Mexico (see figure 1.4). The Sierra de las Navajas, also known as the Pachuca source, was the primary source for obsidian in the development of the Teotihuacan, Toltec, and Aztec states. Unfortunately, quarry sites are rarely studied and little is known about the extraction, production, and distribution of obsidian within and from them. This problem is common to lithic research around the world (Ericson 1984): Archaeologists have tended to assume that prehistoric quarrying was a relatively homogenous process or that research at source areas can reveal little information about economic processes beyond fundamental technological data on how raw material was extracted.

As this contribution will demonstrate, research at source areas like the Sierra de las Navajas can reveal a great deal about the level of demand for obsidian, the intensity of exploitation, and the social organization of craft production. Intensive survey of the source area between 1989 to 1994 (Pastrana 1998:Map 2) reveals that it is possible to identify considerable variation in the intensity of its use over time

despite more than 2500 years of exploitation and reuse of obsidian-rich deposits (Pastrana 1998). Variability in quarrying activity and production is reflected in the areas exploited, the intensity and form of mining activity, the quantity of material removed, the presence or absence of resident workers, the types of production activities taking place at the quarry, the presence of specialized on-site production workshops, and the types of goods produced in them. As discussed in the introduction to this volume, the activities found at Sierra de las Navajas reflect the type of flaked stone processing associated with at-source production locales. Evidence for exploitation from the Middle Preclassic through the Aztec period are presented below to document how obsidian exploitation evolved over time as conditions of demand and the organization of extraction changed within central Mexico.

Middle Preclassic (700–500 BC)

The first clear evidence of mining activity at the quarry dates to the Middle Preclassic period (Spence and Parsons 1972). Evidence for utilization during this period occurs on the top of Cerro Cruz del Milagro in squares 2K-L, 3J-L, and 4J-K (figure 2.1).

The deposits exploited consist of banded blocks of rhyolite and obsidian that comprise the remnants of an ancient volcanic dome. Evidence for mining consists of numerous small pits referred to as *pozos de extraccion*. These are circular pit mines ranging from 3 to 6 m in diameter and 1 to 3 m deep. The remains of extraction and obsidian processing are found around the borders of these pits.

Obsidian-bearing blocks were detached from the lava flow by taking advantage of fractures produced during rapid cooling, which resulted in irregular hexagonal blocks of obsidian. In some instances, erosion separated the obsidian strata into tabular blocks measuring 8 to 12 cm in thick-

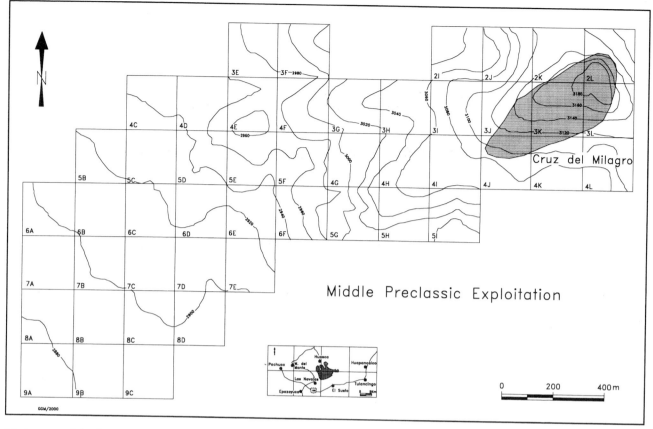

2.1 Areas exploited at Sierra de las Navajas during the Middle Preclassic period. *Illustration prepared by Gerardo Gutierrez. Redrawn from Pastrana 1998:Map 2*

ness and 15 to 20 cm long. Many of these blocks exhibit secondary cortex on all their surfaces. Most extraction took place at an average depth of 4 m below the surface.

The Middle Preclassic sector contains hammers and percussors made of microcrystalline rhyolite. It is possible that wedges of wood were also used to separate the blocks of rhyolite and obsidian. Debitage located around the open pits indicates a diverse rather than specialized range of knapping activities during this period. The products of Preclassic extraction were limited by the form and volume of raw material that was able to be obtained. There is no evidence, for example, that prismatic blade cores were produced. The productivity of mining was relatively limited in relation to the amount of time invested and I believe that extraction was undertaken during intermittent excursions to quarry sources. There is no evidence around pit mines of architectural features or ceramics indicating the presence of permanent facilities used by Preclassic miners.

Classic Period (AD 150–750)

The use of this source by Teotihuacan has been a major topic of discussion over the last three decades because

of the large quantity of Navajas obsidian in the city (Spence 1981). Unfortunately, a clear picture of activities at the source during this period remains elusive. Using surface survey, I have identified the areas directly or indirectly related to Classic-period exploitation. These include squares 4E-G and 5F (figure 2.2).

Unfortunately, study of the Teotihuacan-period exploitation is hindered by low surface densities of Classic material, thick forest cover, and alteration of the landscape by later Toltec and Aztec exploitation. Teotihuacan ceramics are scarce and are related stylistically to those of the Tulancingo area, which remain poorly studied. Excavations will be necessary to recover a Classic-period ceramic sample, identify the form and variety of obsidian extraction, and define the nature of specialized obsidian processing at the quarry.

Early Postclassic or Toltec Period (AD 900–1200)

The area of Toltec exploitation is located at an elevation of 2980 to 3000 msl and is concentrated in squares 4F-G, 5F-G, and 6F (figure 2.3). Square 6F has evidence of knapping areas marked by a high density of debitage and broken artifacts such as scrapers, prismatic blades, and eccentrics. There is also evidence of grinding tools and rhyolite hammerstones. All of these squares have concentrations of Toltec ceramics.

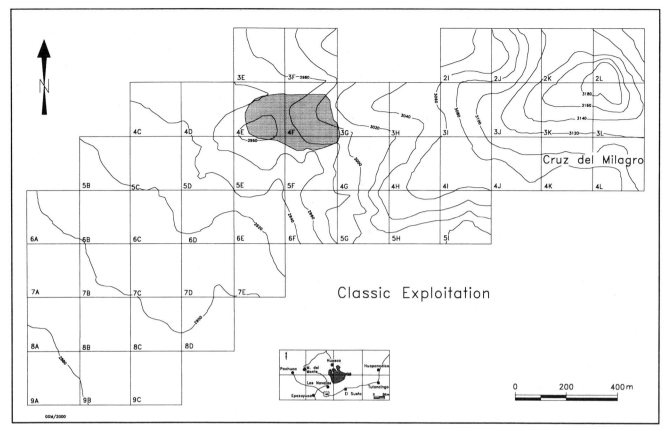

2.2 Areas exploited at Sierra de las Navajas during the Classic period. *Illustration prepared by Gerardo Gutierrez. Redrawn from Pastrana 1998:Map 2*

A stratigraphic pit in this area confirmed the subsurface association of the knapping material and ceramics found in surface contexts. Excavated materials indicate the repetitive and specialized production of scrapers and blade cores. Grinding tools were found that were made out of local raw material. The ceramics recovered were the same as the Toltec-period sherds found on the surface and indicate a direct association of knapping activities with some intermittent domestic occupation at the quarry.

Toltec mines were spaced at 4 to 6 m intervals along a linear north-south exposure of rhyolite. Sixteen shaft mines were encountered that remain open although there is evidence for at least an additional 36 mines that have been partially filled with material from adjacent pits. These shaft mines are referred to as *bocaminas* and have circular openings measuring between 0.8 to 2 m in diameter with straight vertical shafts that may exceed 30 m in depth. The depth of *bocaminas* depends on the location of the mine within the source and the depth where obsidian blocks were found.

The Toltec shaft mines had an average vertical depth of 8 to 10 m. The bottoms of the mines had small irregular chambers. Shaft mines with chambers measuring 2 m in diameter often had one or two lateral tunnels, many of them now filled with material as a result of frequent cave-ins. Some of the tunnel walls exhibit irregular obsidian blocks

found embedded in a matrix of lahar ash and lenses of lapilli. At a depth of 10 m the blocks measure an average diameter of 35 cm. The material removed from the Toltec mines was deposited around their openings. Mixed with the backdirt are obsidian blocks, cortical and interior flakes, and hammerstones of local rhyolite.

The knapping area in square 6F contains obsidian artifacts reflecting the production of narrow stemmed triangular unifaces or scrapers, blade cores, prismatic blades, and eccentrics. The production of scrapers involved the use of cores with semiparallel arrises. These were reduced with direct percussion to remove flakes with one or two dorsal arrises, which were then unifacially retouched to give the uniface a triangular form with a straight or curved distal end. These appear to be preforms rather than finished artifacts and there is no evidence that they were finished at the source. It is possible that they were transported to Tula and other sites where they were knapped into finished products, given that Robert Cobean suggests direct contact with this site on the basis of ceramic pastes. The ceramic similarities and technological continuity in knapping procedures with Tula, however, does not necessarily imply that a

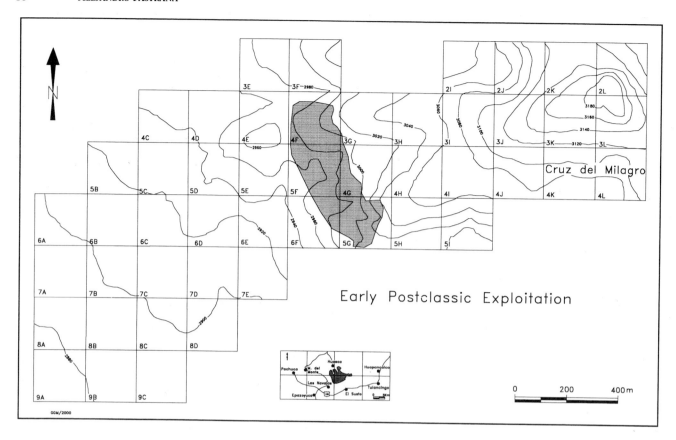

2.3 Areas exploited at Sierra de las Navajas during the Early Postclassic or Toltec period. *Illustration prepared by Gerardo Gutierrez. Redrawn from Pastrana 1998:Map 2*

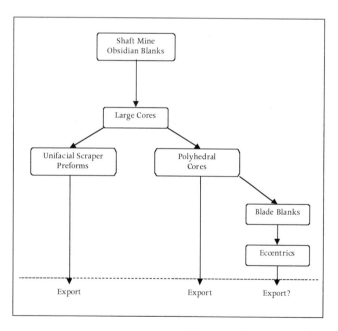

2.4 The Early Postclassic reduction sequence at Sierra de las Navajas, Mexico. *Illustration prepared by Erick Rochette*

population from Tula was directly involved in mining activities at the source.

Blade core and prismatic blade production are two distinct activities at the quarry during this period (figure 2.4). Polyhedral cores shaped by percussion were produced primarily for export. These cores had flat or faceted platforms and were exported to workshops at Tula (Healan et al. 1983). Prismatic blade production provided blade blanks used to make eccentrics at the source. The platforms of these cores were ground and forty-two complete and broken bilobal and trilobal eccentrics were found in surface and subsurface explorations that can be associated with their production.

Late Postclassic or Aztec Period (AD 1350–1521)

Intense mining was conducted during the Aztec period when two major methods of extracting obsidian were used (shaft and open-air pit mines). Aztec *bocaminas* were surveyed that reach 40 m in depth, although many shafts probably were much deeper. Shafts are often filled in as a result of: 1) intentional backfilling by the ancient miners when a shaft was abandoned, 2) natural erosion, 3) intentional backfilling by the modern residents of El Nopalillo, or 4) modern mining of obsidian in the area. As of now, we have identified 187 Postclassic shaft mines or *bocaminas*.

The majority of the Postclassic mines are located in

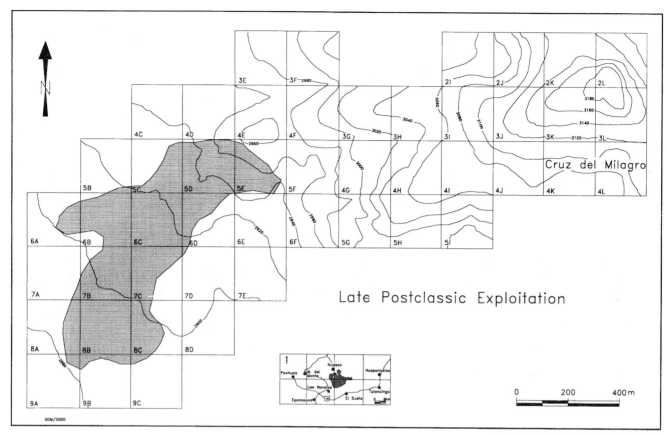

2.5 Areas exploited at Sierra de las Navajas during the Late Postclassic or Aztec period. *Illustration prepared by Gerardo Gutierrez. Redrawn from Pastrana 1998:Map 2*

squares 5C-E, 6C-D, 7B-C with some isolated zones of activity in squares 6A-B, 6E, 7E, 8A-C, and 9B (figure 2.5). In many of these sectors, one can see the remains of both extraction and reduction, indicating that mining and production took place close to each other. An especially high level of production was observed in squares 5C-D, 6C-D, and 7B.

SHAFT MINING

Obsidian blocks are not distributed uniformly throughout the lahar deposit; so, some locations would have yielded more material than others. The spatial proximity of the Toltec- and Aztec-period mines suggest that Aztec miners used the location of Toltec pits as a basis for selecting productive locations to begin mining.

Mines were excavated primarily with picks and hammers to remove the lahar deposit consisting of compact volcanic ash mixed with small fragments of rhyolite and pumice. Shafts average 1 m in diameter making them large enough for a single man to excavate when backdirt is removed using ropes and baskets (figure 2.6). As the mines became deeper, labor investment increased because deposits were more compact and blocks of rhyolite and obsidian became larger. Excavation continued until blocks of obsidian of the desired quality and size were found. For example, in square 5D average shaft depth was about 20 m.

Once the proper depth was reached a chamber would be opened to create enough space for two to three miners to work. From these chambers, tunnels might be excavated to follow obsidian deposits. The direction of the tunnels was determined by the concentration of obsidian blocks. To minimize work, abandoned tunnels were often filled with material removed from another tunnel in the mine. The process of excavation required the coordination of several miners. Illumination was probably provided by torches made of wood covered with local resins such as *ocote*.

When the miners inside the tunnels encountered blocks of obsidian encrusted with ash, they would immediately remove a few flakes to assess their quality. Before being transported to the surface, large blocks of obsidian were broken into fragments with a maximum diameter of 45 cm and a weight of about 25 kg, which facilitated the removal of blocks to the surface.

Descent into the deep mines was dangerous because rocks or fragments of obsidian could fall down the vertical shafts. It was essential, therefore, to keep the surface area around the shaft openings clean of debris. Retention walls were built at some shaft openings to keep surface material from falling into the mines. These walls are usually found

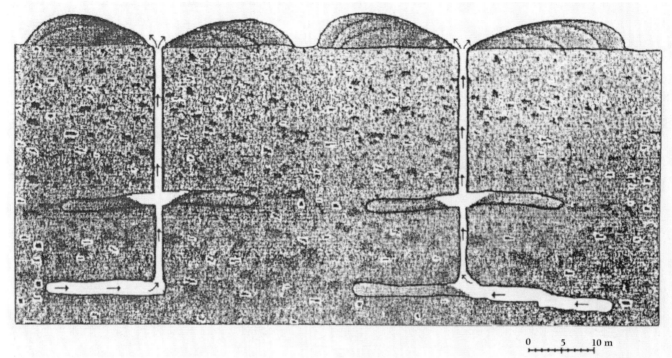

2.6 Schematic representation of the Late Postclassic shaft mines *(bocaminas)* at Sierra de las Navajas, Mexico. *Illustration prepared by the author*

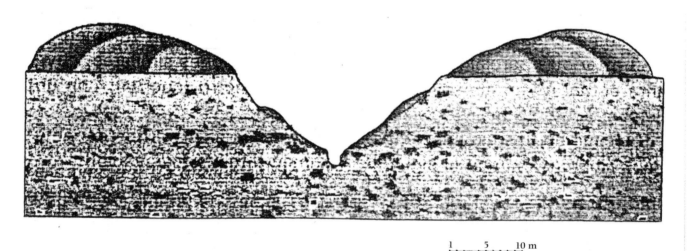

2.7 Schematic representation of a Late Postclassic open-air pit mine *(albercas)* at Sierra de las Navajas, Mexico. *Illustration prepared by the author*

on the upslope sides of shaft openings or where excavated debris had accumulated over a long period of time.

Small cavities placed opposite one another were identified in the walls of several shafts. These paired cavities are separated by an average vertical distance of 60 cm and may have been footholds used for scaling the shaft. Since the shafts averaged 1 m in diameter, vertical movement using these cavities is feasible if one compresses oneself against the walls with their hands and feet. Doing so, however, re-

quires considerable force especially where the vertical distance between the cavities is lengthy. This mode of movement would have been dangerous because it can create small cave-ins. It is likely that some of the miners used these cavities in this manner but probably only for short distances.

Some cavities possibly represent anchors for beams. In one example about 5 m below the surface, a fragment of wood was found embedded in the wall cavity. If these features were beam anchors, they would have held large horizontal wooden beams around 13 cm in diameter that could have been used as a type of ladder when spaced about 1 m apart. During explorations one bocamina was found that had a beam measuring 15 cm in diameter that had been secured on both sides of the shaft with stakes. This beam had a rope fragment slipped around its center, which was probably used to raise and lower baskets of debris as well as miners. The miners would have had to be careful while touching the shaft walls because of the sharp fragments of obsidian or the possibility of causing rock falls.

OPEN-AIR PIT MINING

Another method of Aztec-period mining was the removal of obsidian from large open-air pit mines called *albercas* (figure 2.7). Pit mines were found in squares 4E and 6B and are large semicircular pits measuring up to 35 m in diameter and 15 m deep. This extraction technique may have been used when shaft and tunnel excavations encountered high concentrations of quality obsidian blocks relatively close to the surface. Although pit mining required more excavation, it probably was faster and more efficient than working in the confining bocaminas since more workers could labor simultaneously in an open and safe environment.

Knapping areas associated with pit mining were located in squares 6A and 6B. The debitage in these areas was mixed with the large volume of material removed during excavations. It seems that a considerable portion of the work areas in these sectors were probably covered as a result of the continuous expansion of backdirt piles.

Open-air pit mining may be the earliest type of extraction used at Sierra de las Navajas. Small pits were the mode of extraction used during the Preclassic in the Cruz de Milagro portion of the source. Some larger pits in this area may date to the Early Classic period (Cobean 1991). This technique is also reported at other sources including El Pizarrin and Zacualtipan, Hidalgo, and Zinapecuaro and Zinaparo, Michoacan.

AZTEC-PERIOD REDUCTION AND RAW MATERIAL SELECTION

The primary objective of production at the quarry was to make core preforms for blades, scrapers, bifacial implements, and preforms for a diverse number of ritual objects. These were the principal items exported to workshops in areas of the Basin of Mexico such as Otumba, Texcoco, and Tenochtitlan (Spence and Parsons 1972). Final finishing was carried out by craftsmen in these workshops although the reduction process shows technological continuity with initial preforming undertaken at the source.

The specific reduction processes employed were deter-mined in large part by the relationship between raw material, production techniques, and desired artifact morphology. The general tendency in lithic industries was toward production efficiency using the least amount of raw material. In principal, the physical properties of a piece of raw material strongly affected the type of items it could be used to produce. As a result, it was important to examine the physical properties and size of the raw material within the source area since this determined the knapping techniques employed and the final form an item could obtain (Pastrana 1987a:139–140).

Obsidian deposits within the source area occur in diverse forms and sizes because of the way the original flows of obsidian-bearing lava were fragmented and expelled during the eruption. Obsidian blocks range from laminar or tabular to rounded or subangular in shape. A wide variety of cortex types are found, including thick and abrupt, originating during the cooling of lava; thin and regular, forming along interior fractures from the action of weathering and cooling of lava; and irregular, resulting from erosion associated with fluvial transport. The size of the blocks ranges from 10 cm in diameter with a weight of 2 kg to 1.5 m in diameter and weighing hundreds of kilograms.

Green obsidian from Sierra de las Navajas also varies greatly in terms of its physical properties and can be classified into four types based on overall workability. The first type is *transparent green* without vesicles or crystals. Transparent green obsidian fractures with the most uniformity and was used preferentially for making prismatic blades and ground objects such as ear spools and pendants like those on exhibit in the Teotihuacan and Aztec rooms of the National Museum of Anthropology in Mexico City (Solis 1993). This obsidian is excellent for making any knapped or ground object because of its internal homogeneity and absence of inclusions.

The second type of obsidian is *golden green,* which has elongated microscopic vesicles that aligned themselves with the flow prior to cooling. These vesicles have a parallel and uniform disposition and defract light producing a brilliant golden sheen. When the number of vesicles is low this material was used to make prismatic blades and a variety of ground objects like some recovered in offerings in the Templo Mayor (Athie 2001). When the density of vesicles increases the texture of the obsidian becomes rough, porous, and more difficult to fracture. This type was used primarily to make thick scrapers.

The third type of obsidian is dark or *opaque green,* which is translucent in appearance. Generally, the frequency of microscopic vesicles is low and occurs as a disorganized pattern interspersed with small crystals of plagioclase (Garcia-Barcena 1975, Pastrana 1987b). The concentration of these crystals can alter the direction of the fractures and this type was used to make scrapers and bifacial tools.

The fourth type is reddish-brown, commonly referred to as *meca* obsidian. This type has been altered by the oxidation of its metallic components which are present in abundant crystals. Meca obsidian fractures irregularly and was only used to make some projectile points and ground objects (for more information see Glascock et al. 1994).

In the Aztec mines at Sierra de las Navajas there are large blocks of transparent green obsidian that fracture uniformly as well as blocks that have a mixture of the above characteristics. Obsidian of adequate quality and form was channeled into the production of cores for blades, scrapers, and bifacial implements. The principal technique employed in each reduction process was direct free-hand percussion using a wide array of percussors of various forms and weights.

REDUCTION ACTIVITIES IN QUARRY WORKSHOPS

The blocks of obsidian obtained from mines were brought to the surface and transferred to the work areas by the miners. It appears that there was about one work area for eight or more mines where the knappers specialized in manufacturing different types of products. The largest workshops produced subprismatic cores for blades, scraper blanks, and bifacial blanks. The products transported from the quarry workshops were subprismatic cores, nearly finished bifacial and scraper preforms (figure 2.8), and a limited output of preforms for ritual or status items. Because the terminology from Clark and Bryant (1997) does not accommodate the variation in core form found at the quarry, the term *subprismatic* core has been adopted here. Subprismatic core morphology varied according to what it was used to produce.

Small workshops were also identified close to what are believed to be the miners' domestic camps where knapping debitage and fragments of broken scraper and bifacial preforms can be found. These workshops had a notably low volume of debitage in relation to the large workshops where the cores were prepared for producing preform flake blanks.

The large Aztec workshops are characterized by knapping debitage reflecting different production stages, incomplete preforms, fragments of poor quality obsidian, percussors, and some domestic and ceremonial ceramic material. Generally speaking, they did not produce finished tools but instead prepared preforms that were transported to workshops where artifacts were finished. One of the characteristic aspects of the Aztec workshops, besides their large size, is the repetitive nature of the knapping debitage reflecting constant involvement in production over time using a uniform technology. Persistent activity at workshops is evident in debitage deposits that can be as much as 5 m thick. In stratigraphic cuts at some of the workshops, layers of debitage are interbedded between paleosol deposits reflecting the temporal interruption of production activity long enough to permit the formation of a layer of humus that was later covered by more debitage.

The largest Aztec workshops were located in squares 5D, 6B-D and 7B-7C (figure 2.5). These workshops had discontinuous strata interrupted by soils removed from the adjacent mines or the formation of paleosols. Artifacts from the surface and stratigraphic cuts in these areas reflect reduction activities oriented toward the production of subprismatic blade cores, scraper preforms, and bifacial preforms. The initial phases of these production sequences were similar. Production was initiated with the removal of decortication and block reduction flakes. Decortication flakes removed cortex and impurities from high-quality obsidian and were normally detached using natural planes and surfaces as percussion platforms. Block reduction flakes were removed from blocks that had already had much of their cortex removed. These flakes were used to give a cylindrical form to macrocores and include the flakes used to prepare percussion platforms. In general, decortication and block reduction flakes can both have cortex and similar morphological characteristics.

During initial core reduction it is sometimes necessary to eliminate arrises that run at 90-degree angles to the longitudinal axis of the core. These arrises are generally removed by a flake with a triangular cross section that runs the length of the core. These are called lamacrettes or crested flakes and represent a recurrent technique used in the preparation of prismatic cores.

The next flakes are primary flakes, which can be detached using percussion from either the proximal or distal ends of core preforms. They are used to initiate the formation of semiparallel arrises and to eliminate geometric irregularities. The dorsal surface of these flakes generally have one dorsal arris and run the length of the core's axis. These are followed by secondary flakes that were intended to form parallel and equidistant arrises along the sides of the core. Secondary flakes are also removed by percussion and usually have two or more dorsal arrises.

At this point production diverges into the three separate reduction sequences (figure 2.8). Some of the cores produced were subprismatic scraper blank cores (figure 2.9). These cores are semicylindrical and have at least 70% of their cortex removed. The longitudinal axis typically measures one and a half to two and a half times their diameter. The arrises are straight and inclined at an angle of 10 to 35 degrees. Subprismatic scraper blank cores are principally

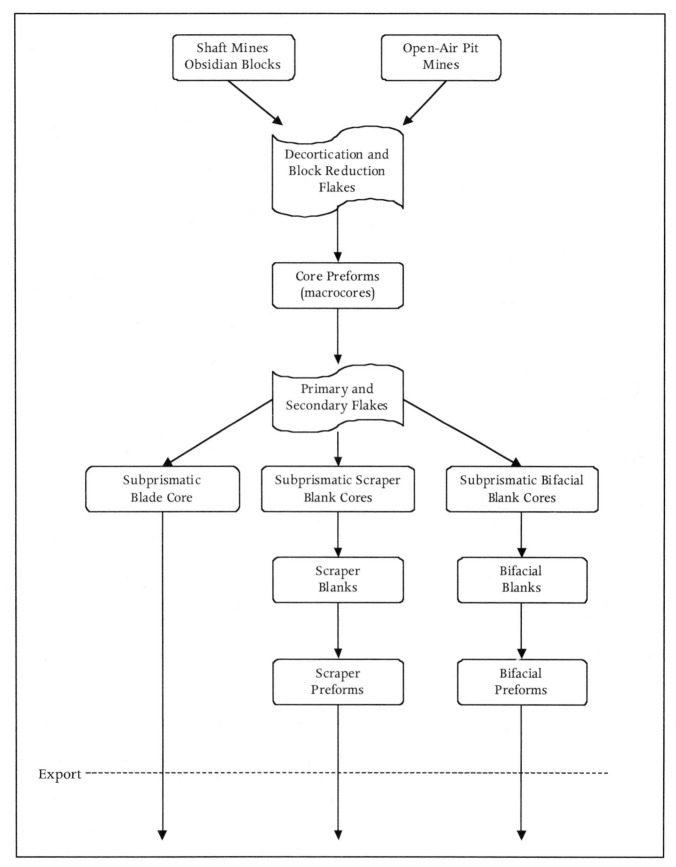

2.8 Late Postclassic reduction sequence at Sierra de las Navajas, Mexico. *Illustration prepared by Erick Rochette*

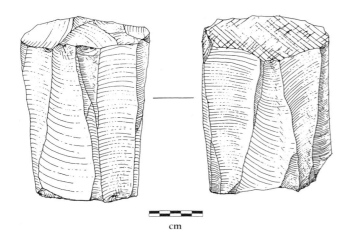

2.9 Subprismatic scraper blank core from Sierra de las Navajas, Mexico. *Illustration prepared by the author*

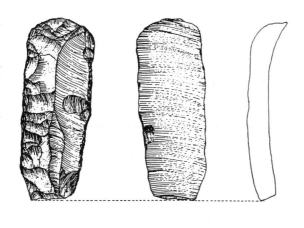

2.10 Scraper preforms produced at Sierra de las Navajas, Mexico. *Illustration prepared by the author*

formed by the detachment of primary flakes. The scars left by these flakes are generally equal to or less than one-eighth the circumference of the core. These cores generally have two platforms allowing for bidirectional flake removal.

Scraper preforms were produced from decortication and interior flakes detached from subprismatic scraper blank cores. The flake blanks selected are regular or semiregular ellipses in plan view and preferably have curved cross sections (figure 2.10). The average weight of these flakes ranged from 80 to 140 grams. These blanks were unifacially shaped through the removal of scraper retouch flakes along their margins forming a working edge on the distal end of the flake that typically is the widest part of the artifact. Afterwards, they would round the distal section by removing parallel flakes in order to finish the scraper preforms, which average from 40 to 110 grams in weight. These flakes are relatively small, measuring less than 2.5 cm in length, and tend to be triangular or elliptical with curved cross sections. The curvature and size of the flakes depends on where they were detached along the margin.

Another type of core produced at the Aztec workshops was the subprismatic bifacial blank core (figure 2.8). These cores are semicylindrical and have 80% or more of their cortex removed (figure 2.11). The longitudinal axis is one and a half to three times their largest diameter. Arrises are straight and semiparallel, formed from the detachment of primary and secondary flakes, which typically average one-sixth of the core's circumference. These cores generally have bidirectional platforms.

Bifacial preforms were made from decortication and interior flakes (figure 2.12). The flake blanks that were used were regular, elliptical, or triangular in cross section. Bifacial retouch flakes were used to bifacely shape and regularize the margins using direct percussion. These flakes are generally less than 3 cm in length, have triangular or fan-shaped plan views, and curved cross sections depending on where they were removed. Generally, the extreme distal portion of the bifacial flake blank was shaped into a sharp point.

The third type of core produced in quarry workshops was the subprismatic blade core (figure 2.13). These were conical in form and had 100% of the cortex removed. The longitudinal axis was one and a half to three and a half times the diameter and the arrises tended to be straight, parallel, and converging at the distal end of the core. These cores were formed by the removal of percussion flakes whose average scar widths were equal to or less than one-tenth of the core circumference. Core platforms were principally produced by percussion. These cores do not necessarily correspond to what Clark and Bryant (1997) call polyhedral cores that are ready for reduction by pressure techniques. Depending on the morphology of the core many still required some additional percussion shaping to produce regular parallel arrises.

Summary and Conclusions

Jonathon Ericson has argued that quarry sites have frequently been neglected in favor of other types of production sites because of the "technical and methodological limitations imposed by a shattered, overlapping, sometimes shallow, nondiagnostic, undatable, unattractive, redundant, and at times voluminous material record" (1984:2). What research at the Sierra de las Navajas source has shown is that quarries are not homogenous areas and careful survey can reveal considerable information on the variability of exploitation. Provisioning constraints did not affect the level of exploitation at quarry sites since obsidian was abundant. Nevertheless, the intensity of exploitation was closely linked to the demand for obsidian at the level of the larger provisioning area. As a result, over time we see changes in the intensity of exploitation, methods of extraction, and whether tools are being processed into preforms in workshop areas at the quarry sources.

Considerable variation was found in the level and intensity of exploitation throughout four pre-Hispanic periods beginning with the Middle Preclassic and continuing into the Aztec period. Intensity of exploitation and mining increased over time reflecting both a greater demand for obsidian as well as changes in the structure of how obsidian was mined and processed. Mining areas shifted from the summit of Cruz de Milagro during the Middle Preclassic, where deposits were relatively close to the surface, to deeper but richer deposits on its lower southwestern slopes during the later periods. Moreover, the quantity of material extracted increased over time. Although not clear from surface remains, it appears that intensive exploitation began during the Classic period when Teotihuacan made extensive use of the source. Mining intensified during the period of Aztec utilization reaching the highest levels of utilization found at the quarry.

Particularly notable is the change in the form of material extraction over time. There is a change from small-pit mining (*pozos de extracción*) reaching only 3 to 6 m in depth during the Middle Preclassic, to shaft mines (*bocaminas*) between 10 to 30 m deep during the Early Postclassic Toltec exploitation. Mining operations increased to their most intensive level during the Aztec period when there is an expansion in both the number of mines and the scale of exploitation. Shaft mining continues (figure 2.6) and is augmented by the addition of open-air pit mining (*albercas*), which opened pits up to 35 m in diameter (figure 2.7). The implementation of open-air pit mining apparently al-

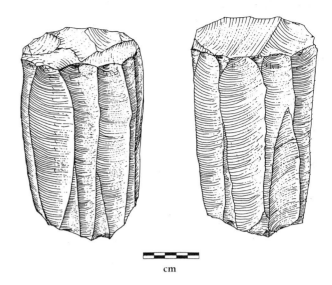

2.11 Subprismatic bifacial blank core from Sierra de las Navajas, Mexico. *Illustration prepared by the author*

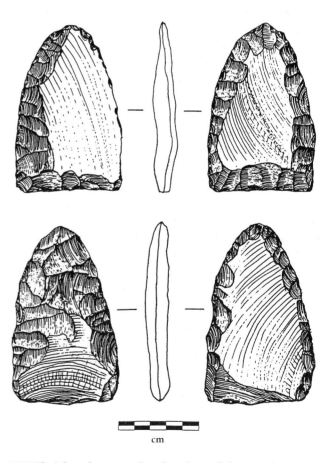

2.12 Bifacial preforms produced at Sierra de las Navajas, Mexico. *Illustration prepared by the author*

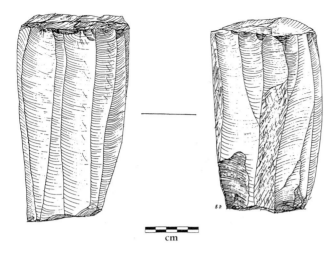

2.13 Subprismatic blade core from Sierra de las Navajas, Mexico. *Illustration prepared by the author*

lowed more material to be extracted at a more efficient or faster pace by expanding the number of miners.

The high level of exploitation during the Aztec period left a considerable amount of undisturbed information. It appears that the period of Aztec exploitation was not only more extensive but also was more specialized than previous periods. Different grades or qualities of obsidian were selected for different types of production with better quality material used for manufacturing blade cores and ceremonial items and lower quality material reserved for biface and uniface production. Domestic camps with well-constructed houses appeared at the quarry, making it easier to date the exploitation of the source. Such construction also suggests an increased number of individuals were involved in mining during this period as exploitation of the source intensified. It is likely that these were part-time residents from the surrounding communities who were specialists in mining and obsidian craft production (Pastrana 1998:Map 6).

Perhaps the most important evidence for greater specialization in exploitation during this period was the appearance of small craft workshops at the quarry that specialized in the production of different kinds of goods. Although production was oriented toward manufacturing preforms rather than finished goods, it is clear that they were linked to high levels of demand within the Valley of Mexico and were part of a broad regional system promoting more efficient and intensive levels of production during the extraction process.

Archaeological data presented here in combination with ethnohistoric documentation at the time of the Conquest make it possible to infer what the sociopolitical conditions of production were during Aztec exploitation. Analysis of ethnohistoric information presented elsewhere (Pastrana 1998:179) indicates a general shift from the collection of obsidian through tribute relations to a state-controlled extraction network sometime after AD 1428. Because of its importance, obsidian fell increasingly under the control of the Triple Alliance, specifically the important city-states of Texcoco and Tenochtitlan. The best ethnohistoric evidence for this shift is the disappearance of references to towns supplying obsidian as a tribute good and its replacement with agricultural products. The absence of obsidian from the Matrícula de Tributos (Corona Nuñez 1968) indicates that it was not considered a tribute good for towns near the source at the time of the Conquest even though the *Relación Geográfica de Epazoyuca* indicates that they previously had paid tribute in obsidian before the reign of Ahuitzotzin (Acuña 1985).

It is also likely that at least a portion of the resident population involved in obsidian extraction during the Aztec period was brought in from outside the region. This can be inferred from the fact that the resident population found around Sierra de las Navajas was ethnically Otomí, composed of semisedentary groups who engaged in a mixed hunting-agriculture mode of subsistence. It is unlikely that a large segment of the Otomí population could be actively involved in full-time or near full-time exploitation of obsidian production and mining since this would conflict with normal scheduling of domestic activities. It is more likely that the large-scale exploitation and specialization found at Sierra de las Navajas was supported by more fully agricultural communities of the Aztec state.

Obsidian sources and quarry areas remain poorly studied in Mesoamerica (Healan 1997:77). The reason may be that they are seen as areas with little variation and with small potential for contributing to a broader study of Mesoamerican production processes. This study has shown that not only is it possible to date areas exploited at quarries over time but that they also reflect a wide array of variability in how obsidian was used and exploited. Investigators will, I hope, turn their attention to more intensive study of source-area exploitation in the future.

CHAPTER THREE

Producer Versus Consumer

Prismatic Core-Blade Technology at Epiclassic/Early Postclassic Tula and Ucareo

Dan M. Healan

Current understanding of Mesoamerican prismatic core-blade technology is a legacy of several decades of research including the pioneering application of technological classification to archaeological assemblages (Hester, Jack, and Heizer 1971), replicative experimentation (Crabtree 1968, Sheets and Muto 1971; Clark 1982), and the formulation of sequential behavioral-typological models of lithic reduction sequences often conceptualized as flow charts (Collins 1975; Sheets 1975). Today such charts commonly accompany studies of core-blade as well as other industries and often include illustrations of typical specimens of each major category (Clark and Bryant 1998:Fig. 3). While providing succinct characterizations of the behavioral-topological approach, such charts also reveal three assumptions about the technology.

First, the reduction sequence is conceptualized as a basically continuous process in which behavioral shifts and concomitant morphological changes produce discontinuities, hence points of reference, in what might otherwise be a purely clinal phenomenon. One such shift, indeed a major watershed in most current models, involves the change from a percussion mode of force to pressure in the latter part of the reduction sequence. In the past I and others have in fact used these terms in typological nomenclature (for example percussion core versus pressure core, percussion blade versus pressure blade).

Second, illustrations of idealized cores indicate a general assumption that prismatic core reduction is typically *unidirectional*, featuring conical cores with a platform at one end. Indeed, present data support this assumption, one result of which is the popular but technically incorrect convenience of referring to *proximal* and *distal* portions of cores that is thoroughly embedded in the literature (including the present chapter), but such would not be the case if bidirectional blade cores were common.

Third, the complete reduction sequence, usually spanning raw material to exhausted cores, has rarely if ever been encountered at any one locality. Indeed, it is usually conceded that the first steps would be found only at sites located near the sources themselves. The sequence is thus an abstraction of activities normally performed at two or more distinct localities.

This chapter compares two core-blade industries at sites that constitute the initial and terminal nodes of one obsidian exploitation system of pre-Hispanic Mesoamerica. Specifically, the sites involve Tula, Hidalgo, a major consumer and possible distributor of obsidian from two key sources in highland Mexico, and various habitation and quarry sites at Ucareo, Michoacan, one of these two sources (figure 3.1). In general, the production activities found at Ucareo reflect those common at other *at-source* locations in Mesoamerica. The discussion of the core-blade technology found at Tula reflects production at a *proximate source* locale situated at some distance from the obsidian quarry (see chapter 1). Though based on information gained from analysis still in progress, the comparative technological information provides valuable insights into two temporally overlapping core-blade industries that exhibit striking variations on a number of basic technological themes, any of which appear to be a function of differences in raw material availability.

Core-Blade Technology at Tula

Tula is located on the northwestern fringes of the Basin of Mexico (see figure 1.5). Recent archaeological investigations indicate Tula began as a modest settlement during the Epiclassic period (AD 700–900) and subsequently grew to a city at least 12 km^2 in area, with a maximum estimated population of around sixty thousand during the Early Postclassic period (AD 900–1200).

3.1 Location of Ucareo
and Tula in central
Mexico. *Illustration
prepared by the author.
Adapted from Raisz
(1959)*

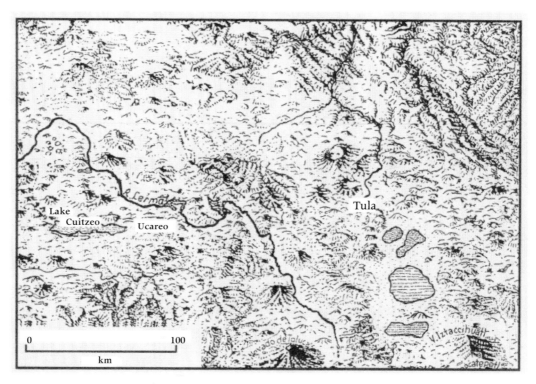

Obsidian is abundant at Tula. Nearly sixteen thousand obsidian artifacts were recovered in surface survey of less than 1% of the ancient city, for which over 98% of identifiable artifacts are clearly core-blade derived (Healan 1989). Over twenty-five thousand obsidian artifacts were recovered from excavation of two residential compounds, of which nearly 99% consisted solely of prismatic blade segments (Benfer 1974; Healan 1989). These are not the result of accident but rather intentional breakage of whole blades into two or more segments. Many specimens exhibit patterned edge damage, some of it indicative of use and/or haft wear (Healan 1993:Fig. 2).

Concentrated core-blade surface debitage was encountered in the extreme eastern portion of the ancient city and was interpreted to indicate the presence of intensive artifact production facilities, or workshops. Exploratory excavations in this area encountered a portion of one such facility, which was revealed to be a complex of juxtaposed residential, lithic working, and refuse dumping areas that embodies the model of a preindustrial craft workshop wherein artisans both lived and worked (Healan et al. 1983). Over five hundred and eighty thousand obsidian artifacts were recovered in the excavation that, excluding small, fragmentary debris, comprised an assemblage of about four hundred and thirty-five thousand macroscopic artifacts, hereafter referred to as the *macroassemblage*.

THE MACROASSEMBLAGE: GENERAL CHARACTERISTICS

Virtually all identifiable artifacts in the macroassemblage clearly pertain to prismatic core-blade production. Not-

withstanding this impressively large quantity of material, this breaks down to a rather modest estimated output of less than one core per day of its estimated 150-year occupation (Healan 1993). A low level of production is likewise suggested by refuse deposits consisting of mixed domestic and low-density workshop refuse.

It is clear, however, that core-blade reduction regularly took place at specialized localities and comprised a highly systematized set of activities. Geochemical and visual analysis revealed that obsidian at both the workshop and the site of Tula in general came mainly from two sources: Pachuca, Hidalgo and Ucareo, Michoacan (see figure 1.4), the latter of which is one of three distinct flows that make up the Ucareo-Zinapecuaro source area (Healan 1997). Stratigraphic and other data indicate a diachronic city-wide pattern in which source utilization shifted from being primarily Ucareo during Tula's initial Epiclassic settlement to primarily Pachuca during its Early Postclassic Tollan-phase apogee.

The workshop reduction sequence began with the importation of *polyhedral cores*, presumably made in workshops located near the obsidian sources (figure 3.2). Relatively little direct evidence of polyhedral cores was recovered, but extant remains suggest an average length of about 90 mm and a platform width ranging from 50 to 100 mm. If these dimensions are both accurate and representative, these cores would generally have been about the same length as whole prismatic cores in the macroassemblage and would have had a rather chunky appearance.

It is evident that a significant proportion of the im-

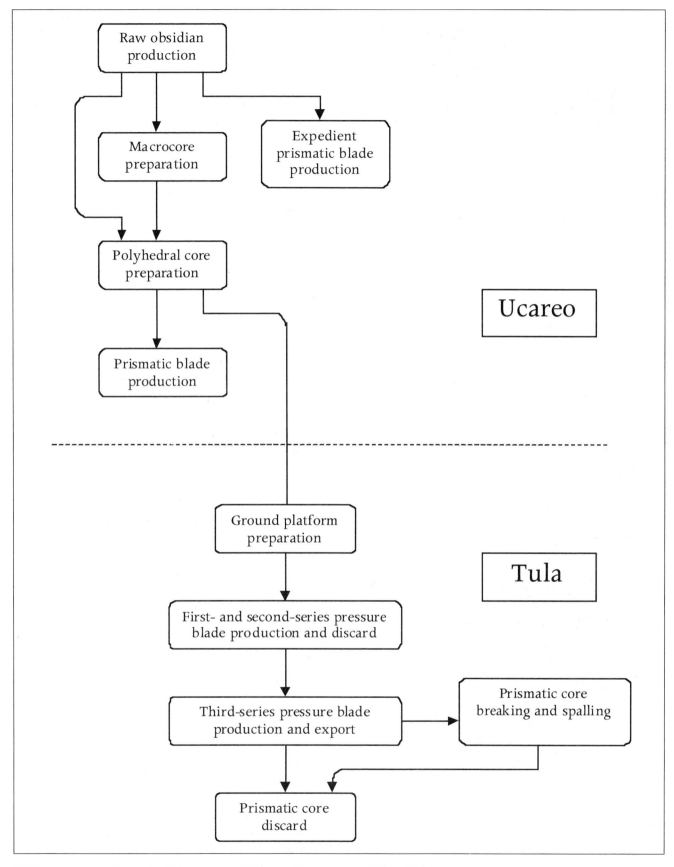

3.2 Flow diagram of the reduction sequence at Ucareo, Michoacan, and Tula, Hidalgo.
Illustration prepared by Erick Rochette

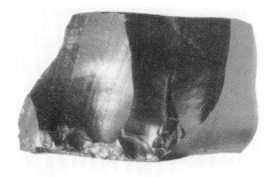

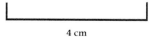

3.3 Distal portions of plunging blades derived from cylindrical, bidirectional polyhedral cores. *Illustration prepared by the author*

3.4 Distal portion of unidirectional prismatic core with flat bottom that had probably previously been bidirectional. *Illustration prepared by the author*

ported polyhedral cores, perhaps one-third or more, were bidirectional. This assertion is based on evidence that includes a number of percussion plunging blades (figure 3.3) whose distal heel is not the tapering point or wedge typical of unidirectional cores but rather a flat surface whose rim exhibits both initiating and terminating blade facets and thus cylindrical rather than conical in form, with a co-platform at each end.

It appears, however, that this bidirectional character was not maintained since none of the prismatic cores in the workshop were bidirectional. Indeed, the shift from bidirectional to unidirectional blading is preserved in distal fragments of three prismatic cores from relatively early in the third-series blade stage, which exhibit terminating blade facets encroaching upon what appears to be the remnants of a former co-platform (figure 3.4). As seen in figure 3.4, the facets are parallel-sided even at the distal end and exhibit a squared, slightly concave rather than pointed termination, a function of the more cylindrical form and flat termination surface provided by the former co-platform. Such generally rectangular blades would have had advantages for certain applications, and the ability to produce them may have been one reason for importing bidirectional cores. Indeed, Taube (1990) notes that Sahagun depicts a merchant whose wares include what appear to be two prismatic blades, one a pointed lancet form and the other a parallel-sided blade with a squared concave tip (see figure 4.3).

GROUND PLATFORM PREPARATION

One of the first workshop activities involved preparation of the distinctive ground platform that characterizes prismatic cores and blades at Tula and Postclassic sites (figure 3.5). This appears to have been a three-stage process, beginning with flaking of the polyhedral core platform to produce a multifaceted surface of overlapping flat, shallow scars and intervening arrises. Since it appears that the polyhedral cores already had multifaceted platforms when they arrived at the workshop, the additional faceting may have been performed in order to render a more regular surface. The multifaceted surface was then lightly struck or pecked all over, probably with a small, relatively hard hammerstone, thus obliterating most of the ridges and covering the surface with tiny impact fractures that have the appearance of cracked ice. The final step was the actual grinding, which appears to have been accomplished by rubbing the platform against a hard, flat surface covered with an abrasive agent. Incompletely ground platforms often bore traces of all three stages of the grinding process, in areas where relatively low-lying facets did not come into complete contact with the grinding surface (figure 3.6).

Although the abrasive agent has not been identified, a large number of basalt slabs were recovered both in excavation and on the surface of the workshop locality that appear to have been used in the grinding process. These slabs, distinctive in appearance from the ubiquitous domestic metate, appear restricted to the workshop locality and display a rotary wear pattern rather than the reciprocal pattern characteristic of metates. Other stone slabs believed to have been involved in the grinding process contained one or more depressions measuring approximately 3 to 5 cm in width and approximately 1 to 3 cm in depth. I have also encountered both these kinds of slabs at a core-blade workshop that featured ground platforms near the Ucareo obsidian source, as described below, as has Hirth at core-blade workshops in Xochicalco (chapter 7).

It is important to note that preparation of the multifaceted platform produces a distinctive flake, which I call *platform-facet flakes* (figure 3.7). Over sixty-five thousand specimens were recovered, thus comprising a large part (at least 16%) of the obsidian recovered from the workshop and up to 12% of its total weight. This total does not include the weight of obsidian that had left the workshop, which is conservatively estimated to equal roughly the weight of what was left behind. Thus, as much 6% of the mass of obsidian imported by the workshop was discarded almost immediately as a by-product, not of blade manufacture, but of platform preparation.

PRISMATIC BLADE PRODUCTION

It might be recalled that early replicative experiments in prismatic blade production by Crabtree (1968) and by Sheets and Muto (1971) used cores consisting of sawn blocks of obsidian, whose perfectly straight corners provided guiding ridges that ensured nearly perfectly parallel-sided blades early on, if not from the very beginning. Although sawn cores saved time and thus allowed Crabtree and his students to concentrate upon the production of fine prismatic blades themselves, this product of industrial technology did not shed much light on how Mesoamerican blade makers came to derive such prismatic blades from comparatively coarse polyhedral cores. Since then, the process has been well documented both archaeologically and experimentally, the essence of which is that fine blades result by establishing a pattern of fine scars on the core face (which results from prior removal of fine blades). What appears to be a technological catch-22, however, is simply a matter of positive feedback in which blades become increasingly more regular in form and consequently leave increasingly more regular scars to guide subsequently regular blades. Although this is a continuous, repetitive process, several factors permit its subdivision into three distinct and

3.5 Overhead view of prismatic core with ground platform. *Illustration prepared by the author*

3.6 Overhead view of prismatic core with incompletely ground platform, showing low-lying facets and impact scars from pecking. *Illustration prepared by the author*

3.7 Examples of platform-facet flakes. *Illustration prepared by the author*

Table 3.1 Percussion and pressure blades at Tula, Hidalgo

Blade type	a Whole	b Fragments	c Total	d Whole (%)	e Estimated # of individuals	f Individuals per core
Percussion	1,332	14,369	15,701	8.5	4,549	2.4
First/second series	5,244	196,010	201,254	2.7	70,107	36.9
Third series	157	54,580	54,737	0.3	11,354	6.0

sequential activities, each yielding a distinctive subtype of blade generally referred to today as first, second, and third series (that is, Clark 1997). This tripartite blade sequence is clearly evident in the Tula workshop, which, indeed, provided some of its earliest documentation (Healan et al. 1983).

As the first round of blades removed by pressure from a polyhedral core, first-series blades typically bear the scars of previous percussion blades on their dorsal surface. Most are irregular in outline and terminate relatively high on the core face. Second-series blades, which constitute one or more subsequent rounds, generally terminate at or near the other end of the core, hence often bear remnant percussion scars on their distal portion. Though longer and more regular than first-series blades, second-series blades tend to have relatively irregular margins and dorsal arrises compared to subsequent, third-series blades which have extremely regular margins and arrises, and epitomize what are commonly thought of as fine prismatic blades.

From the perspective of the core, the sequence of first- to third-series blade removals results in the imposition of numerous, closely spaced, small facets and ridges over a preexisting topography of wider facets and relatively massive ridges left by percussion blading. Thus a fundamental distinction between prismatic and polyhedral cores is one of topography, with "prismatic" referring to a particularly regular, fine-grained pattern of polyhedral topography.

A small but significant number of percussion blades are also present in the macroassemblage. Fully 75% removed hinge scars and other potential impedances to pressure blading and were removed rather early in the reduction sequence given the absence of any specimens exhibiting prismatic topography on the dorsal surface. On the other hand, nearly half exhibited platforms on which grinding was underway or complete, a process that must have begun almost immediately upon arrival at the workshop.

In column e of table 3.1, I have estimated the number of individuals for each blade type in the macroassemblage based on the number of whole specimens in column a plus an estimate of the number of individuals represented by the fragmentary specimens in column b. The latter estimation was accomplished using one or more of the following methods: the number of proximal blade sections among fragmentary specimens; dividing total weight of fragmentary speci-

mens by mean weight of whole specimens; and dividing total "running length" of fragmentary specimens by the mean length of whole specimens. First- and second-series blades have been combined because of difficulty in consistently differentiating the two.

Collectively, first- and second-series blades (N=201,254) account for nearly half (46%) of the macroassemblage (N=435,000), while third-series blades and blade fragments account for only about 13%. In column f, the number of individual blades is divided by the estimated number of about 1,900 individual prismatic cores (see below) in order to estimate the number of blades per core in the macroassemblage for each blade type. The exceedingly low ratio (6:1) of third-series blades per core indicates that most are missing and presumably constituted the workshop's output. By comparison, the combined estimate of about 37 first- and second-series blades per core does not appear to be unusually low and would suggest that both tended to remain at the workshop. First- and particularly second-series blades are quite usable, and the very low percentage (2.7%) of whole specimens for the two combined suggests that they may have been utilized for domestic and/or workshop tasks. This is also true of third-series blades in the macroassemblage, whose percentage of whole specimens is even smaller. By comparison, a much larger percentage (8.5%) of percussion blades occur as whole specimens, perhaps reflecting a less accidental or intentional breakage because of their larger size and/or pattern of use.

About 394 whole and 3,742 transverse segments of prismatic cores were recovered, together with 1,916 miscellaneous core spalls and fragments (see below). Together these whole and fragmentary specimens represent an estimated 1,900 individual cores. Most whole specimens were approaching exhaustion, given average platform and body diameters of around 16 mm and 23 mm, respectively. Most whole and segmentary cores are full round, that is, exhibit blade facets around the entire circumference. A small number lack prismatic topography in one area of the core face, often where a material flaw, massive hinge scar, or other anomaly hampered effective blade removal. Such cores were typically flat or tabular in cross section because blades could not be removed from all faces. Most cores with unbladed faces appear to have been a consequence of unavoidable circumstances rather than an intentional pattern of blading.

Most of the 3,742 prismatic core segments—consisting of about 30% proximal, 41% medial, and 29% distal specimens—were derived by breaking the core by one or more blows to the face. A yet undetermined number of segments, perhaps 18% or more, exhibited modification on the truncated surface similar to the procedures for preparing a ground platform, including faceting and/or abrasion. Unlike true ground platforms, however, the abraded surfaces were uneven and patchy, and none had pecked surfaces. Relatively few such platforms exhibit subsequent pressure blading, although most exhibit one or more of the percussion spall scars described below.

Nearly half of the whole cores and at least as many core segments exhibit scars from one or more anomalous percussion spalls removed from either end and, in some cases, from the face. These are often massive removals that leave a hinge or plunging termination on the piece. About 1,700 of the spalls themselves were recovered.

Various explanations can be offered for this peculiar pattern of systematic breakage, occasional faceting and/or abrasion of truncated surfaces, and subsequent percussion spalling that occurred on a majority of cores after blading was halted. One is that it represents a systematic attempt to recover usable material from exhausted cores, a common characteristic of prismatic blade assemblages, though its occurrence within the workshop is surprising. One would expect to encounter such an industry outside of the workshop, perhaps in a context associated with those who might have scavenged the workshop dumps. Another explanation, that it is the work of novices or even child's play, could account for its occurrence within the workshop confines, though it seems too systematic a practice to have resulted at the hands of such idiosyncratic agents. Moreover, the fact that there are far fewer spalls than spall scars in the macroassemblage suggests a significant proportion may be missing and thus may indeed represent systematic efforts to recycle exhausted cores.

As noted above, most of the workshop obsidian was imported from the Pachuca, Hidalgo, and Ucareo, Michoacan, sources. Although Ucareo was initially the principal source, Pachuca was the principal source during its apogee. Pachuca thus accounts for about 85% of the workshop obsidian and is easily distinguishable by its green color. The relative proportion of green and grey (mostly Ucareo) obsidian varies markedly by debitage category but in a clearly patterned manner. Specifically, categories of debitage derived from early in the reduction sequence consistently show disproportionately greater amounts of grey obsidian than debitage from later stages. This suggests that grey, chiefly Ucareo, polyhedral cores arrived in a state that required more pre-

liminary reduction than did the Pachuca cores.

Core-Blade Production in the Ucareo-Zinapecuaro Source Area

Sourcing studies over the last twenty-five years have identified obsidian from flows near Zinapecuaro and Ucareo, Michoacan, at sites widely distributed in time and space. The more recent of these studies suggest that Zinapecuaro and Ucareo are chemically distinct but similar obsidian sources within a larger source area and that the vast majority of obsidian artifacts that have been attributed to this source area are specifically from the Ucareo source. These findings are fully supported by recent field investigations (Healan 1997), which indicate considerably greater exploitation occurred at Ucareo rather than at the Zinapecuaro source. During the Epiclassic and Early Postclassic periods, Ucareo comprised a major, if not the principal, source for a number of sites in central Mexico including Xochicalco and Tula as well as sites in Oaxaca and northern Yucatan (Healan 1997:Table 1).

There is evidence of intensive polyhedral core production at many quarry sites in the Ucareo region, including one immense quarry with production loci situated atop terraces constructed of pure core-blade debitage (Healan 1997:Figs. 20, 21). Prismatic cores and blades also occur at quarry sites (figure 3.2) and appear to have been produced on site for local use. At most habitation sites in the Zinapecuaro-Ucareo source area, prismatic cores and blades are not as common as expedient cores and small, polyhedral flake/blade cores that make use of the ubiquitous obsidian cobbles. This is particularly true of sites in the Zinapecuaro region, where prismatic cores are not common until the late Postclassic Tarascan period. The few sites where prismatic core-blade artifacts occur in abundance are found in the Ucareo region and appear to be specialized production loci.

Prismatic cores from sites in the Ucareo region tend to be quite large, often exceeding 220 to 230 mm in length compared to the average of 90 mm at Tula. Ucareo blades and cores commonly exhibit pronounced rippling of the proximal region (figure 3.8) that is rarely seen at Tula. Jeffrey Flenniken and Gene Titmus (1999) believe that this attribute relates to differences in the application of force possibly necessitated by considerable core length. This characteristic is also seen on prismatic cores of Ucareo-Zinapecuaro obsidian (probably specifically Ucareo) of comparable size from Villa Morelos in southeastern Michoacan (Hester 1978b:Figs. 1,3).

Aside from their large size, one of the most intriguing characteristics of prismatic core-blade industries in the Ucareo region is the use of single-facet and multifaceted platforms rather than ground platforms, which do not seem to appear until the Late Postclassic period when the region

3.8 Prismatic cores from the Ucareo region showing pronounced rippling at the proximal end. *Illustration prepared by the author*

3.9 Blocky nodule of Ucareo obsidian exhibiting corner blade removals at four corners (only one corner shown). *Illustration prepared by the author*

was under Tarascan domination. The persistence of single-facet platforms on prismatic cores—long after this method of platform preparation had been replaced by ground platforms—is perplexing, considering the systematic preparation of ground platforms at Tula and elsewhere on polyhedral cores that may have been fabricated by these very artisans.

At many of the quarry workshops, the majority of visible and excavated debitage is derived from activities associated with transforming nodules and flow fragments into polyhedral cores with multifaceted platforms like those imported by Tula. It often appears that this process was accomplished without the initial creation of macrocores described by Clark and Bryant (1997). As noted above, prismatic cores and blades are also found at quarry sites, most of which were fabricated on site, presumably for local use. Many of these prismatic cores have the appearance of ad-hoc manufacture with prismatic topography confined to one part of an otherwise unmodified nodule, as if blade makers literally picked up a nodule and began producing prismatic blades almost immediately. Evidence of how these expedient prismatic cores may have been produced is provided by two kinds of artifacts: extremely regular corner blades derived from blocky nodules whose perfectly straight ridges permit the removal of near perfect blades almost immediately and blocky nodules that bear the scars of straight corner blade and subsequent removals (figure 3.9). Here then is a reduction strategy that involves neither preformed cores nor intermediate series of blades and virtually duplicates in nature the very cores and reduction strategy used by Crabtree and his students in the early replicative experiments mentioned above.

Prismatic cores and blades with ground platforms do not appear in the Ucareo-Zinapecuaro source area until Late Postclassic times and appear mainly associated with domestic assemblages. One specialized production facility was encountered near Ucareo that engaged almost exclusively in platform grinding. Like the Tula workshop, this facility imported polyhedral cores with multifaceted platforms from nearby quarry sites and used much the same three-step process of faceting, pecking, and grinding. Indeed, both kinds of stone slabs believed to have been used in platform grinding at the Tula workshop were found in abundance here as well. Unlike the Tula workshop, this facility showed no evidence of prismatic blade production, and hence was engaged exclusively in preparing ground platforms on polyhedral cores, which were apparently exported to other localities, perhaps within the Tarascan heartland for further reduction. Moreover, in contrast to the Tula workshop with its refuse dump containing mixed domestic and low-density workshop refuse, the Ucareo production facility was situated apart from any settlement and its refuse dump was a single mound measuring some 20 m in diameter and several meters in height and consisting of pure platform flake and percussion blade debitage.

Discussion

Comparison of Tula's prismatic core-blade industry with that of sites in the Zinapecuaro-Ucareo source area provides an opportunity to examine two nodes at opposite ends of an obsidian exploitation system from a unique perspective. The comparative technological perspective provides valuable insights into two partly contemporaneous overlapping core-blade industries that exhibit striking variations on a number of basic technological themes.

The abundant prismatic core material at Tula reflects a widespread trend, beginning perhaps as early as the Middle to Late Classic period, of prismatic blades coming to dominate chipped-stone industries in western Mesoamerica. Indeed, they did so almost exclusively in a single guise, that of intentionally snapped segments of blades used individually or hafted as composite tools and weapons, the best-known example being the Aztec *macuahuitl* (obsidian-edged wood sword). Not only could such composite tools assume functions previously performed by conventional unifaces and bifaces but blade segments themselves often were also used as blanks for making points and other unifacial and bifacial objects. This degree of dependence upon a single but highly versatile artifact has not heretofore been fully appreciated.

It may be no coincidence that this banalization of the prismatic blade (Darras ND) occurred at roughly the same time that a significant innovation in core-blade technology, the ground platform, replaced previous modes of prismatic core platform preparation to the extent that its presence or absence is often used as a chronological marker. The importance of the ground platform is aptly illustrated by the degree to which its preparation dominated the Tula workshop activity and the amount (up to 20% of total mass) of obsidian it diverted from blade production. Various explanations have been offered for the widespread popularity of ground platforms, including the ability of the textured surface to prevent the force tip from slipping during blade removal (Crabtree 1968). Additionally, the extensive fracturing effected by pecking and grinding may facilitate crack initiation and propagation on the platform surface, a process Crabtree compared to breaking the surface tension of a liquid. Finally, in addition to being slip-proof and pre-fractured, ground platforms are remarkably flat surfaces, a characteristic that can be truly appreciated only after attempts to produce such a surface through replicative experimentation. As Clark (ND) once noted, this near-perfect

flatness is enormously advantageous in maintaining a consistent platform-to-face angle and thereby facilitating successful blading. Collectively, these explanations suggest that ground platforms made blade production easier, faster, and subject to fewer errors. Thus, its initial adaptive advantage may have been, in modern parlance, to promote technology transfer, specifically to facilitate the spread of prismatic blade technology as both a cause and effect of the growing dependance upon prismatic blades seen at such sites as urban Tula. That this innovation apparently had little impact in the Ucareo-Zinapecuaro region may be a consequence of several factors, the most obvious of which is the low value of labor-intensive versus material-intensive strategies within a supply zone (Parry and Kelly 1987). In this region not only did prismatic blade technology enjoy a more restricted occurrence vis-à-vis expedient core technology, but blade makers could also manipulate their choice of raw material, for example, choosing blocky nodules to initiate prismatic blading directly on nodules and thereby blurring the distinction between prismatic and expedient core technology. The resulting technological disjunction between producer and consumer nodes would mean that if the polyhedral cores of Ucareo obsidian that the Tula workshop imported were made at sites in the Ucareo-Zinapecuaro source area, then they were made by persons who did not themselves use ground platforms. This may explain why Ucareo polyhedral cores generally required more preliminary preparation at the Tula workshop than did those from Pachuca.

Finally, it is interesting to note the appearance of ground platforms and, indeed, a platform grinding workshop, in the Ucareo region in the late Postclassic period. Even then, however, the use of ground platforms appears restricted to a few sites where they co-occur with single-facet platforms. Ethnohistorical and archaeological data (Pollard et al. 1990) indicate that the Ucareo-Zinapecuaro source area was under Tarascan control and supplied the majority of the empire's obsidian, mostly in the form of prismatic blades with ground platforms. Thus it appears that ground platforms were mainly being prepared for core-blade workshops in the Tarascan heartland rather than for local consumption, which is consistent with both the highly specialized and intensive nature of the Ucareo platform grinding workshop. Regarding the latter, the massive and highly dense nature of the Ucareo workshop refuse deposits compared to the sparser, mixed (with domestic refuse) nature of the Tula workshop refuse provides a succinct distinction between what may be a true factory on the one hand and a cottage industry on the other. This distinction may be of considerable use in contemplating questions of production rates and degree of occupational specialization.

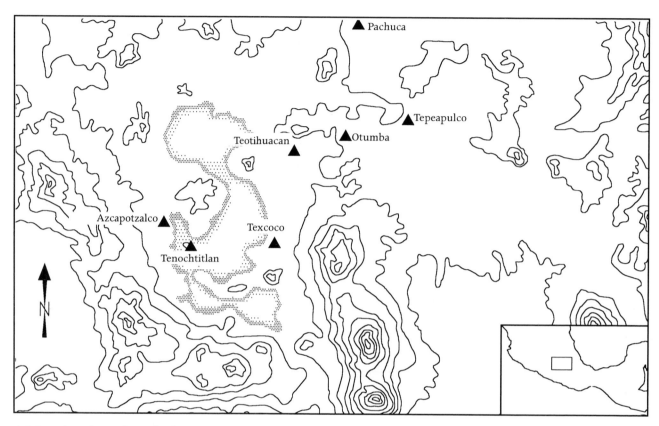

4.1 Location of Otumba and other Late Postclassic archaeological sites in the Basin of Mexico. *Illustration prepared by Bradford Andrews*

CHAPTER FOUR

Aztec Blade Production Strategies
in the Eastern Basin of Mexico

WILLIAM J. PARRY

THE MANUFACTURE OF OBSIDIAN PRISMATIC BLADES HAS been a topic of discussion for hundreds of years. The first Europeans to witness blade production were both amazed and perplexed by the process. One Spanish priest commented, "to see them produced from stone is a great marvel, and a thing worthy of much admiration, and the talented person who invented this art is greatly to be praised" (Torquemada, translated by Fletcher 1970:210). Another priest admitted, however, that "no one who has not seen how they make these knives can understand how they do it" (Motolinía 1950:79).

Modern scholars, seeking to understand "how they did it" have often focused on ethnohistorical accounts purporting to describe the production of blades by the Aztecs in the Basin of Mexico, combined with attempts to replicate the production of blades experimentally. In at least some cases, the resulting descriptions of blade technology have tended to be overly normative, implying that a single generalized blade technology was universally present throughout Mesoamerica and that the technology employed in the Basin of Mexico during the Late Aztec period was a typical (or even stereotypical) example.

As this volume demonstrates, however, there was tremendous variation among Mesoamerican prismatic blade technologies, in response to differing social and environmental conditions. Late Aztec blade technologies in the Basin of Mexico were not necessarily typical. Rather, they were in some ways unique, just as other aspects of Aztec economy and society differed from those of other cultures in Mesoamerica.

This chapter will describe a Late Aztec blade industry from the eastern Basin of Mexico and point out some of the distinctive attributes of this technology. It is suggested that the most atypical features of this technology may have been determined by production constraints, particularly the interplay of highly specialized production to meet the demands of highly specialized consumers. Production constraints appear to have overridden provisioning constraints, resulting in what might otherwise appear to be inefficient and uneconomical use of raw materials.

My reconstruction of Late Aztec blade production is based primarily on the results of recent investigations at the site of Otumba (TA-80), directed by Thomas H. Charlton, Deborah L. Nichols, and Cynthia L. Otis Charlton (Charlton et al. 1991; Charlton and Otis Charlton 1994; Otis Charlton et al. 1993; Parry 1990, 2001). Production activities at Otumba (figure 4.1) reflect its *proximate source* location, which, as discussed in chapter 1, is within a 100 km radius of its utilized obsidian source. Several blade workshops at Otumba were investigated through systematic surface collections and small-scale test excavations. This archaeological evidence, supplemented by the available ethnohistorical accounts, provides a relatively complete picture of Late Aztec blade manufacturing in the eastern Basin of Mexico.

Ethnohistorical Accounts of Blade Manufacture

There are several ethnohistorical accounts of blade manufacturing, written by Spanish priests during the second half of the sixteenth century. These have been summarized and analyzed by Clark (1982, 1989a, 1989c) and others (Fletcher 1970; Feldman 1971; Hester 1978a); so, I will not go into detail here. The most important are accounts by Hernández (1959:406–407), Sahagún (1977:148), Motolinía (1950:79–80), and Mendieta (1870:406–407; copied by Las Casas and Torquemada, the latter translated by Fletcher [1970:210]).

Each of the accounts describes only the last stage of manufacture of prismatic blades. Starting with a preformed

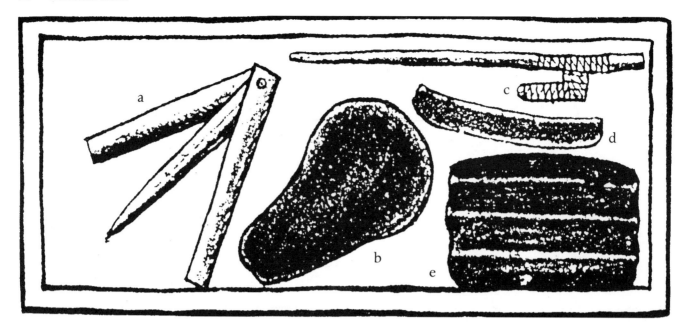

4.2 Aztec obsidian tools, as depicted in the Florentine Codex (about 1579): *a*, European lancet; *b*, a large endscraper of obsidian; *c*, a wooden pressure-flaking tool used to produce blades; *d*, prismatic blade of obsidian; *e*, blade core of obsidian. *Reprinted from Sahagún 1963:226–227*

4.3 Goods carried by Aztec vanguard merchants, as depicted in the Florentine Codex (about 1579): *a*, rectangular obsidian blade; *b*, pointed obsidian blade. *Illustration prepared by author and redrawn by Bradford Andrews from Sahagún 1959:8, 17*

core, the knapper sat with the core held between his feet and pressed on the edge of the platform with a special wooden tool (figure 4.2), removing prismatic blades by pressure. Motolinía describes the core: "They cut a piece of the stone...about the length of a span [*palmo*] or a little less, and shape it round [*rollizo*] and as thick as the calf of the leg" (1950:79). A nearly identical description is found in Mendieta (1870:406) and Torquemada: "a piece of black stone...a span [*palmo*] long, or a little more, and as thick as one's leg, or a little less, and round [*rollizo*]...the front of the stone is also smoothed and trimmed [*llano y tajado*]" (translation in Fletcher 1970:210).

Only one Spanish account says anything about the stages of manufacture that preceded the removal of prismatic blades. According to Hernández, stones are "taken from the mines...they are divided into medium-sized pieces and sharp corners [are removed] and they are rubbed with small but very rough stones" (1959:406–407, translated by Feldman 1971:214). It is not clear if the last comment refers to abrasion of the platform edges to remove overhangs or to the grinding of the platform surface.

In addition to the Spanish accounts, there is also one account in Nahuatl (Sahagún 1961:85, 1963:226–227). Sahagún's Aztec informants described the process of blade making by listing seven different Nahuatl verbs, accompanied by illustrations of cores, blades, and other artifacts (figures 4.2, 4.3). In a section discussing obsidian (*itztli*), two verbs are mentioned (*nitztetlapa, niqueva, in itztli*) that are translated by Anderson and Dibble as "I shatter an obsidian nodule; I flake the obsidian" (Sahagún 1963:227). In another section on obsidian sellers (*itznamacac*), Sahagún lists five other verbs (*tlauipeoani, tlauipeuhqui, itzuipeuhqui, itzuipeoa, tlapaneoa*). Although the first four verbs used by Sahagún in this section probably had different meanings, they are all translated by Anderson and Dibble as "he forces off blades." The last verb is translated differently as "he breaks off flakes" (Sahagún 1961:85). Unfortunately, none of these verbs are defined, but it appears that they are technical terms representing at least five different activities or stages in the production of obsidian blades. Only one or two of these five (or more) stages is described in the Spanish accounts.

Archaeological Evidence from Otumba

In order to understand all of the procedures and stages of manufacturing obsidian blades, it is necessary to turn to the archaeological record. The most detailed evidence comes from the Late Aztec town of Otumba (TA-80), located about 10 km east of Teotihuacan in the eastern part of the Basin of Mexico (see figure 1.5). This site has abundant evidence of craft production, including the manufacture of figurines and other ceramic items, fiber processing and spinning, manufacture of basalt implements, lapidary work (obsidian ear spools, lip plugs, and beads), and the production of obsidian prismatic blades and cores (Charlton et al. 1991; Charlton and Otis Charlton 1994; Otis Charlton et al. 1993).

Dense concentrations of debris from the manufacture of obsidian cores and blades are found in at least seven locations at Otumba (Parry 1990, 2001). Although Otumba is located in close proximity to a source of gray obsidian, only one of the concentrations of debris is composed of gray Otumba obsidian. All of the others are almost entirely (90% or more) of green obsidian from the famous Sierra de Pachuca (Sierra de las Navajas) source, located about 50 km north of Otumba (Charlton and Spence 1982). Finished blades from consumers' households at Otumba show a comparable mix of raw materials, being about 85% green Pachuca obsidian and 15% gray Otumba obsidian.

Although both green and gray obsidian were used to produce blades (employing similar technologies and core forms for both materials), the green obsidian was clearly preferred in most workshops. This preference is surprising, given that the green obsidian source was relatively distant, whereas the local gray obsidian appears to have been available and usable (although perhaps slightly inferior in workability). It is not clear whether the intensive use of gray obsidian in one workshop was the result of an idiosyncratic preference or of differences in availability or access to the nonlocal green obsidian. It appears, however, that provisioning constraints had a significant impact on the selection of raw materials, although both materials were subsequently employed in similar technologies.

For the purposes of my description of Late Aztec blade production, I focus on artifacts from several excavated contexts at Otumba. The first of these, designated operation 2, was located within one of the obsidian concentrations. This area included a large midden, about 50 meters in diameter and 20 to 40 cm deep, containing abundant obsidian debris intermixed with equally abundant ceramics of Late Aztec and Early Colonial types. This appears to be a dump of refuse derived from a blade workshop (Healan et al. 1990). Table 4.1 summarizes the obsidian artifacts from a 1 x 1 m test unit in this dump (unit N27W7, levels 2–4).

Excavations to the south of this dump exposed a smaller midden (designated feature 1), associated with an altar foundation and postholes (Healan et al. 1990), in what appears to be a patio area, probably in close proximity to a residence. This midden included numerous intact blade cores and other obsidian debris, intermixed with abundant Late Aztec and Early Colonial ceramics, animal bones, and other domestic refuse. The midden also included fragments of painted plaster walls and floors from a demolished structure (Healan et al. 1990). The blade cores from this midden (unit S6-18E6-9) will be discussed later.

Only 100 to 150 meters north of the operation 2 obsidian dump are two large mounds that appear to be the ruins of monumental elite residences built on adobe platforms. Test excavations in these mounds were designated operations 9 and 10. These excavations recovered artifacts from the construction fill of both platforms. Excavations in operation 9 exposed: "an undisturbed deposit of domestic refuse with a depth of almost 1 m... [including] lenses of ash and large fragments of pottery.... Above the undisturbed deposits were the remains of a now destroyed large and well-made structure with rock walls and floors of plaster" (Charlton 1990: 150). The ceramics are post-Conquest in date represented by a mixed deposit of Aztec III and Early Colonial (Aztec IV and monochrome glaze) ceramics. "The artifacts, including...part of the costume of a jaguar warrior...suggest that the inhabitants were members of the elite" (Charlton 1990:150). The unusual number of core fragments will be discussed later.

Table 4.1 Summary of obsidian artifacts from operation 2, unit N27W7, levels 2 to 4 (debris from a blade workshop)

White chert	3 (0.1%)
Gray (Otumba) obsidian	88 (3.0%)
Green (Pachuca) obsidian	2860 (96.9%)

Green obsidian	Total (%)	With dorsal cortex (%)
Prismatic blade (intact/proximal)	118 (4.1%)	6 (5.1)
Prismatic blade (distal/medial)	369 (12.9%)	44 (11.9)
Percussion blade (intact/proximal)*	83 (2.9%)	19 (22.9)
Percussion blade (distal/medial)*	65 (2.3%)	15 (23.1)
Crested blade (intact/proximal)	3 (0.1%)	1 (33.3)
Crested blade (distal/medial)	21 (0.7%)	4 (19.0)
Blade core frag./rejuv./recycl.	32 (1.1%)	3 (9.4)
Flake core or chunk	5 (0.2%)	1 (20.0)
Platform-faceting flake (intact/proximal)**	19 (0.7%)	0 (0.0)
Platform-faceting flake (distal/medial)**	5 (0.2%)	0 (0.0)
Flake (intact/proximal)	877 (30.7%)	46 (10.9)
Flake (distal/medial)	1263 (44.2%)	134 (10.6)
Total	2860 (100.0%)	323 (11.3)

*Includes macroblades, small percussion blades, and first-series pressure blades
**Undercounted

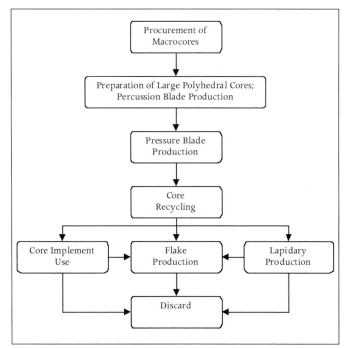

4.4 Obsidian core-blade reduction sequence from Late Postclassic Otumba, Mexico. *Illustration prepared by Erick Rochette*

Table 4.2 Summary of obsidian artifacts from operation 10, unit E18N18.44, levels 3 to 10 (refuse from an elite residence)

White chert	0 (0.1%)
Gray (Otumba) obsidian	24 (9.4%)
Green (Pachuca) obsidian	230 (90.6%)

Green obsidian	Total (%)	With dorsal cortex (%)
Prismatic blade (intact/proximal)	42 (18.3)	0 (0.0)
Prismatic blade (distal/medial)	99 (43.0)	5 (5.1)
Percussion blade (intact/proximal)*	12 (5.2)	4 (33.3)
Percussion blade (distal/medial)*	13 (5.7)	2 (15.4)
Crested blade (intact/proximal)	1 (0.4)	0 (0.0)
Crested blade (distal/medial)	0 (0.0)	0 (0.0)
Blade core frag./rejuv./recycl.	21 (9.1)	4 (19.0)
Flake core or chunk	0 (0.0)	0 (0.0)
Platform-faceting flake (intact/proximal)**	2 (0.9)	0 (0.0)
Platform-faceting flake (distal/medial)**	0 (0.0)	0 (0.0)
Flake (intact/proximal)	25 (10.9)	2 (8.0)
Flake (distal/medial)	15 (6.5)	1 (6.7)
Total	230 (100)	18 (7.8)

*Includes macroblades, small percussion blades, and first-series pressure blades
**Undercounted

A 2 x 2 m unit in operation 10 (E18N18.44, levels 3–10) revealed rubble from razed domestic structures and a deposit of domestic refuse and rubble sealed below a layer of yellow clay adobes. The ceramics were entirely Late Aztec (Aztec III), and it appears that this deposit is an unmixed pre-Conquest one (Charlton 1990). Table 4.2 summarizes the obsidian artifacts from this unit, representing a domestic context that contrasts with the workshop deposits.

In addition to the specimens from Otumba, I have also examined surface collections of blade-manufacturing debris from two other Aztec city-states in the eastern Basin of Mexico. One of these is from a workshop in the vicinity of Tepeapulco, located about 20 km northeast of Otumba (Charlton 1978), and the other is from an Aztec workshop at San Mateo, located in the southeastern corner of Teotihuacan (Spence 1985). These collections from Tepeapulco and San Mateo both appear to be essentially identical to the blade-manufacturing debris from Otumba (Parry 2001).

Blade Manufacturing and Consumption at Otumba

Not all stages of reduction are represented in the blade-manufacturing debris at Otumba (figure 4.4). Large decortication flakes and macroflakes are rare at Otumba, indicating that the first stage of reduction was done elsewhere, probably at the quarry. The material was subsequently imported to Otumba in the form of roughly shaped blocks or what Clark has termed macrocores (Clark 1986; Santley et al. 1986). This is indicated by both the proportions of various artifact types (Parry 1998), as well as the presence of significant numbers of macroblades (large percussion blades) and other artifacts diagnostic of the reduction of macrocores. Recent work by Pastrana (1993, 1994, 1998, and this volume; Cruz 1994) at the Sierra de las Navajas (Pachuca) source, however, indicates that later stages of reduction were also sometimes completed at the quarry.

At Otumba, macrocores were reduced by the removal of one or more rings of large percussion blades (macroblades) and small percussion blades, resulting in cylindrical cores, similar to what Clark (1986) has termed *large polyhedral cores*. Platform preparation took place at this stage of reduction. Unlike the Classic-period industries described by Clark (1986), the platform of the macrocore (originally formed by a single large flake scar) was subsequently modified. During the removal of percussion blades, several series of small flakes were also removed from around the circumference of the platform (extending about halfway across the surface of the platform), creating a level but multifaceted platform. The distinctive flakes (figures 4.5, 4.6) that were removed during this process have been termed *platform-faceting flakes*

(Healan 1986; Kerley 1989).

After the platform had been flattened and leveled by this process, the entire surface was then pecked and ground smooth. At Otumba, no further modification of the platform occurred after grinding had begun. There are no platform-faceting flakes with ground facets, and core tablets or other types of platform rejuvenation flakes are extremely rare.

Percussion blades continued to be removed throughout the process of platform preparation and grinding. About 25% of macroblades, and nearly half (46%) of all percussion and first-series pressure blades, had partially or fully ground platforms. Grinding was, however, substantially completed before the removal of prismatic blades: 85% of (rejected?) prismatic blades from workshop deposits had partially or fully ground platforms, whereas 98% of the prismatic blades that were exported from the workshops had fully ground platforms (table 4.3).

Both prismatic blades and cores were the desired end products, and both commodities were exported from the workshops. In fact, core fragments are proportionately more abundant in residential contexts (9.1%) than in workshop deposits (1.1%) (tables 4.1, 4.2). Many cores were used as implements (for unknown purposes) and exhibit abrasion on their faces perpendicular to their ridges. At Otumba, some core segments were recycled by lapidary workers into polished earspools and lip plugs (Otis Charlton 1993). Other cores were used as a source of expedient flake tools or smashed for some other purpose, often by bipolar reduction. Whatever the reason, the cores were literally consumed, and most of them were reduced to small, nondescript flakes and fragments. Intact cores, or segments of cores, are extremely rare.

There are, however, two excavated proveniences at Otumba that contained examples of intact cores or of large fragments that preserved the entire circumference. A midden in operation 2 (feature 1), in close proximity to a blade workshop, included a number of intact cores (figures 4.7, 4.8). A 2 x 2 meter unit in another midden in an elite residence (operation 9, E6N39.2) produced an unusual number of core segments (figure 4.9 b, c). Both of these proveniences probably represent post-Conquest (Early Colonial) deposits, and it is possible that cores were not recycled as thoroughly after the Conquest as they had been in earlier periods.

All of the cores from these units, as well as the identifiable fragments from other Aztec proveniences in Otumba and in Tepeapulco, are similar in size and form. In every case, prismatic blades have been removed only from half of the circumference of the core. In cross section, the cores are

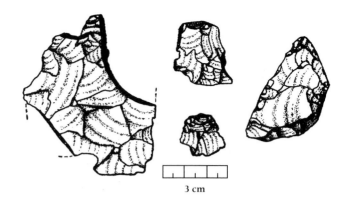

4.5 Platform-faceting flakes from Late Aztec or Early Colonial sites. All are of green (Pachuca) obsidian. The three specimens on the left are from a deposit of blade-manufacturing debris at Otumba (TA-80, operation 2, N27W7, level 3), the specimen on the right is a surface find near Tepeapulco (Tep. VII, SU340-1). *Illustration prepared by William J. Parry and Bradford Andrews*

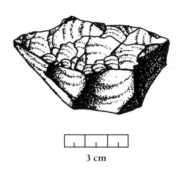

4.6 Fragment from the platform of a large polyhedral core, of green (Pachuca) obsidian from a Late Aztec lapidary workshop at Otumba (TA-80, operation 11, W10S10, level 5). The knapper first removed macroblades from the circumference of the core, then removed a series of platform-faceting flakes to flatten the platform. During the removal of the platform-faceting flakes, the core broke along an internal flaw. *Illustration prepared by William J. Parry and Bradford Andrews*

Table 4.3 Platform preparation of blades

I) Workshop debris (operation 2, N27W7, levels 2–4)

	Ground	Partly ground	Unground
Prismatic blades	93 (79.5%)	6 (5.1%)	18 (15.4%)
Percussion blades	23 (28.8%)	14 (17.5%)	43 (53.7%)

II) Residential midden (operation10, E18N18.44, levels 3-10)

	Ground	Partly ground	Unground
Prismatic blades	41 (97.6%)	0 (0.0%)	1 (2.4%)
Percussion blades	3 (23.1%)	2 (15.4%)	8 (61.5%)

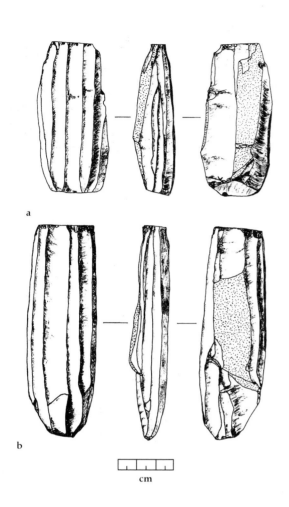

a

b

cm

4.7 Two intact blade cores, with ground platforms, from a Late Aztec or Early Colonial midden associated with a blade workshop at Otumba (TA-80, operation 2, feature 1): *a*, S6E9, level 4, item 3; *b*, S6E9, level 4, item 4A. Both are of green (Pachuca) obsidian. *Illustration prepared by William J. Parry and Bradford Andrews*

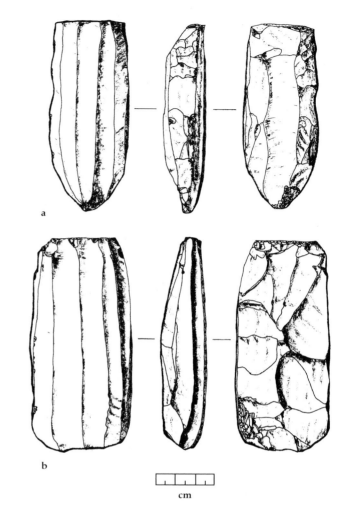

a

b

cm

4.8 Two intact blade cores, with ground platforms, from a Late Aztec or Early Colonial midden associated with a blade workshop at Otumba (TA-80, operation 2, feature 1): *a*, S6E9, level 3, item 3; *b*, S12E6, level 3. The top specimen is of green (Pachuca) obsidian, the bottom specimen is of gray (Otumba) obsidian. *Illustration prepared by William J. Parry and Bradford Andrews*

oval or rectangular, rather than circular, and blades have been removed only from one of the two wide faces. The other face bears only cortex or percussion scars (figures 4.7–4.9). In plan view, the cores are nearly rectangular in outline, tapering only slightly toward the ends. The average length of the exhausted cores is 89 mm (range 72–108), average width is 40 mm (range 31–64), and average thickness is 21 mm (range 12–33) (table 4.4).

The few intact prismatic blades are similar in length to the exhausted cores (range 52–97 mm), as are the intact macroblades and small percussion blades. None are longer than 100 mm (10 cm), indicating that the discarded cores are about the same length as the original large polyhedral

cores. This observation, combined with the near absence of core tablets or other platform rejuvenation flakes (or of blades removed from truncated cores), suggests that platforms were almost never rejuvenated by truncating the proximal ends of the cores. In fact, most of the discarded cores do not appear to require rejuvenation, as they retain adequate platforms, and do not exhibit hinge fractures or other fatal errors. In most cases, it seems that a few more blades could have been removed and that the cores are not truly exhausted.

Although the platforms were not rejuvenated, many of the cores have been trimmed or truncated at their distal ends (figures 4.7a, 4.9a). This trimming does not appear to

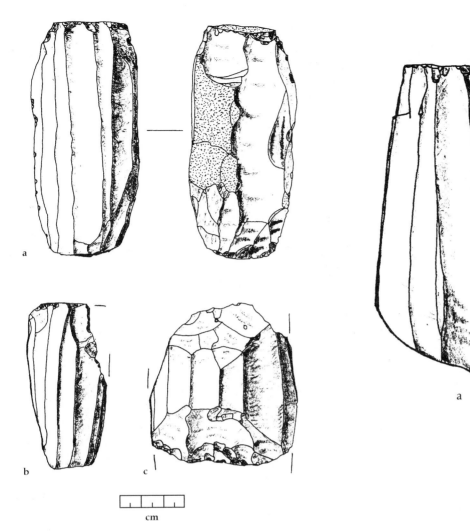

4.9 Obsidian artifacts: *a*, intact blade core, with ground platform, a Late Aztec or Early Colonial surface find from Otumba (TA-80, field 21, square 407); *b, c*, fragmentary blade cores, from an Early Colonial midden associated with an elite residence (operation 9) at Otumba (TA-80, Op. 9, E6N39.2). All are of Pachuca obsidian. *Illustration prepared by William J. Parry and Bradford Andrews*

4.10 Two intact Pachuca obsidian blade cores and a core tablet from the surface of a Late Toltec (Mazapan) mound near Otumba (TA-39, square 31, mound 122): *a*, large core rejuvenated on both ends, resulting in a single-facet (unground) platform; *b*, small core with a ground platform. *Illustration prepared by William J. Parry and Bradford Andrews*

have been done to remove hinge fractures (to rejuvenate the core) but rather to maintain the rectangular outline of the core, trimming off a pointed tip. It is possible that this shape was preferred for the cores intended use or reuse. Note that the idealized core depicted by Sahagún's informants had the same shape (figure 4.2e); however, it is also possible that this trimming was done in order to control the size and shape of the blades. These cores, with their flattened cross sections and squared distal ends, would have yielded relatively wide blades with parallel edges and squared terminations. This core shape precluded the formation of narrow, tapering blades with pointed tips. Coincidentally, it also precluded the formation of plunging blades.

The complete absence of plunging blades in the collections from both Otumba and Tepeapulco confirms that cylindrical cores with pointed distal ends were not being used at these sites.

Sahagún's Aztec informants explicitly distinguished rectangular obsidian blades from pointed ones, both in text (Sahagún 1959:8, 17; 1961:85) and in illustrations (figure 4.3a, b). This distinction was repeated by Sahagún in his Spanish text, which contrasts [rectangular] blades used for shaving and little pointed blades used for bloodletting (*"navajas ... para raer los cabellos, y otras navajitas de punta para sangrar"* [Sahagún 1977: 29]). A similar distinction was made by Motolinía, who observed that "they will get over

Table 4.4 Dimensions of green obsidian blade cores from Otumba

Unit	Level	Item	Condition	L (mm)	W (mm)	T (mm)
Operation 2, S6E9	3	5	Intact	73	33	17
Operation 2, S6E9	4	1	Intact	77	32	23
Operation 2, S6E9	4	3	Intact	78	37	24
Operation 2, S12E8	4	-	Intact	83	34	18
Operation 2, S6E9	4	2	Medial	-	41	21
Operation 2, S6E9	4	6	Intact	90	42	25
Operation 2, S18E6	3	1	Intact	91	36	21
Operation 2, S6E9	3	3	Intact	92	40	21
Operation 2, S6E9	3	6	Intact	94	40	19
Operation 2, S18E6	3	5	Intact	105	33	22
Operation 2, S6E9	4	4A	Intact	108	36	20
Operation 2, S6E9	4	4B	Distal	-	48	17
Operation 9, E6N39.2	4	-	Proximal	-	31	17
Operation 9, E6N39.2	1	-	Almost int.	72	34	12
Operation 9, E6N39.2	5	-	Proximal	-	34	25
Operation 9, E6N39.2	7	-	Proximal	-	40	19
Operation 9, E6N39.2	-	R'	Medial	-	46	21
Operation 9, E6N39.2	3	-	Medial	-	51	19
Operation 9, E6N39.2	3	-	Medial	-	64	33
Surface square 407	-	-	Intact	99	46	24
Means				89	40	21

two hundred knives from one stone, and some lancets for bloodletting as well" (1950:80).

It appears that the blade makers at Otumba and Tepeapulco deliberately avoided manufacturing small pointed blades but restricted their production to rectangular blades. To ensure this standardized output, cores were likewise restricted to a particular size and shape. As soon as the core was too narrow, too tapered, or too convex to reliably produce wide blades with square terminations, it was discarded or recycled, even though the core could still yield some small, tapering blades.

The rectangular blades were probably intended for use in utilitarian, domestic tasks. Many blades were used without modification, but some of them were retouched. In particular, many of the blades have been retouched on their distal ends to form tiny endscrapers. The blades produced at Otumba and Tepeapulco are ideally shaped to use as blanks for these small endscrapers.

Since the documentary accounts mention small, pointed blades, it must be assumed that there were *some* Aztec workshops that produced such blades, even though they were not manufactured at Otumba or Tepeapulco. A possible candidate for such a workshop is the Plaza Banamex site, an Early Colonial blade workshop located in close proximity to the Templo Mayor in Mexico City (Cassiano 1991; García and Cassiano 1990). According to published descriptions, the blades from this site include both rectangular blades *(navajillas)* and small pointed blades *(micronavajas)*. Although the majority of cores are similar to those from Otumba, at least some of them were reduced further, obtaining a cylindrical shape, tapering to a point. There is also more evidence of platform rejuvenation at this site than there is at Otumba (Cassiano 1991).

Variation Over Time

Although there appears to be some diversity among Aztec blade workshops, there were even greater differences between Aztec (Late Postclassic) blade technologies and those of earlier periods in the Basin of Mexico. Blade cores from the Late Toltec period (Early Postclassic) have ground platforms, prepared by the removal of platform-faceting flakes, just like the Aztec cores (Healan 1986; Healan et al. 1983; Kerley 1989; Santley et al. 1986). The majority of Toltec cores, however, have circular cross sections and have blades removed from their entire circumference. The resulting exhausted cores are cylindrical or conical in shape and are often smaller than the Aztec cores (figure 4.10). Also, the Toltec cores were frequently rejuvenated by truncating their proximal ends, removing a core tablet. Both core tablets and plunging blades are common at Late Toltec sites (Healan 1986; Kerley 1989; Santley et al. 1986), but they are virtually absent at Late Aztec sites such as Otumba.

Small cylindrical cores, core tablets, and plunging blades are also characteristic of Early Toltec (Epiclassic) and Classic

(Teotihuacan) sites in the Basin of Mexico. Platform grinding begins during the Early Toltec period in this region; Classic-period cores have unground platforms formed by a single large flake scar. It is clear that platform preparation techniques, as well as core forms, changed over time, and probably also varied somewhat among contemporary sites (particularly during the Epiclassic period).

Raw material usage also changed over time. At Teotihuacan, most blades were made from gray Otumba obsidian during the Terminal Formative period (through Tzacualli phase). During the Early Classic period, use of green Pachuca obsidian increased dramatically, until 90% or more of prismatic blades were made from green obsidian by the Late Tlamimilolpa phase (Ruiz 1981; Spence 1981, 1984). This emphasis on green Pachuca obsidian probably declines during the Coyotlatelco (Early Toltec) phase (Garcia Chávez et al. 1990:230) but again is characteristic of blade industries in the Basin of Mexico during the subsequent Late Toltec and Aztec periods.

Conclusions

It would appear that the Aztec core forms and reduction strategies, as represented at Otumba, are the exception rather than the norm for blade industries in the Basin of Mexico. When compared to earlier industries in the Basin (or contemporary ones in other regions of Mesoamerica), the Aztec blade technology displays a number of distinctive attributes. These include removal of blades from only one face of the core, trimming of the core tip (preventing plunging blades), lack of platform rejuvenation, and discard or recycling of the core when it was still relatively large. All these factors resulted in cores that were constrained to a relatively narrow range of sizes and shapes.

The desired cores were rectangular in outline, with flattened cross sections and squared distal ends, and would have yielded relatively wide blades with parallel edges and squared terminations. Cores that no longer conformed to this standard (being too small, too cylindrical, or too tapered) were discarded or recycled. Even though they were not exhausted in the sense that blades could still be removed from them, they could no longer yield blades of the desired size and shape.

In general, the distinctive attributes of the Aztec blade industry most likely resulted from production constraints. At Otumba, at least, highly specialized producers were manufacturing a single, standardized form of tool (or blank) in large quantities, presumably to meet the demands of other highly specialized consumers. This demand for blades of a specific, restricted size and shape appears to have determined many of the decisions about core-reduction strategies, rejuvenation, and discard or recycling.

Provisioning constraints appear to have been less important than production constraints. Although local material was available, the majority of the blades were made from nonlocal material (Pachuca obsidian), which was transported in bulk form from sources located a significant distance from the workshops. Even though such material would presumably be relatively costly and less readily available than local material, blade cores of this nonlocal material were not reduced any more extensively or rejuvenated any more than the cores of local material (as we would expect if provisioning constraints had been important). In fact, the use of raw material in the blade industry appears somewhat wasteful and inefficient. When viewed within the production constraints imposed by the Aztec economy and the restricted nature of demand, however, the technology probably was not uneconomical within its context. The variability in Mesoamerican blade technologies can only be understood in the context of the society's broader social and economic conditions.

ACKNOWLEDGMENTS

I thank Thomas H. Charlton, Deborah L. Nichols, and Cynthia L. Otis Charlton, for the opportunity to study the obsidian artifacts from Otumba. All field and laboratory research was carried out under permits issued by the Consejo de Arqueología of the Instituto Nacional de Antropología e Historia and was partially funded by research grants to Charlton from the National Endowment for the Humanities and to Charlton and Nichols from the National Science Foundation. I received a PSC-CUNY Research Award from the City University of New York. I also thank Kenneth Hirth and Bradford Andrews for their helpful comments on an earlier draft of this chapter.

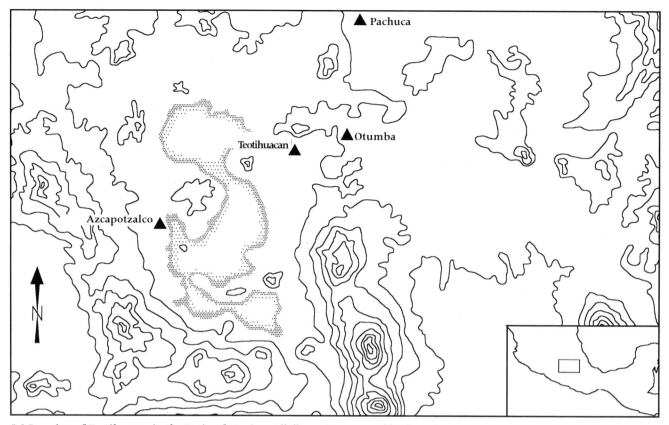

5.1 Location of Teotihuacan in the Basin of Mexico. *All illustrations prepared by the author*

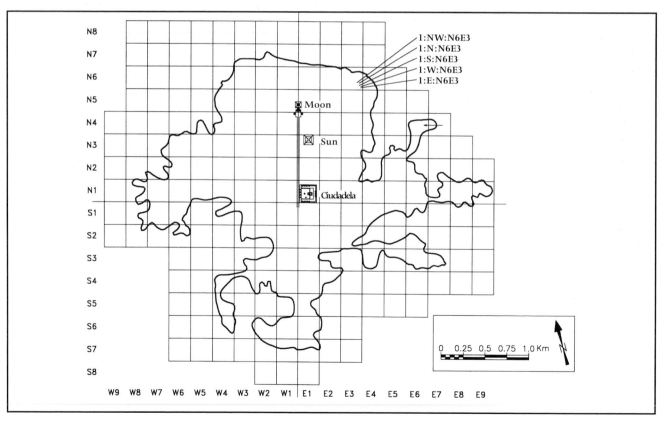

5.2 Locations of the San Martin obsidian tool workshop complex within Teotihuacan.
Illustration prepared by Peter Van Rossum. Redrawn from Millon et al. 1973:Fig 13a

CHAPTER FIVE

Stone Tool Production at Teotihuacan

What More Can We Learn from Surface Collections?

BRADFORD ANDREWS

THE PRODUCTION OF STONE TOOLS AND THE NATURE OF craft specialization at Teotihuacan have been topics of great interest to archaeologists for many years. These topics have also provoked more than a little controversy (Clark 1986). Teotihuacan was the largest Classic-period (AD 150–700) center in the highlands of Mexico (see figures 1.5, 5.1) and stone tool production is believed to have been an important component of its craft economy (Sanders and Santley 1983, Santley 1984, Santley et al. 1995, Spence 1967, 1981, 1987). Unfortunately, just how complex this dimension of the economy was remains obscure.

The principal reason for our limited understanding of stone tool production at Teotihuacan is that virtually all of the interpretations are based on unsystematic surface collections of artifacts from areas believed to have been workshops (Clark 1986). Despite the limitations of these data, however, artifacts recovered from surface contexts can provide useful information about stone tool production in the Classic-period city.

The primary objective of this chapter is to outline inferences about the form in which obsidian was imported into the San Martin workshop complex located on the northeast side of Teotihuacan (figure 5.2). These inferences are supported by a careful examination of the production debitage contained in surface collections recovered from this complex. Different scenarios of raw material import are evaluated for consistency with this surface data. As discussed in chapter 1, Teotihuacan represents a *proximate source* production context because most of the obsidian used here came from quarry areas less than 100 km from the city. This analysis addresses how the type and form of raw material may have resulted in a production linkage relationship, which is one source of technological variation outlined in chapter 1 (figure 1.3).

The secondary objective of this chapter is to investigate the level of product specialization that characterized stone tool production at the San Martin complex by examining the array of stone tool industries represented in the workshop collections. Such information can be used to infer whether the San Martin craftsmen emphasized either core-blade or biface production or had a general proficiency in both.

This effort should not be regarded as a grand synthesis of Teotihuacan's lithic industries. This is impossible with the data available. It would be foolish to assume that unsystematic surface collections represent comprehensive samples of debitage from their respective workshops. Furthermore, my information comes from only one production area at the site. Instead, my intent is to formulate some reasonable hypotheses about the process of stone tool production in one workshop area using the lithic technology approach (Collins 1975, Sheets 1975).

The following discussion first describes the San Martin complex and the size of its study sample. Next, the earlier interpretations of Teotihuacan's core-blade and biface industries are reviewed and then the technological framework used for this analysis is described. The expected types of workshop debitage given different scenarios of raw material import are then discussed. Subsequently, the artifactual content of the San Martin surface data is described and then evaluated to see how Pachuca and Otumba obsidian may have been imported and used in this complex. The final section briefly examines what the data indicate about the level of product specialization at San Martin.

San Martin Complex and Study Sample

The San Martin surface data were collected during the Teotihuacan Mapping Project (Millon et al. 1973). Spence (1981) classified the locality as a large regional workshop area that may have supplied consumers not only

5.3 San Martin workshop complex showing the location of the five workshop areas. *Illustration prepared by Bradford Andrews. Adapted from Spence 1986*

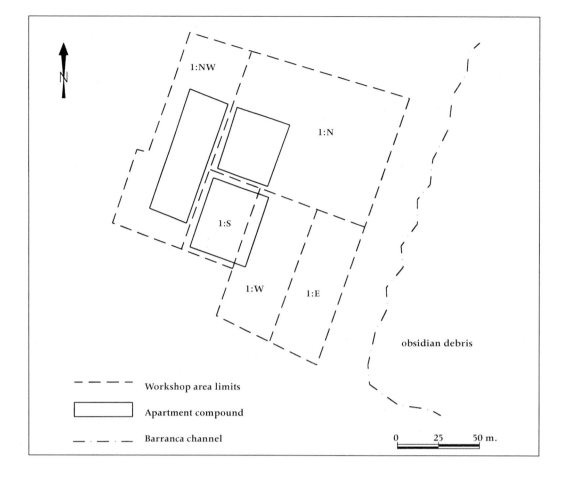

in the city but also in distant areas elsewhere in highland Mexico. The San Martin complex consists of a large mounded feature covering about 2 ha. It appears to represent the remains of three separate residential compounds occupied by an estimated 140 to 300 people (Spence 1986). Spence (1986, 1987) divided the complex into the Northwest, North, South, West and East workshops (figure 5.3). Based on the close spatial association of these five workshops, Spence (1986:3) suggested that the craftsmen here were cooperatively organized.

Although the status of many of Teotihuacan's proposed production areas are uncertain (Clark 1986), the San Martin Complex appears to have been an intensive setting of stone tool production during the Classic period (AD 150–650). Its dense surface and subsurface deposits of obsidian artifacts can definitely be associated with residential architecture (Andrews 1999:276–281, Spence 1986). Although the site has never been excavated, holes for planting *nopal* cactus and a *barranca* cut along its eastern margin make it possible to observe the association of obsidian craft by-products with domestic house features. The available evidence provides strong support for Spence's (1967, 1981, 1986) contention that the San Martin complex was a specialized domes-

tic workshop area with a high output.

The study sample consists of five extensive surface collections, one from each San Martin workshop (figure 5.3), and one intensive surface collection from the West workshop. The five extensive collections represent artifacts recovered from sampling units of unstandardized dimensions. They were retrieved by simply gathering a sample of artifacts visible on the surface of each of the five workshops. As a result, the items in these collections tended to be relatively large. The sample from the five extensive collections consists of 11,120 artifacts, of which 5,161 are technologically diagnostic (table 5.1). The nondiagnostic majority (N = 5,959) represent flakes,

Table 5.1 Counts of total and diagnostic artifacts from the San Martin extensive and intensive artifact collections

	Pachuca	Otumba	Total
EXTENSIVE			
Diagnostic	3,509	1,652	5,161
Total	6,850	4,270	11,120
INTENSIVE			
Diagnostic	1,065	274	1,339
Total	2,253	1,882	4,135

flake fragments, chunks, and shatter that could not be assigned to a specific production stage.

The intensive collection was obtained by picking up every visible piece of obsidian in a 1 m² area where subsurface material had been brought to the surface by animal activity. This collection consists of a total of 4,135 artifacts, of which 1,339 are technologically diagnostic (table 5.1). This collection is important because it contains the entire size range of artifacts, including extremely small pieces of debitage that were missed by the extensive collections. I do not assume that this sample is representative of the lithic activities that went on in the West workshop, let alone the entire complex. The importance of this dense sample, however, is that its small artifacts reflect knapping activities not evident in the extensive collections. Such information highlights the need for future stratigraphic collections that are size-range comprehensive.

The San Martin collections contain a total of 6,500 diagnostic artifacts. To my knowledge, this is the largest and most technologically comprehensive sample from any of Teotihuacan's workshop areas. It provides, therefore, a valuable body of technological data that can be used to support inferences about stone tool production in the complex.

Teotihuacan's Core-Blade and Biface Industries

Before the data is reviewed, it is useful to frame the analysis in terms of previous conclusions about stone tool production at Teotihuacan. Early interpretations suggested that there were two major traditions at the site referred to as the core-blade and biface industries (Spence 1967, 1981). Craftsmen involved in core-blade production were viewed as specialists who used pressure techniques to make prismatic blades of Pachuca obsidian (Spence and Kimberlin 1979:4, Spence et al. 1984:98), the source for which is located 50 km northeast of Teotihuacan in the state of Hidalgo, Mexico (figures 1.5, 5.1). Obsidian from Pachuca was obtained in large blocks suitable for a wide range of reduction strategies (see chapter 2). This model of a specialized core-blade industry supported the proposal that Pachuca obsidian was imported as polyhedral or prismatic cores immediately suitable for making pressure blades (Clark 1983, 1986).

In contrast, craftsmen involved in the biface industry were viewed as those who used percussion and pressure techniques to make biface and unifacial implements (Spence and Kimberlin 1979:1, Spence 1981:776, Spence et al. 1984:97). It was suggested that most of these tools were made of Otumba obsidian whose source is located 16 km west of Teotihuacan (figures 5.1, 1.5). Obsidian occurs in both block and cobble form at Otumba (Spence 1981:776).

Table 5.2 Technological sequences of the core-blade and bifacial industries at Teotihuacan

PERCUSSION CORE-BLADE
  Macroflakes
  Macroblades
  Small percussion blades
PRESSURE CORE-BLADE
  Prismatic cores
  Prismatic core fragments
  Prismatic core rejuvenation debitage
  Prismatic blade sections
BIFACIAL
  Biface fragments
  Uniface fragments
  Bifacial edge preparation flakes
  Bifacial thinning flakes

The block obsidian at Otumba was acquired in large pieces suitable for the production of macrocores, which were subsequently reduced to make macroblades. It has been suggested that craftsmen at Teotihuacan used these large Otumba macroblades as blanks to make large biface and unifacial tools (Spence 1986:7).

The cobbles of Otumba obsidian are water-born material carried from the source by the Rio San Juan, which passes through Teotihuacan. As a result, these materials are available along the length of this river and were probably acquired by dredging its alluvial deposits within the city. Because of their small size, cobbles were primarily used to make smaller biface and unifacial tools (Spence 1981).

Technological Framework of the Study

During analysis of the Teotihuacan workshop material, I used a technological classification based on the core-blade and biface traditions outlined by previous researchers. This enabled me to separate the artifacts into two reduction industries (table 5.2). These include: the core-blade industry, with its corresponding percussion and pressure stages, and the biface industry. The terminology used for the core-blade artifacts follows that of Clark and Bryant (1997) described in chapter 1 (see figures 1.1, 1.2).

The percussion and pressure stages of core-blade production represent the opposite ends of a broadly defined reduction sequence. The artifacts related to initial percussion reduction (see figure 1.1) include decortication flakes, large initial platform preparation flakes, platform-faceting flakes, macroflakes, macroblades, small percussion blades, crested blades and a wide variety of angular debris associated with the formation and reduction of macrocores. Aside from percussion blades, the polyhedral core was an important end product of this reduction stage.

The pressure core-blade stage primarily involved the use of pressure techniques associated with the reduction of polyhedral and prismatic cores (see figure 1.2). Artifacts related to this stage include pressure-derived initial, or first-series blades, second-series blades, third-series blades, exhausted cores, core fragments (from platform rejuvenation, alteration, or terminal processing), and errors such as nacelle flakes (Inizan et al. 1999:37) and *outrepasse* (plunging blades).

The biface industry involved the use of percussion and pressure techniques necessary for thinning bifacial and unifacial implements. Artifacts related to this industry include bifacially and unifacially worked fragments and various flakes associated with bifacial thinning. The latter category may consist of bulb removal flakes, edge preparation flakes, margin removal flakes, percussion bifacial thinning flakes, and pressure bifacial thinning flakes. In the following discussion, references to the biface industry refer to the manufacture of both bifacial and unifacial implements.

The artifacts listed above encompass the general array of items that can be associated with each reductive industry. The items actually recovered using surface collection procedures, however, can vary according to at least two important factors. First, unsystematic surface collections would tend to obtain samples with primarily large artifacts. This major methodological shortcoming of the extensive collections is partially offset by the intensive collection. Second, and perhaps most important, the types of artifacts associated with a given industry depend on how raw material was imported and subsequently reduced. Although the first factor limits the reliability of this analysis, I can still explore questions about the form of raw material import and the reduction strategies practiced at the complex. This exploration requires a careful evaluation of the technological variation reflected by lithic artifacts, one of the major objectives of this volume.

Raw Material Import Models

Raw material acquisition is an important component of any production system (Brumfiel and Earle 1987, Costin 1991, Torrence 1986). The nature of acquisition for a given system can vary in an infinite number of ways, ranging from organization (for example, the number of specialists and the amount of task segregation) to the specific items that were produced. These factors are often interrelated.

The following discussion outlines the expected types of artifacts that should be present in workshop assemblages given alternative forms in which raw material could have been imported. These expectations provide the basis for my analysis of the San Martin data. I have separated the discussion of the core-blade industry from that of the biface industry because of the distinctive features of these reductive strategies.

Core-Blade Reduction

Obsidian entering Teotihuacan for use in core-blade production could have been imported in a number of different forms. For example, it could have arrived as relatively *unaltered* material. In this case, workshop assemblages would look similar in some respects to those near quarry areas where core-blade production was carried out (for example, Sierra de las Navajas, see chapter 2). One distinct diagnostic feature of these assemblages would be relatively high frequencies of primary and secondary decortication flakes associated with initial raw material reduction. There would also be artifacts indicative of macrocore shaping including initial platform preparation flakes, large platform-faceting flakes, and macroflakes with platform to face angles of roughly 90 degrees.

The material also could have been imported as already shaped macrocores that were produced elsewhere. In this case, workshop assemblages would contain little to no decortication debitage or large flakes associated with the initial shaping of macrocores. Instead, one should find a few macroflakes, in addition to macroblade fragments, small percussion blade fragments, and angular debris associated with macrocore reduction. The specific range of items would depend on how the macrocores had been shaped prior to import. For example, if they entered workshops after most macroblades had been removed, assemblages would contain a greater percentage of small percussion blade fragments and debris related to final macrocore reduction.

Finally, obsidian for core-blade production also could have been imported as *polyhedral* or *prismatic* cores ready for pressure reduction (Clark 1986:70). In this case, except for core maintenance and/or rejuvenation, percussion core-blade artifacts should not be found in workshop assemblages. Areas that imported polyhedral cores should have assemblages containing some first- and second-series pressure blade artifacts associated with the production of more refined prismatic cores. In contrast, areas that imported prismatic cores should have assemblages that contain few first- and second-series blades.

Biface Reduction

Like core-blade reduction, obsidian used for biface reduction could have entered workshops in unaltered form as either blocky or cobble material. Once again, the clearest evidence for this would be an assemblage with a high percentage of decortication flakes and angular debris. Many of these items should be relatively large artifacts. Larger pieces of unaltered material as well as primary and secondary decortication flakes might have been processed into flake and/or blade blanks. Consequently, some of the decortication flakes will have characteristics consistent with bifacial thinning flakes (for example, dorsal platform grinding and platform-to-face angles significantly less than 90 degrees). In addition, bifacial thinning flakes produced during blank reduction should be prevalent. These should have dorsal attributes reflecting remnant flake or blade blank ventral detachment scars or dorsal arrises. There should also be bulb removal, edge preparation, and margin removal flakes associated with biface blank reduction.

In contrast to larger pieces of unaltered raw material, smaller cobbles also could have been imported. In this case, one option would have been to forgo blank reduction and simply process cobbles into bifacial and unifacial artifacts. As a result, assemblages should have decortication material with incipient cone cortex and bifacial thinning flakes lacking the attributes associated with flake or blade blank reduction.

Besides unaltered raw material, obsidian for biface reduction also could have been imported as *flake* and/or *macroblade blanks* produced at the quarry. Accordingly, production deposits should contain only flake or blade fragments trimmed or broken during bifacial thinning activities, and bifacial thinning flakes with attributes diagnostic of blank reduction. The tool fragments and the bifacial thinning flakes should exhibit distinct attributes depending on whether they were produced from flake blanks or more uniform blade blanks. An assemblage of flake-derived tool fragments should have more overall variation in terms of size, width, and thickness. In contrast, an assemblage with macroblade-derived tool fragments should have more overall uniformity in terms of these attributes. Macroblade-derived fragments may also have trapezoidal to lunate cross sections and evidence of dorsal arrises running parallel to their lateral margins. Consequently, the initial bifacial thinning flakes should have remnants of blank dorsal arrises oriented roughly parallel to their platform margins.

At sites like Teotihuacan where core-blade and biface reduction were important, it is possible that raw material import was structured in such a way that it linked these industries. One of the options I discussed for core-blade reduction was the import of macrocores. In this form, workshops could have produced blanks made from percussion blades that could be used by the biface industry. The macrocores from which these percussion blades were removed could be subsequently processed into polyhedral cores suitable for pressure core-blade reduction. This system would provide a good reason for importing raw material as large macrocores. It should produce assemblages with evidence of macrocore reduction, bifacial implements made from percussion blades (blanks), bifacial thinning debitage indicative of percussion blade reduction, and artifacts associated with prismatic blade production. This would place the core-blade and biface industries in a single linked sequence production relationship.

Data from the San Martin Complex

The previous discussion provides criteria for identifying what workshop assemblages might contain given specific scenarios of raw material import. Comparing the artifacts in the surface collections to these different models makes it possible to infer the form in which obsidian was imported into the San Martin complex.

The first thing the collections indicate is that very little unaltered obsidian appears to have entered this production area. For Pachuca obsidian, material with cortex consisted of only 304 (4.4%) out of the 6,850 artifacts in the extensive collections and only 11 (0.5%) out of the 2,253 artifacts in the intensive collection (table 5.3). Likewise, Otumba material with cortex consisted of only 198 (5%) of 4,270 artifacts in the extensive collections and only 12 (0.6%) of the 1,882 artifacts in the intensive collection. These low percentages indicate that the obsidian imported into the San Martin complex had most of its cortex removed elsewhere.

The extensive collections from each workshop contained diagnostic artifacts from both the core-blade and biface industries, although the frequencies vary according to workshop and obsidian type (table 5.4). The intensive collection contains a similar pattern of artifact frequencies (tables 5.5, 5.6). The following discussion will review the diagnostic data for the core-blade and biface industries separately.

CORE-BLADE DATA

Both the extensive and intensive collections contained more Pachuca core-blade artifacts than those of Otumba (tables 5.7, 5.8). Pachuca obsidian accounted for 91.6% of the core-blade artifacts in the extensive collections and 95.6% in the intensive collection. Pachuca obsidian was therefore the most important material for the core-blade specialists in the

Table 5.3 Percentages of cortex-bearing artifacts in the extensive and intensive collections

	Pachuca		Otumba	
	Qty	%	Qty	%
Extensive with cortex	304	4.4	198	5.0
Total artifacts	6,850	100.0	4,270	100.0
Intensive with cortex	11	0.5	12	0.6
Total artifacts	2,253	100.0	1,882	100.0

Table 5.4 Core-blade and bifacial diagnostic artifacts in the five extensive collections

Workshop	Pachuca	Otumba	Overall
NORTH			
Percussion core-blade	49 (30%)	19 (7%)	68 (16%)
Pressure core-blade	34 (20%)	1 (<1%)	35 (8%)
Bifacial	82 (50%)	253 (93%)	335 (76%)
Workshop total	165 (100%)	273 (100%)	438 (100%)
SOUTH			
Percussion core-blade	97 (59%)	11 (16%)	108 (47%)
Pressure core-blade	34 (21%)	0 (0%)	34 (14%)
Bifacial	32 (20%)	57 (84%)	89 (39%)
Workshop total	163 (100%)	68 (100%)	231 (100%)
NORTHWEST			
Percussion core-blade	85 (32%)	22 (12%)	107 (24%)
Pressure core-blade	125 (46%)	10 (6%)	135 (30%)
Bifacial	60 (22%)	146 (82%)	206 (46%)
Workshop total	270 (100%)	178 (100%)	448 (100%)
WEST			
Percussion core-blade	618 (41%)	36 (9%)	654 (34%)
Pressure core-blade	675 (44%)	42 (10%)	717 (37%)
Bifacial	226 (15%)	334 (81%)	560 (29%)
Workshop total	1,519 (100%)	412 (100%)	1,931 (100%)
EAST			
Percussion core-blade	594 (42%)	81 (11%)	676 (32%)
Pressure core-blade	537 (39%)	41 (6%)	578 (27%)
Bifacial	261 (19%)	598 (83%)	859 (41%)
Workshop total	1,392 (100%)	721 (100%)	2,113 (100%)

Table 5.5 Percussion and pressure core-blade diagnostics from the intensive surface collection at the West San Martin workshop

	Pachuca	Otumba
PERCUSSION REDUCTION		
Primary flake		1
Secondary flake		3
Macroblade proximal		2
Macroblade mid-section	2	
Macroblade distal with cortex	1	
Macroblade distal	1	
Small percussion blade proximal with cortex	1	
Small percussion mid-section	14	
Small percussion distal	10	
Early interior flake/single-facet platform	12	4
Late interior flake/single-facet platform	3	2
Total	44	12
PRESSURE REDUCTION		
Core top–bipolar removal	1	
Core top fragment		1
Core section–bipolar and percussion removal		1
Initial series proximal	7	
Initial series mid-section	3	
Proximal section-single-facet platform	271	6
Mid-section with cortex	5	
Mid-section	402	7
Distal section	38	1
Rejuvenated core–first series proximal	8	
Flex tablet	1	
Snapped blade fragment	7	
Distal section plunging	1	
Notched blade fragment	2	
Blade notch flake	3	8
Eccentric fragment	2	1
Total	751	25

San Martin complex. These percentages are in line with those reported by Spence (1981:Table 2) for other workshops throughout the city.

The San Martin data indicate that the initial shaping of macrocores probably occurred before Pachuca obsidian entered the city. There are no decortication flakes, large initial platform preparation, or platform-faceting flakes in the samples. There are, however, percussion core-blade artifacts indicating that already shaped macrocores were reduced in at least some of the San Martin workshops.

The extensive collections contain thirty-six Pachuca macroflakes and a large number of macroblade and small percussion blade artifacts (table 5.9). The frequencies of the percussion blade artifacts are especially noteworthy. There are significantly more small percussion blade artifacts (N=858) than their macroblade counterparts (N=549). Data on the experimental reduction of macrocores indicates a 1:1 (Clark 1986:Fig. 6) to 2:1 (Clark 1988:213) ratio of small percussion blades for every macroblade removed. My own replication experience produces frequencies closer to the 2:1 ratio.

A 2:1 ratio of small percussion blades to macroblades is, I believe, a realistic indication of macrocore reduction for two reasons. First, small percussion blades are removed during the entire sequence of macrocore reduction. They are used to set up arrises for detachment of specific macroblades and to correct such problem spots as hinge fractures on the face of the core. As a result, they are produced during both the early and late percussion core-blade stages. Second, small percussion blades usually comprise the majority of blades removed during the latter stages of macrocore reduction as they near polyhedral form.

It is possible that Pachuca small percussion blades and macroblades could have been imported in the quantities that would produce this 2:1 ratio. I find the similarity between the extensive collection percentages and my replication experiments, however, to be too close to dismiss as simple coincidence. Moreover, fifteen of the small percussion blade artifacts in the collections were reverse sections. These are usually detached from a core's distal end to remove severe hinge fracture scars below the proximal platform. I find it unlikely that the San Martin craftsmen imported percussion blades with severe hinge fracture attributes. Furthermore, the few macroflakes in the West and East workshops may relate to the early stages of macrocore reduction (table 5.9).

The intensive collection contains a total of forty-four Pachuca percussion core-blade artifacts (table 5.5). Although the sample size is small, the small percussion blade artifacts outnumber their macroblade counterparts as they do in the extensive collections. In addition, twelve early interior and three late interior flakes were identified (figure 5.4c,d).[1] These items may reflect the removal of platform overhang carried out during macrocore reduction. Given the types and frequencies of Pachuca percussion core-blade artifacts in both the extensive and intensive collections, it is likely that a significant amount of this obsidian entered the complex in macrocore form.

In contrast to the Pachuca material, the limited number of Otumba percussion core-blade artifacts in the extensive collections suggests that macrocores were not reduced in the San Martin workshops (table 5.9). The percentages for Otumba small percussion blades (N=54) and macroblades (N=113) produce a ratio of 1:2, which is exactly opposite that of the Pachuca material. This frequency appears to be more consistent with the selective import of large percussion blades rather than on-site reduction of Otumba macrocores, which was probably related to the needs of the biface industry discussed below.

Regarding pressure core-blade material, there were 230 pressure core fragments and 1,175 pressure blade sections made of Pachuca obsidian in the extensive collections (table 5.10). These quantities are in marked contrast to the 17 core fragments and 77 pressure blade sections made of Otumba obsidian. Of the 776 pressure core-blade artifacts in the intensive collections, 751 were Pachuca obsidian (table 5.5, figure 5.5). Many of these were prismatic blade fragments ranging from large, irregular first-series blades to small, thin prismatic sections. Furthermore, most of them were probably too short for effective use and probably were discarded for this reason. The presence of Pachuca first-series blades supports the notion that polyhedral cores were being reduced by pressure techniques in the West workshop. These cores could have been imported in ready-made polyhedral form and/or produced from macrocore reduction in the workshops.

There were far fewer Otumba pressure core-blade artifacts than those affiliated with the percussion core-blade stage (tables 5.4, 5.5), which appears to relate to the physical characteristics of Otumba obsidian. Spence et al. (1984:97) have suggested that a secondary fracture pattern

Table 5.6 Bifacial diagnostics from the intensive surface collection at the West San Martin workshop

	Pachuca	Otumba
Bulb removal	3	2
Bifacial thin.–edge prep. w/detach. scar	4	12
Bifacial thin.–margin removal		2
Bifacial thin.–alternate flake	3	
Percussion bifacial thin. w/macroblade dorsal attributes	8	2
Percussion bifacial thin. w/macroblade detach. scar	11	8
Percussion bifacial thin.	28	18
Early pressure bifacial thin. w/detach. scar–r		1
Early pressure bifacial thin. w/detach. scar–l		10
Early pressure bifacial thin.–r	72	49
Early pressure bifacial thin. –l	35	45
Late pressure bifacial thin.–r	76	50
Late pressure bifacial thin.–l	24	25
Notch flake	3	
Biface	1	
Bifacial fragments-macroblade prox.		1
Bifacial fragments-macroblade mid-section		1
Bifacial fragments-macroblade distal		4
Worked macroblade fragment		1
Bifacial fragment		2
Utilized flake fragment	2	4
Total	270	237

r = flake swings to the right of its platform margin; l = flake swings to the left of its platform margin

Table 5.7 Core-blade diagnostics in the extensive collections

	Qty	%
PACHUCA		
Percussion	1,443	46.4
Pressure	1,405	45.2
OTUMBA		
Percussion	169	5.4
Pressure	94	3.0
Total	3,111	100.0

Table 5.8 Core-blade diagnostics in the intensive collection

	Qty	%
PACHUCA		
Percussion	44	5.3
Pressure	751	90.3
OTUMBA		
Percussion	12	1.4
Pressure	25	3.0
Total	832	100.0

Table 5.9 Pachuca and Otumba percussion core-blade artifacts in the extensive workshop collections

	North	South	Northwest	West	East	Total
PACHUCA						
Macroflakes	0	0	0	33	3	36
Macroblade and macroblade fragments	28	28	44	260	189	549
Small percussion blades and small percussion blade fragments	21	69	41	325	402	858
OTUMBA						
Macroflakes	0	0	0	0	2	2
Macroblade and macroblade fragments	18	8	13	17	57	113
Small percussion blades and small percussion blade fragments	1	3	9	19	22	54

Table 5.10 Pressure core-blade artifacts in the extensive workshop collections

	Pachuca	Otumba
Core fragments	230	17
Pressure blade fragments	1,175	77

Table 5.11 Extensive collection artifacts associated with the bifacial industry

	Qty	%
Pachuca	661	32
Otumba	1,386	68
Total	2,047	100

Table 5.12 Otumba and Pachuca bifacial and unifacial artifact fragments in the extensive collections

	Total	%
OTUMBA		
Flakes or cobbles	563	46
Macroblades	654	54
Total	1,217	100
PACHUCA		
Flakes	197	40
Macroblades	299	60
Total	496	100

Table 5.13 Dimensions of blade-derived bifaces and unifaces and macroblades made of Otumba obsidian in the extensive collections

	Blade-derived tool fragments (N = 47)	Macroblades (N = 90)
Width	37.0 mm (σ 7.1)	34.0 mm (σ 6.6)
Thickness	7.1 mm (σ 2.4)	6.6 mm (σ 2.4)

Table 5.14 Width and thickness of blade-derived bifaces, unifaces, and macroblades made of Pachuca obsidian in the extensive collections

	Blade-derived tool fragments (N = 42)	Macroblades (N = 340)
Width	32.0 mm (σ 6.8)	28.0 mm (σ 5.9)
Thickness	8.8 mm (σ 1.8)	7.5 mm (σ 2.3)

created by stress prior to final solidification makes the Otumba material difficult to reduce with pressure techniques.

If Otumba macrocores were imported, the higher frequency of percussion versus pressure core-blade artifacts would indicate that very few of them were used to make third-series pressure blades. Such a scenario should have produced assemblages with a number of exhausted macrocores discarded after the percussion blades were removed. There were no artifacts in any of the collections that were consistent with such a category. More likely, most of the Otumba obsidian entered the complex as percussion blades destined for biface reduction rather than as macrocores destined for core-blade reduction.

BIFACIAL DATA

In the five extensive collections from San Martin, 68% of the artifacts related to biface production are made of Otumba obsidian (table 5.11). Likewise, all but one of the finished bifacial tools in the intensive collection are made of Otumba, although there were slightly more Pachuca bifacial thinning flakes (table 5.6). These data indicate that Otumba was the material of preference for the biface industry.

Most of the bifacial artifacts in the extensive collections are bifacial and unifacial tool fragments. The low number of small thinning flakes probably relates to the use of an unsystematic surface collection strategy. The Otumba tool fragments appear to have been made from cobbles, flake blanks, and macroblade blanks. The Pachuca bifacial tool fragments are made from either flake or macroblade blanks since this material does not occur in cobble form (table 5.12). Many of the flake-derived and cobble tool fragments are small and show a wide range of variation in both width and thickness.

Macroblade blanks of both types of obsidian were the preferred form for biface production. At least 54% of the Otumba tool fragments and 60% of their Pachuca counterparts are made from macroblade blanks (table 5.12). The number of blade-derived bifacial and unifacial tool fragments was probably higher but the removal of dorsal (arrises) and ventral (detachment scars) macroblade attributes makes a precise estimate impossible.

These tool fragments have trapezoidal cross sections, evidence of ventral detachment scars, and remnants of one or more dorsal arrises (figures 5.6, 5.7). Many of them made from proximal macroblade sections have thick single-facet platforms. In addition, their widths and thicknesses are similar to the Otumba and Pachuca macroblades in these collections (tables 5.13, 5.14).

The intensive collection contains a significant number of bifacial thinning flakes that were not found in the extensive collections (table 5.6). Many of these flakes also indicate the bifacial reduction of macroblade blanks. The six Otumba bifacial fragments (table 5.6) appear to have been made from macroblades because of their shape and ventral detachment scars (figure 5.8). There are also bulb removal flakes, edge preparation flakes with remnant detachment scars, margin removal flakes, and one macroblade proximal section with its bulb removed (figure 5.9).

Bulb removal flakes are unique because they have bulbs on both their ventral and dorsal surfaces. They were produced by removing the bulbs of force on flake or blade blanks during the initial stages of thinning. Edge preparation flakes with detachment scars were removed to give curvature to the flat ventral surfaces of macroblades. Imparting curvature to this surface is necessary for the successful removal of subsequent thinning flakes. The margin removal flakes represent errors because they eliminated more of a blank's margin than the knapper had probably intended. Most of the remaining Otumba bifacial artifacts were percussion and pressure bifacial thinning flakes (table 5.6, figures 5.10, 5.11).

The Pachuca bifacial artifacts are similar to those made from Otumba obsidian (table 5.6). One Pachuca biface in the collection is probably made from a macroblade judging from its slightly trapezoidal cross section and small remnant macroblade detachment scar (figure 5.12a). There are also two bulb removal flakes, edge preparation flakes, and percussion and pressure bifacial thinning flakes (figures 5.13, 5.14).

Percussion bifacial thinning flakes are generally larger than the pressure flakes. Some of these percussion flakes appear to exhibit evidence of either a remnant dorsal arris or the dorsal lateral facet of a macroblade (figures 5.10, 5.13). Others exhibit remnant detachment scars that may represent the ventral surface of such blades. These data indicate that large blades were initially flaked with percussion enabling the removal of their dorsal arrises. Along with edge preparation flakes, percussion bifacial thinning also was effective for imparting curvature to the ventral surface of these large blades.

Bifaces were further thinned with early and late-stage pressure flakes (figures 5.11, 5.14). These were not removed in a strictly sequential fashion, although this generally may have been the case. Both the early and late pressure flakes have distal ends that either sweep to the right or left of the platform margin. Assuming the use of a consistent pressure flaking technique, I suggest that this is evidence that there were right- and left-handed knappers in the San Martin workshops. Experimental flint knapping has shown that right- and left-handed people using the same technique will produce pressure flakes that sweep in opposite directions.[2]

It is possible that the San Martin knappers could have pressure flaked by following the ridges established during percussion bifacial thinning. This would result in pressure flakes with random platform to distal end orientations. Such a practice, however, was probably unlikely. The few bifacial fragments in the collections appear to have been flaked systematically. Furthermore, many of the pressure flakes consistently sweep either right or left and have only one dorsal ridge running parallel to their lateral margins. Such morphological characteristics are consistent with sys-

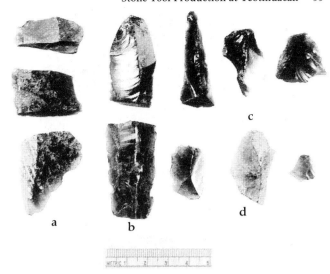

5.4 Pachuca percussion core-blade artifacts in the intensive collection: *a*, three macroblade fragments; *b*, two small percussion blade fragments; *c*, three early interior flakes; *d*, three late interior flakes

5.5 Pachuca pressure core-blade artifacts in the intensive collection: *a*, bipolared core top; *b*, plunging blade section; *c*, six third-series pressure blade sections; *d*, three rejuvenated core first-series sections; *e*, three blade notch flakes

5.6 Bifacial fragments made from proximal macroblade sections in the extensive collections from the west San Martin workshop: *top row*, ventral surface; *bottom row*, dorsal surface

5.7 Bifacial fragments made from macroblade distal sections in the extensive collections from the west San Martin workshop: *top row,* **ventral surface;** *bottom row,* **dorsal surface**

5.8 Otumba biface fragments in the intensive collection

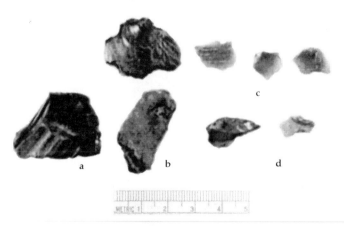

5.9 Otumba bifacial artifacts in the intensive collection: a, macroblade proximal with bulb removed; b, two bulb removal flakes; c, three edge preparation flakes; d, two margin removal flakes

tematic flaking.

Given the foregoing discussion, it seems that most of the Otumba obsidian at the complex was imported from the quarry in the form of macroblade blanks that were made into large bifacial and unifacial tools (figure 5.15). Otumba cobbles probably were not heavily used by the San Martin craftsmen because they were too small; Spence (1981:776) reports that Otumba cobbles rarely exceed 12 cm in maximum diameter. Cobbles of this size are not big enough for making macroblade blanks.

Evidently, many of the Pachuca bifacial and unifacial implements were also made from macroblades. It is possible that these Pachuca macroblades were imported directly from the quarry. As I suggested above, however, it is also possible that the San Martin craftsmen may have imported Pachuca macrocores that were made into polyhedral cores that yielded macroblades in the process. I refer to this scenario as the linked-sequence model of production because it would have tied the core-blade and biface industries together (figure 5.16).

The linked-sequence model assumes that there were craftsmen who removed percussion blades from macrocores at both the quarry and in Teotihuacan's workshops. This raises the question, why not conduct all of the percussion reduction at the quarry and then import suitable macroblades and polyhedral cores into Teotihuacan (figure 5.17)? While this is a good question, the reverse is also worth considering. If macrocore reduction results in both macroblades for bifaces and polyhedral cores for pressure blades, then why not import Pachuca macrocores?

I suggest that there were craftsmen who could perform percussion core-blade reduction at the Pachuca quarry and Teotihuacan during the Classic period. Based on my experience, the 2:1 ratio of small percussion blades to macroblades is consistent with on-site reduction of macrocores. Unfortunately, the Classic-period deposits at the Pachuca source have not been studied enough to determine the form in which cores were exported (see chapter 2). The lithic material reflecting Late Postclassic exploitation, however, indicates that relatively large blade cores were a primary item of export (Pastrana 1998). These were suitable for either percussion or pressure reduction depending on the shape and regularity of a core's lateral arrises (Alejandro Pastrana, personal communication, March 2000).

There is evidence from other workshop contexts in Mesoamerica that macrocores were commonly imported. Parry (chapter 4) reports that most of the Pachuca obsidian which entered Otumba's Postclassic workshops arrived in macrocore form. Likewise, Santley and Barrett (chapter 8) suggest that black obsidian macrocores were the major object entering sites throughout the Tuxtla and Hueyapan regions of the southern Gulf lowlands. In west Mexico, Spence et al. (chapter 6) report that macrocores were imported into the Classic-period site of Teuchitlan and the Postclassic site of Las Cuevas. This information indicates that percussion core-blade reduction carried out in both quarry and workshop locales may have been common throughout highland Mesoamerica.

Furthermore, personal experience has shown me that macrocore shaping and subsequent macroblade removal involve slightly distinct percussion techniques. According to the preceding discussion, therefore, it seems reasonable that there were craftsmen who formed macrocores at the Pachuca quarry and craftsmen who reduced them in Teotihuacan. If this was true, it appears that Teotihuacan's system of acquisition and production was highly specialized.

Product Specialization at the San Martin Complex

The San Martin surface collections also allow us to evaluate the nature of product specialization within the complex. My reanalysis of the data supports Spence's (1986:4) original contention that Pachuca macrocores were imported to produce several types of products. These included prismatic cores, bifacial and unifacial tools, prismatic blades, and a wide variety of small prismatic blade tools such as projectile points and eccentrics.[3] The range of techniques necessary to make these products suggests that the San Martin craftsmen were generalized specialists. The Northwest, West, and East workshops displayed similar percentages of artifacts related to the percussion and pressure core-blade and the biface reduction (table 5.4). These areas appear to have been loci where the entire range of activities associated with the core-blade and biface industries were carried out.

Only the North and South workshops had relatively low numbers of pressure core-blade artifacts (table 5.4). In these areas, the emphasis appears to have been placed on the percussion core-blade and bifacial sequences of reduction. Accordingly, even the craftsmen in the North and South workshops do not appear to have specialized in only core-blade or biface reduction. Instead, the San Martin data indicate a diversified strategy of technological specialization. It appears that even at one of Teotihuacan's most intensive production contexts, craftsmen did not specialize in only one set of reduction techniques.

Conclusions

While most archaeologists would agree that surface data are limited in their ability to support archaeological interpretations, such data do provide a basis for for-

5.10 Otumba percussion bifacial thinning flakes in the intensive collection: *top row*, percussion flakes; *bottom row*, percussion flakes with remnant macroblade detachment scars

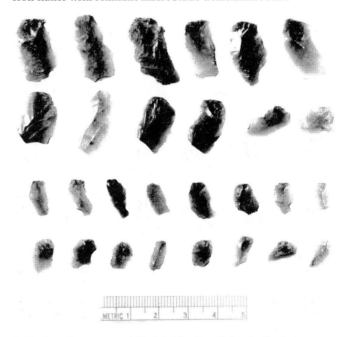

5.11 Otumba pressure bifacial thinning flakes in the intensive collection: *top two rows*, early pressure flakes; *bottom two rows*, late pressure flakes

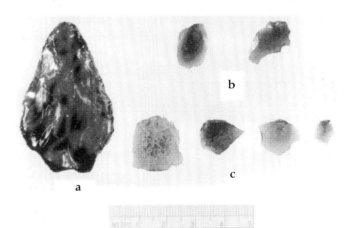

5.12 Pachuca bifacial artifacts in the intensive collection: *a*, biface tool; *b*, two bulb removal flakes; *c*, four edge preparation flakes

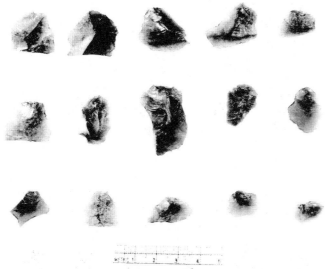

5.13 Pachuca percussion bifacial thinning flakes in the intensive collection: *top row*, percussion flakes with remnant macroblade dorsal attributes; *middle row*, percussion flakes with remnant macroblade detachment scars; *bottom row*, percussion flakes

5.14 Pachuca pressure bifacial thinning flakes in the intensive collection: *top two rows*, early pressure flakes; *bottom two rows*, late pressure flakes

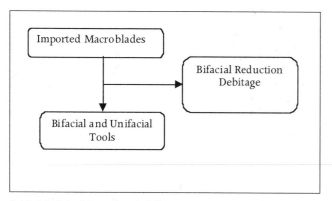

5.15 Model of Otumba obsidian procurement and reduction

mulating testable hypotheses, which can be addressed by future stratigraphic investigations. This has been, after all, the logical progression of field research over the last thirty years. Unfortunately, studies of Teotihuacan's lithic industries have not yet addressed the issues I have raised here with stratigraphic investigation.

What is fortunate, however, is that use of the lithic technology approach makes it possible to use surface collections to make reliable inferences about how obsidian was imported and reduced in the San Martin complex. As it stands now, we can only use the data we have at hand. The San Martin collections discussed in this chapter are complete enough to inform us not only about the industries represented, but also how the physical properties of the stone affected its use.

The form in which Pachuca obsidian was imported is a question that cannot be satisfactorily answered at this time. Nevertheless, the surface data indicate that it was used for the entire range of core-blade and bifacial manufacturing activities. The key question is whether the percussion reduction of Pachuca macrocores took place in the San Martin workshops. I have argued that the types and frequencies of percussion core-blade artifacts are consistent with this suggestion. If so, it would seem that at least some Pachuca macrocores (as opposed to polyhedral or prismatic cores) were imported into the complex.

The San Martin surface collections indicate that Pachuca obsidian was used for both pressure core-blade and biface reduction. Furthermore, I think that many of the Pachuca bifacial and unifacial tools were made from Pachuca macroblades. Accordingly, Clark (1986:70) has suggested that Pachuca obsidian was imported as polyhedral cores for the core-blade specialists (Clark 1986:70) and macroblades for the bifacial specialists (figure 5.17).

It is also possible, however, that the import of Pachuca macrocores could have supplied the San Martin craftsmen with polyhedral cores and macroblades (figure 5.16). This would have tied the core-blade and biface industries together in what I have called the linked-sequence model of production. Both the polyhedral-macroblade and macrocore import scenarios were possible and are not mutually exclusive.

The San Martin data indicate that Otumba obsidian was used primarily for biface reduction. The artifacts in the collections indicate that the core-blade reduction of Otumba obsidian was relatively unimportant. This may relate to the physical properties of Otumba obsidian that make it unsuited for reduction with pressure core-blade techniques (Spence et al. 1984:97). Most of the Otumba material, therefore, was probably imported from the

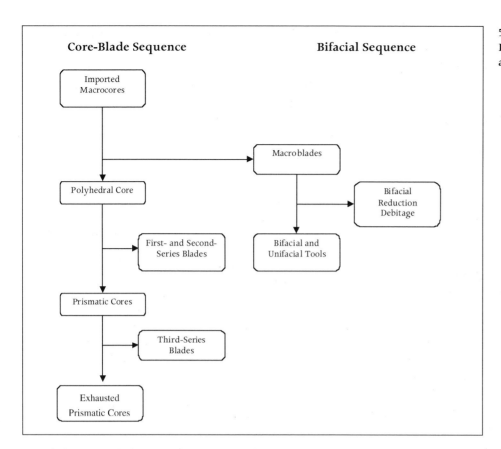

Core-Blade Sequence   **Bifacial Sequence**

Imported
Macrocores

Macroblades

Polyhedral Core

Bifacial
Reduction
Debitage

First- and Second-
Series Blades

Bifacial and
Unifacial Tools

Prismatic Cores

Third-Series
Blades

Exhausted
Prismatic Cores

5.16 Linked sequence model of Pachuca obsidian procurement and reduction: Scenario 1

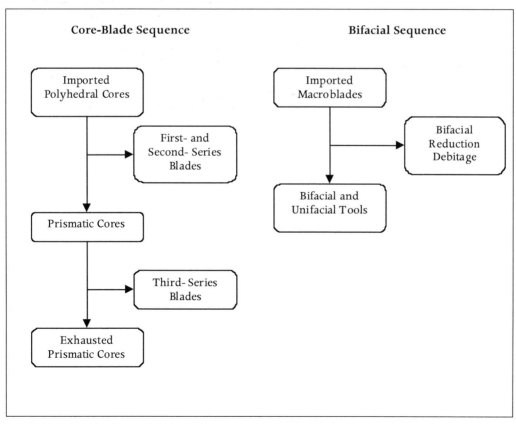

Core-Blade Sequence   **Bifacial Sequence**

Imported
Polyhedral Cores

Imported
Macroblades

First- and
Second- Series
Blades

Bifacial
Reduction
Debitage

Prismatic Cores

Bifacial and
Unifacial Tools

Third- Series
Blades

Exhausted
Prismatic Cores

5.17 The separate sequence model of Pachuca procurement and reduction: Scenario 2

quarry in the form of macroblades (figure 5.15). These were used to make the large bifacial and unifacial tools. The Otumba cobbles do not appear to have been intensively used in the San Martin complex because they were too small for making macroblades.

The San Martin data also indicate that the craftsmen in each workshop were involved in both the core-blade and biface industries. This would indicate a generalized strategy of stone tool manufacture, where craftsmen did not specialize in only one set of reduction techniques. The other workshop collections I have examined from Teotihuacan indicate that this may have characterized the skills of many stone tool craftsmen in the city (Andrews 1999).

Although the lithic technology approach allows us to draw inferences from surface collections, future excavations of the Teotihuacan workshops are an absolute necessity. Models of raw material import and production cannot be satisfactorily evaluated until we have collected technologically representative samples from subsurface contexts. In addition, more technological studies of the Classic-period artifacts at the Pachuca quarry are needed. Only then can we begin to reconstruct a comprehensive understanding of obsidian craft production at Teotihuacan.

ACKNOWLEDGMENTS

First and foremost, I thank Kenneth Hirth for his patience and diligent review of the previous versions of this manuscript. In addition, I am indebted to Michael W. Spence for providing access to the intensive artifact collection and permitting me to continue a project he started many years ago.

I also appreciate the support of George Cowgill, Pedro Baños, and Seferino Ortega, who enabled me to analyze the extensive collections in San Juan Teotihuacan. The valuable help provided by Gerardo Gutierrez on the maps is also greatly appreciated. Also, many thanks to Alejandro Sarabia for photographing the biface artifacts. Finally, I thank Neil Murray and Timothy Murtha for the Photoshop wizardry they applied to the figures.

NOTES

1. Interior flakes are usually associated with the early stages of macrocore shaping and are used to remove prominent ridges in preparation for blade removal. Early interior flakes exhibit thick triangular to rhomboidal cross sections and are generally linear to irregular in plan view. Late interior flakes have thinner often undulating rhomboidal cross sections and more regular to expanding plan views.

2. Many of the flakes may have been removed by left-handed knappers if the Mesoamerican pressure flaking technique replicated by Gene Titmus (personal communication, June 1996) was used at the San Martin complex. Using this technique, left-handed knappers would have produced flakes that sweep to the left. If this is true, then as much as 44% (N=80) of the Otumba and 28% (N =59) of the Pachuca early and late bifacial thinning flakes may have been removed by left-handed knappers (table 5.7). If these percentages reflect the "handedness" of the San Martin craftsmen, the number of left-handed individuals would have been high compared to the 10% that is typical of most human populations (McKeever 2000).

3. Prismatic core fragments and spent cores have been reported in non-workshop contexts at Teotihuacan. Storey (1985) suggests that these were obtained from the workshops and may have been reduced by craftsmen who went door to door making blades from cores curated at individual compounds.

CHAPTER SIX

Production and Distribution of
Obsidian Artifacts in Western Jalisco

Michael W. Spence, Phil C. Weigand, and
Maria de los Dolores Soto de Arechavaleta

The highland lake basins of western Jalisco (figures 6.1, 6.2) have been the scene of a number of important cultural developments (Weigand 1974, 1985, 1993a, 2000). Although now largely extinct, these lakes in the past formed the focal points for a large indigenous population that was concentrated along their margins and on the first few terraces above them. From west to east they include the Laguna de San Marcos, Laguna de Palo Verde, Laguna de Etzatlan (or Magdalena), Laguna Colorada, and Laguna de Teuchitlan (or La Vega). Each offered an important set of aquatic resources and would also have served as a medium for canoe-born communication and exchange among the surrounding communities. The rich land around them provided the agricultural basis for increasingly large and complex societies.

Obsidian was an important resource and was readily available throughout the highland basins of western Jalisco. The type of obsidian processing found at sites in the region reflects what Hirth and Andrews (chapter 1) refer to as *proximate source* production activity. Obsidian procurement, processing and distribution played a significant part in local economic systems, and in some periods it became a major item in external trade. This chapter examines the development of obsidian production systems in the region over twenty-five centuries. The technological variation visible over time and space will be described, and the factors contributing to it will be discussed. Particularly important among these factors are the location and quality of the sources, the role of regional elites in production and distribution, the training and experience of the knappers (and, for that matter, of the consumers), and the size and distribution of the consuming population.

The material described here derives from numerous surface collections made by Weigand and his associates during their extensive survey of the region. The collections were analysed by Spence in 1977–1979 and 1987. However, understanding of the large feature 83 workshop of Teuchitlan is based largely on the survey and excavation conducted there by Soto de Arechavaleta (1982, 1990). A preliminary assessment of our findings has been published

6.1 Archaeological sites and areas of west Mexico.
Illustration prepared by Michael Spence and Kate Dougherty

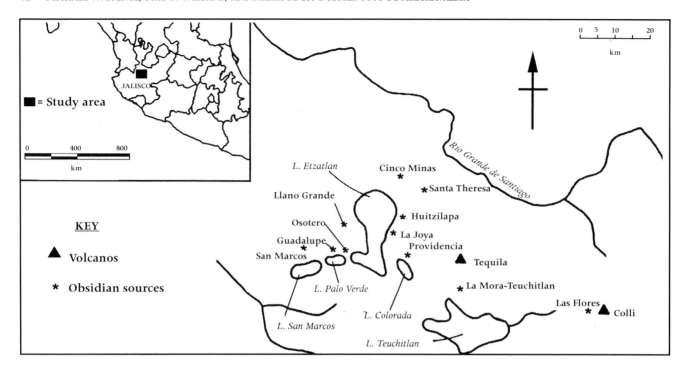

6.2 Pre-Hispanic lakes and obsidian sources of the highland lakes region, Jalisco. *Illustration prepared by Michael Spence and Kate Dougherty based on an original by Phil Weigand*

(Spence et al. 1980; see also Weigand 1993a:203–209).

The chronology followed here has been discussed in more detail elsewhere (Weigand 1989, 1990a, 1990b, 2000). The Formative period is represented by the San Felipe (1000–300 BC) and El Arenal (300 BC–200 AD) phases. These are followed by three Classic period phases: Ahualulco (200–4200 AD), Teuchitlan I (400–700 AD), and Teuchitlan II (700–900 AD). The Postclassic period includes the Early Postclassic Santa Cruz de Barcenas phase (900–1250 AD) and the Late Postclassic Etzatlan phase (1250 AD–Conquest). Because the collections are from the site surfaces they frequently encompass material from more than a single phase. Much of the discussion will thus be in terms of the periods, though reference will be made where possible to particular phases in order to clarify developments within a period.

Obsidian Sources in Western Jalisco

There are a number of different obsidian sources in the region (Cárdenas García 1992:47; Weigand and García de Weigand 1994). Surveys have identified over thirty obsidian outcrops, of which at least twelve show pre-Hispanic exploitation. Michael Glascock of the University of Missouri Research Reactor Center has chemically characterized most of these, some quite extensively, and has developed a data bank that will play an important role in further studies

of the region (for example, Darling and Glascock 1998). However, our source assignments of the materials discussed here are based largely on visual criteria rather than on any form of technical analysis. Fortunately, some sources produce obsidian that is distinctive enough to allow reliable visual identification. One such source is the La Mora-Teuchitlan deposit (group T), located just beyond the Teuchitlan habitation zone (figure 6.2; Breton 1902). This major source produces a high-quality obsidian (here termed group T) that was widely used in the Classic period (table 6.1). The quarry area includes a lot of debris, many hammerstones, and a number of large core preforms and macrocores, but very few refined cores or other products. Analyses of the chemical structure of this obsidian have been presented by Cobean et al. (1971:Table 2), Cobean et al. (1991), Zeitlin and Heimbuck (1978), Trombold et al. (1993:257–258, Table 1), Pollard and Vogel (1991), Weigand and García de Weigand (1994:Figs. 5-6), and Darling and Glascock (1998).

The La Joya source (group J) produces an equally fine obsidian, one that can also be visually identified with some confidence (table 6.2). It is located on the east side of the Laguna de Etzatlan basin and extends over a considerable distance, with well over a thousand distinct exploitation loci (figures 6.1, 6.2; Weigand and Spence 1982; Weigand and García de Weigand 1994). Most of these are open quarry operations, but actual mines with chambers may also occur. The principal items found there are core preforms and macrocores. The only pre-Hispanic architecture in the quarry area is a small platform at its southern

Table 6.1 Obsidian groups and sources

Group	Source	Associated major workshop	Characteristics
T	La Mora-Teuchitlan	Feature 83	Fine quality: semitranslucent blue black
J	La Joya	Las Cuevas	Fine quality: semitranslucent golden brown
B	Unknown	Unknown	Fine quality: semitranslucent green
G	Various	Unknown	Variable quality: grey, black, red and black

edge, overlooking the lake. The concentration of core preforms and macrocores near the platform suggests that it was a collection point for material intended for shipment to the associated island workshop at Las Cuevas. The source has been extensively analysed by J. Michael Elam and Michael Glascock of the Missouri University Research Reactor (Weigand and García de Weigand 1994:Fig 4). Pollard and Vogel (1991) have also analysed samples.

A fine, dark green obsidian (group B) appears in minor quantities at a number of sites but appears to have come from beyond the region. Its distribution in archaeological sites suggests a source somewhere in eastern Nayarit or northwestern Jalisco. Stross et al. (1976:Table 13.1) refer to it as the "San Blas" variety, and characterize it chemically on the basis of site rather than source samples. Pollard and Vogel (1991) analysed a number of specimens that they describe as green, but none of their identified sources correspond to this material; it may be of their "unknown 3" or "unknown 4" group. Ericson and Kimberlin (1977) identify a green variant at Amapa and assign it to a source near Magdalena, Jalisco, but more evidence is needed before this can be accepted. Group B obsidian is visually similar to, but somewhat more opaque than, the material from the Pachuca source area of central Mexico.

Besides the group T and group J fine obsidians, there are a number of grey, black, and red-black obsidians occurring naturally at several points in the region. Although suitable enough for the production of unifaces, bifaces, and even some cores and blades, they are often not of fine enough quality for the consistent and reliable pressure manufacture of prismatic blades. Since we are unable to visually distinguish them with any reliability, we shall refer to them here collectively as group G. Sources included in this group are San Marcos, Osotero, Llano Grande, Providencia, and Santa Theresa, among others (figure 6.2). There is evidence of exploitation, often extensive quarrying, at many of these sources. Several have been characterized by composition analyses (Stross et al. 1976; Cobean et al. 1971; Cobean et al. 1991; Ericson and Kimberlin 1977; Zeitlin and Heimbuck 1978; Pollard and Vogel 1991).

The wide distribution of obsidian sources in the region means that there would have been a deposit within reach of

Table 6.2 Blade widths (mm) of the 1987 sample of J material

	N	Range	Mean	sd
PERCUSSION BLADES				
All	238	11–82	34.5	12.1
Subset with cortex	27	11–58	37.9	12.3
PRESSURE BLADES				
All	105	10–42	18.6	4.9
First-series	32	14–42	22.1	5.6
Second-series	3	22–25	23.7	1.5
Third-series	70	10–25	16.8	3.5

most of the inhabitants, one that they could exploit either directly or through relatively close and secure trade relationships. Only two of these deposits, the sources of groups T and J, however, produced obsidian good enough for the consistent manufacture of fine prismatic blades. Accordingly, the limited availability of these obsidians presented the region's inhabitants with a situation in which a few strategically located communities could restrict access to an important natural resource. Nevertheless, this potential economic advantage was not always exploited as effectively as it could have been.

Obsidian Typology

The artifact categories emphasized in the analysis are waste, cores, blades, bifaces, and unifaces. Waste is rather broadly defined. It consists largely of the discarded by-products of obsidian artifact manufacture and refinement. However, it also includes some expedient tools created by using, and sometimes casually retouching, amorphous pieces of obsidian. Bifaces include knives, projectile points and drills produced by bifacial working or by the careful edge trimming of selected flakes or blades. The uniface category comprises a variety of well-formed scrapers, gravers and gouges created by edge retouching or by more extensive working over one face (figure 6.3a-c).

Blades have been divided into two major categories; flake blades and fine blades. They are defined largely on the basis of their dorsal morphology. Flake blades are more roughly formed and generally broader, with somewhat

6.3 Obsidian artifacts: *a-c,* endscrapers/gravers (group T obsidian); *d-e,* exhausted prismatic cores (group J obsidian); *f,* fine blade (group J obsidian); *g-i,* side-notched points on fine blades (group J obsidian). Sites represented: *a,* Teuchitlan; *b-c,* Ahualulco; *d,* Cruz de Cristo Rey; *e,* Las Cuevas; *f-h,* Etzatlan; *i,* Santiaguito. *Illustration prepared by Joseph Parish.*

irregular edges and dorsal arrises. Fine blades are narrower and highly regular in form, with linear dorsal arrises (figure 6.3f). This distinction is intended to facilitate classification of the fragmented and highly incomplete blades that form the bulk of the surface-collected blade material.

Some collections were reanalyzed in 1987 applying the technologically based framework developed by John Clark

and others (Clark 1990a, 1997; Clark and Bryant 1997; Sheets 1975; Healan et al. 1983; Santley et al. 1986). Clark's replicative experiments demonstrate that the various stages of core manufacture and reduction create identifiable products. The initial working of blocks or nodules produces decortication flakes (largely covered on one surface by the original cortex) and macroflakes. As reduction and refinement proceed, fewer pieces show cortex, the area of cortex diminishes on those pieces that do have it, and the flake scars on the core face become more closely and regularly spaced. Reduction during this stage is by percussion flaking, with the blades so produced becoming progressively narrower and more linear. These blades were all placed in our flake blade category. They have the somewhat irregular edges and dorsal faces that are the criteria for the category, and ventrally show the large bulbs, eraillure flakes, and rippled surfaces that characterize percussion reduction.

Eventually the core reaches the polyhedral stage, when it has been refined sufficiently to allow a shift from percussion to pressure flaking. The first ring of blades removed at this point, first-series blades, will display the characteristics of pressure removal on their ventral faces (should these be complete enough to characterize) but dorsally will still retain the scars of prior percussion-removed blades. Most of these were thus also placed in our flake blade category, based as it is on the dorsal characteristics of the blades. First-series blades do not run the full length of the polyhedral core, and so tend to be shorter than other blades.

The next rings produce second-series blades. These extend the full length of the core and are characterized dorsally by the presence of the irregular percussion blade facets only on their more distal segments, those not removed by the preceding first-series blades. Second-series blades can therefore be quite difficult to identify in highly fragmented surface collections. They probably appear in both our flake blade and fine blade categories.

The succeeding third-series blades were usually the ultimate goal of the process. Their dorsal surfaces display only the highly regular and linear facets left by the pressure removal of previous blades. These, and probably some of the second-series blades, would fall in our fine blade category.

The 1987 reanalysis included 633 obsidian items from fourteen of the Postclassic surface collections. All of the reanalyzed material is of group J and there were 354 blades in this material. The reanalysis established that our flake blade category includes all of the percussion blades produced from the early stages of core reduction to the polyhedral core stage. It also includes the first-series blades constituting the initial ring of blades to be removed by pressure.

The second-series blades are more difficult to identify as mentioned above. Some would have been included in the flake blade category, whereas others would have been placed with the fine blades. In fact, only three of the sample of 354 blades in the 1987 reanalysis were identified as second-series. This is clearly far less than would be expected and reflects the difficulty of recognizing this artifact in fragmented surface collections. In sum, then, our flake blade category includes all the blades produced by percussion and the first ring produced by pressure, with perhaps some of the second-series pressure blades. Our fine blade category has no percussion blades but most of the pressure blades, probably including most of the second-series blades. To a considerable extent, therefore, our flake blade/fine blade morphological distinction parallels the percussion/pressure technological distinction.

The metric data on the blades reanalyzed in 1987 are presented in table 6.2. Because the material was recovered from surface collections, only four complete blades were found: three percussion blades with lengths of 86, 117 and 188 mm, and one first-series blade 37 mm long. Consequently, the table 6.1 data only reflect information on blade width. As expected, these show a progressive reduction in width from percussion through third-series blades. In the percussion category, those exhibiting dorsal cortex reflect a greater width indicating that they may have been removed earlier in the sequence of core refinement.

Two observations are relevant for table 6.2. First, the collections come from a variety of sites occupying different points in the Postclassic production and distribution networks; some sites may have received more refined materials than others. Second, only the group J material was reanalyzed. It is possible that other materials, with other qualities, would produce somewhat different measurements (for example, Clark 1990a: Table 11).

Formative Period

Only two small collections can be assigned to the San Felipe phase (1000–300 BC). One is from the San Felipe site, to the west of the Laguna de San Marcos, and the other is from the Laguna Colorada site, near the southwest edge of the Laguna Colorada (figure 6.4). The artifacts include flake blades and bifaces. Fine blades are not present, though this may merely be owing to the small size of the collections.

The projectile points include stemmed, convex base, and lenticular forms. The striking platforms of the flake blades have level, single-facet surfaces indicating that core platforms were created by single or, at most, a few large flake scars. None of the pecking or grinding of core platforms observed in later periods was present in these collections, though again the small size of the samples may be responsible.

Even in this early period, the group J obsidian was being circulated in the region. It formed the bulk of the material from the Laguna Colorada site, not surprising in view of the site's proximity to the La Joya source (figures 6.2, 6.4). Even the bifaces there were made from J flake blades. However, J obsidian also formed a respectable minority of the San Felipe collection, accounting for two of the three flake blades and 17% of the waste. At San Felipe it seems to have been channelled preferentially into core-blade production, while the prevalent group G obsidian was used for point production. The group B obsidian forms only a minor part of the material from this phase, represented by two waste pieces from the San Felipe site.

The only collection that can be assigned to the following El Arenal phase (300 BC–200 AD) is the one from the surface of the El Arenal site in the Laguna de Etzatlan basin (figure 6.4; Corona Nuñez 1955). Among the 75 pieces of obsidian collected are end and side scrapers, convex base and lenticular points, and two flake blades. Group J obsidian is minor, accounting for only about 5% of the waste (but also one of the two blades and one of the three bifaces). Group B obsidian formed 9% of the waste and one of the four unifaces. The rest of the material was group G, probably from one or more of the sources in that part of the region.

El Arenal phase tombs have produced evidence for the production of a variety of ground obsidian ritual items or ornaments (Weigand 2000:49). Among other forms, these include crosses, lunates, circles, pendants, beads, earspools, and probable mirror backs. The skill involved in their manufacture implies the presence of specialists.

Protoclassic Period

At a number of sites materials from the El Arenal phase and the following Early Classic Ahualulco phase (200–400 AD) are mixed on the surface. Continuities in settlement location and cultural traits, for example shaft tomb architecture, make it difficult to assign materials from these sites to a specific phase. This led to the creation of a distinct taxonomic category, the Protoclassic period. Although its applicability in other respects is unknown, it does serve as a convenient unit for the discussion of these mixed lithic collections. Included are materials from the Aguacero, Limoncillo, Osotero, and other sites, and from some parts of the Oconahua, Laguna Colorada, and San Juanito sites (figure 6.4).

The artifacts include cores, flake blades, fine blades, bifaces, and unifaces. The platforms of the flake blades are generally single-facet surfaces. However, a few pecked-and-ground platforms occur. Stemmed and lenticular point forms are most common, but side notched, straight base and convex base specimens are also present. Most of the unifaces are endscrapers. Group J obsidian is dominant on sites in the Laguna Colorada area and is present as a minor variety on many of the other sites. It was circulated to some degree as unaltered raw material but more commonly in blade form. Group B obsidian is absent.

Two obsidian concentrations, both small and not very dense, were identified on the surface of the Laguna Colorada site. One of these was oriented toward the processing of a poor-quality group G obsidian, which may have come from the Providencia source. In the other concentration, located in a different part of the site, group J obsidian was the principal material. Also, in some of the Protoclassic elite shaft tombs of the region macrocores or large polyhedral cores are found, usually three or four per tomb. One tomb at Las Cuevas produced the skeleton of an elderly male, a set of figurines, and seven cores of group J obsidian (Weigand and Spence 1982:183). The largest of the cores was about 45 cm high by 25 cm in diameter at the platform.

The size and low density of the obsidian concentrations indicate that specialization in obsidian working was on a small scale, probably by individual part-time knappers. The presence of cores in elite tombs further suggests that these knappers may have been attached to the households of some of the regional elite, producing goods for exchange with other communities or for distribution within their own. Furthermore, some new procedures are now in evidence. In some cases core platforms are being heavily pecked and ground. These techniques were being employed in the El Arenal phase in the production of the obsidian ornamental/ritual items described above. It is possible that at that time they were also being applied to cores, though our small sample from that period offers no examples. In any case, this was certainly happening in the Protoclassic period, that is to say, by the following Ahualulco phase, if not in the El Arenal phase.

The appearance of platform grinding in the region is much earlier than in central Mexico, where it does not occur until the Postclassic period (compare Santley et al. 1986:126–129). Hirth and Andrews in chapter 1 (figure 1.3), suggest that one of the technological factors that may affect obsidian artifact production is the presence in the group's repertoire of suitable techniques that were being applied to other media or other tasks. Unfortunately, in the case of

Jalisco, our data are not yet sufficient to say whether grinding was first done on the ornamental/ritual items and then transferred to core production, or vice versa. In either event, it was well established in the repertoire of specialists by the Protoclassic period.

There is another consideration here: The pecking and grinding of platforms adds additional time and effort to the process of core manufacture. On the other hand, it breaks the surface tension of the obsidian, which would facilitate the removal of blades and provides a textured surface that permits seating of the pressure tool on the core platform (Crabtree 1968; Sheets 1978). This increased control over the process of blade removal may be most crucial in the pressure reduction stage. An experienced specialist may not require this sort of advantage. The cores that left the workshops, however, were probably being reduced after that point by less skilled knappers, perhaps even by ordinary members of the community whose experience with obsidian working was comparatively limited. The prepared core platforms would undoubtedly have improved their chances of successfully producing good prismatic blades. Specialists, then, may have added this step to their procedures for the sake of the consumers, rather than to facilitate their own work. Viewed in this light, platform grinding may be an indicator of a well-developed system of specialized production for relatively unskilled consumers.

Classic Period

In the Teuchitlan I phase (400–700 AD) there was a major population shift into the basin of the Laguna de Teuchitlan. Much of this expanded settlement was in the form of habitation zones, areas of dispersed but essentially continuous occupation that extended for several kilometers. These contrast with the smaller and more nucleated habitation sites that characterized earlier and later periods. The Teuchitlan habitation zone is an extensive area of diffuse occupation that forms an arc along the north side of the lake (figure 6.4; Ohnersorgen and Varien 1996:Fig. 2). Weigand (1990a:39) suggests a population of twenty to twenty-five thousand for the zone. It includes a number of widely dispersed precincts of civic-ceremonial architecture, each of which probably served as the ritual and administrative center for the population immediately around it. Foremost among these is the Guachimonton precinct in the west end of the zone. The extent and scale of the Guachimonton architecture indicates its political primacy within the zone and perhaps also in the larger polity that may have existed in the highland lake basin region at that time (Weigand 1990a; Beekman 1996, 2000; compare Ohnersorgen and Varien 1996).

The source of group T obsidian lies only about three kilometers northwest of the Guachimonton precinct (Weigand 1990a:49). As the nearest major precinct in the Teuchitlan habitation zone, Guachimonton would have controlled access to this obsidian deposit vis-à-vis other precincts located further to the east. Immediately west of, and associated with, the Guachimonton precinct is feature 83, an area of 0.6 ha with a cover of debris of group T obsidian (Weigand 1996: Fig.4). The data in table 6.3 are from a surface collection of feature 83 by Weigand. More recent intensive investigation by Soto de Arechavaleta (1982, 1990) has provided a much larger body of material and a better understanding of the feature 83 workshop. The various artifact categories tend to cluster differentially in the site, suggesting that several specialists had worked obsidian there (Soto de Arechavaleta 1990). The raw material entered the site in the form of macrocores (*sensu* Clark and Bryant 1997). Decortication flakes are relatively rare in the assemblage, but macroflakes, macroblades and blades are numerous. The workshop output consisted of cores, refined to the point of prismatic blade production, but also of macroflakes, macroblades and blades (figure 6.5). Some of these were intended for use without further modification while others were exported as preforms for a variety of tools (Soto de Arechavaleta 1982:128–130). Finished bifaces and unifaces were produced from them in only one small part of the workshop, area E (Soto de Arechavaleta 1990:240).

The blades show a variety of platform treatments (Soto de Arechavaleta 1982:145, Fig. 26). Platforms of cortex are a minority, representing only 4% of the combined surface collected and excavated material. Single-facet platforms are found on 21% of the blades, while multifacet platforms are found on 37% of them. The *picoteado-abrasado* category, which combines pecked and ground platforms, represents another 37% of the total.

Pecking and grinding are usually sequential, not alternative, procedures of core platform preparation. The cortex of the obsidian blocks sometimes formed a suitable platform, at least for the initial reduction of the core. More often, though, a platform was prepared by a lateral blow, creating a single large flake scar (Clark 1990a: Fig. 1, nos. 2,3; Clark and Bryant 1997:113). This was apparently done at the quarry. In some cases the platform was either created by, or further refined by, multiple percussion flaking to produce a multifacet platform. It is also possible that some of what we call multifacet blade platforms are actually pecked, the platforms offering too small a field to determine the precise nature of the alteration. Also, the use of these procedures may vary somewhat from knapper to knapper,

Table 6.3 Sources of obsidian in the Teuchitlan habitation zone

	Feature 83		Guachimonton area		Other areas	
	T	G	T	G	T	G
Waste	35	1	73	4	59	44
Cores	6		9		2	2
Flake blades	126	1	191	8	63	39
Fine blades	114		155	1	78	3
Bifaces	6		15	5	28	46
Unifaces	8		19	1	45	31
Bifaces on blades	5		8		7	5
Bifaces on flakes	1		1			2
Unifaces on blades	4		12	1	35	25
Unifaces on flakes	3		5		7	6

the "idiosyncratic artisan practices" noted by Hirth and Andrews in figure 1.3. Their differential distribution in the feature 83 workshop is consistent with this interpretation (Soto de Arechavaleta 1990:227).

In any event, pecking of the platform started relatively early in the process of core reduction and seems to have been done to further level the platform and to prepare it for grinding. The grinding took place later in the sequence (figure 6.5). A sample of flake blades of group T obsidian from throughout the Teuchitlan habitation zone has a mean width of 53.6 mm (N=27) for those with pecked platforms and 38.1 mm (N=7) for those with ground platforms. Soto de Arechavaleta (1982:135) noted that pecking and grinding were sometimes confined to the margins of the core platform. Also, fine blades have mostly ground platforms. Although a few pecked fine blade platforms were observed, none are cortex, single-facet, or multifacet.

Most of the ceremonial precincts of the Teuchitlan habitation zone include minor obsidian concentrations that suggest localized craft activity. For example, at one point on the platform of the Caldera de los Lobos precinct, there is a concentration about 5 m in diameter (Weigand 1976:206, Fig. III). The small size and moderate density of the concentration suggest a single specialist, probably attached to the local elite household. Most of the collected material is group T obsidian: nine waste pieces, eleven blades (eight flake, three fine), four bifaces and two unifaces. Most of the blades show use, and so any obsidian working that was done here may have been incidental to some other activity. The material entering the site, and the similar concentrations noted in some of the other precincts, probably came through the Guachimonton precinct from the feature 83 workshop in the form of cores, flake blades,

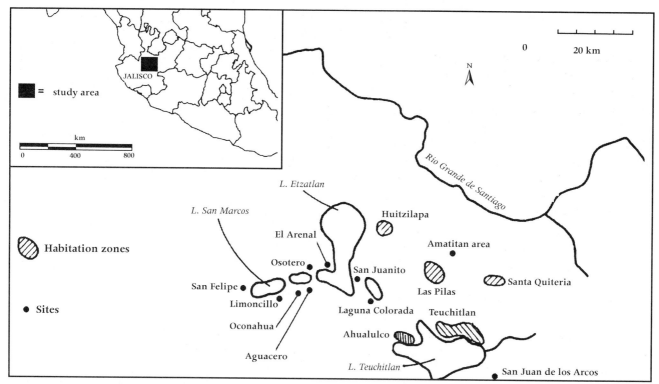

6.4 Habitation zones and sites of the highland lakes region, Jalisco, during the Formative and Classic periods. *Illustration prepared by Michael Spence and Kate Dougherty based on an original by Phil Weigand*

and fine blades. The bifaces and unifaces in the other sectors are usually manufactured from flake or fine blades (see table 6.3, but note figure 6.3a, an endscraper and graver on a waste piece of T). The majority of these blade preforms are flake blades; only about 10% of the unifaces and bifaces on blades were made from fine blades.

Guachimonton, however, did not totally dominate the supply of obsidian to the other parts of the Teuchitlan habitation zone. There is a significant amount of group G obsidian in these other areas, contrasting with its rarity in the Guachimonton area, suggesting that they had independent access to other sources, albeit not always of as high-quality as the group T material (only 4 of the 51 group G blades from Teuchitlan are fine blades). Weigand has located one exploited G source south of the San Juan de los Arcos site. Variants of group G material are also available at the north end of the group T source area and at a number of other points around the Tequila volcano (figure 6.2).

The presence of the obsidian concentrations in the civic-ceremonial precincts indicates that the distribution of group T obsidian in the Teuchitlan habitation zone was conducted through the elites of the various precincts. The elite of Guachimonton, which was closest to the source and

which included the rich feature 83 workshop, would have controlled this system. Hence, obsidian may have played an important role in the political structure of the community (Weigand 1976:214). The major qualification here is that we do not know how the group G material was circulated. It may have passed through the same elite system, reinforcing elite control, but there is reason to believe that the two distribution systems were not totally isomorphic. Group G material forms 38% of the obsidian in the areas of the Teuchitlan zone beyond Guachimonton but only 19% of the material in the Caldera de los Lobos precinct concentration and only 3.9% in the Guachimonton area.

There are several other Classic-period habitation zones in the region beyond the Teuchitlan zone. One of these, the Ahualulco zone, covers 586 ha and lies to the west of the Teuchitlan zone (figure 6.4; Weigand 1974; Ohnersorgen and Varien 1996: Fig. 2). Its major occupation was during the Ahualulco and Teuchitlan I phases, overlapping to a considerable degree with that of the Teuchitlan zone. The residents of Ahualulco relied primarily on group T obsidian (table 6.4). The only other obsidian used in any quantity there was group J material, which accounts for only about 8% of the total (82 of 1,004 artifacts at Ahualulco) and was apparently imported as unprocessed raw material.

Ahualulco may have had relatively free access to the La Mora-Teuchitlan source. Although the Teuchitlan habitation zone was closest to the source and physically controlled access to it, there is no indication that this advantage

Table 6.4 Sources of Classic period artifacts by habitation zones

	Teuchitlan			Ahualulco			Santa Quiteria			Las Pilas			Amatitan area			Magdalena			San Juan de los Arcos		
	T	G	J	T	G	J	T	G	J	T	G	J	T	G	J	T	G	J	T	G	J
Waste	132	48		542	9	64	20	52		28	12			31	4		5	12		8	
Cores	11	2		21							1							1			
Flake blades	254	47		142	3	10	13	21		22	8			6	2			3		6	
Fine blades	233	4		35	1	1	2	2		2										1	
Bifaces	43	51	3	22	6	3	3	4		1	3				1			1		2	
Unifaces	64	32		61	5	2	9	4		6	1			3	1		1	2		2	
Bifaces on blades	15	5	1	5				1		1											
Bifaces on flakes	1	2		5																	
Unifaces on blades	47	26		19	2		4	3		4				3	1			1		1	
Unifaces on flakes	12	6		41	3	2	3	1		2							1	1			
Total	812	223	4	893	29	82	54	88	0	66	25	0	0	43	9	0	7	21	0	20	0

was exploited. Technological data indicate that the Ahualulco obsidian was not processed through the feature 83 workshop. There are considerable quantities of waste at Ahualulco, including a number of large pieces and a limited amount of decortication material. The obsidian was probably processed into macrocores at the quarry, then moved to Ahualulco for further refinement. Whether this initial processing and transport was done by people from the Teuchitlan zone or by people travelling to the source from Ahualulco is unknown.

The refinement at Ahualulco did not follow the same sequence of procedures as in feature 83. The core platforms were treated differently. Twenty-one cores were collected from the Ahualulco zone, all of which were still in the percussion stage of reduction (table 6.4). Eleven had identifiable platforms, of which two were partially faceted with some cortex, eight had single-facet platforms, and one had a multifaceted platform; none are pecked or ground (table 6.5). This is similar to the treatment of the flake blade platforms, which include only one pecked (hammered) and no ground specimens. The platforms of only five fine blades were identifiable, all of which are ground. Apparently, therefore, the Ahualulco core platforms were not usually pecked as a separate stage in the reduction sequence and were ground only when they became polyhedral cores reduced with pressure.

The edge of the core platform was also altered at both Teuchitlan and Ahualulco. The negative scar of the bulb of percussion, created by the removal of a blade, left an overhang or lip at the edge of the platform. This lip was often removed to ensure fuller control over subsequent blade removal. In the earlier stages of core reduction, when the percussion technique that was employed left extensive overhangs, a relatively forceful technique was used to remove them. Blade platforms from this stage often show the results of battering and heavy flaking at their dorsal edges (table 6.6). As the blades became smaller and more regular, with less pronounced overhangs, the platform edges were either left unaltered or were removed by a more controlled technique, abrasion or retouching. The Guachimonton area blades show this shift through the percussion reduction of the core. In the Ahualulco zone, on the other hand, the more controlled abrasion was applied later in the sequence, when small flake blades and prismatic blades were being produced, and often no removal of the overhang was attempted during percussion reduction (table 6.6).

The more casual core reduction procedures displayed at Ahualulaco may reflect the presence there of less skilled, and less specialized, obsidian workers. This is suggested also by the more irregular form of Ahualulco cores and the low ratio of fine to flake blades (table 6.4). No workshop concentrations have been identified in the Ahualulco zone, and the artifact forms vary somewhat from one sector to another through the zone (figure 6.3b-c). Obsidian working was probably still a household activity there, rather than

Table 6.5 Classic period core-blade technology for group T and group G obsidian

	Teuchitlan		Ahualulco		Santa Quiteria		Las Pilas	
	T	G	T	G	T	G	T	G
CORE PLATFORMS								
Cortex	1	1						
Cortex and facets			2					
Single facets	1		8					1
Multiple facets			1					
Hammered	1							
Ground	1							
FLAKE BLADE PLATFORMS								
Cortex	6	2	11		3		2	
Single facets	7	7	52	1	5	7	7	2
Multiple facets	1		9		1		6	4
Hammered	32		1		1		1	
Ground	22				1			
FINE BLADE PLATFORMS								
Cortex					1			
Single facets								
Multiple facets								
Hammered	3						2	
Ground	12		5		1			

Table 6.6 Classic period platform overhang treatment

	Guachimonton		Ahualulco	
	Qty	%	Qty	%
FLAKE BLADES				
Battered	9	40.9	22	40.7
Unaltered	4	18.2	20	37.0
Abraded	9	40.9	12	22.2
FINE BLADES				
Battered				
Unaltered	3	16.7		
Abraded	15	83.3	5	100.0

being done by specialists.

Santa Quiteria and Las Pilas are extensive Classic-period zones to the north of the Teuchitlan area in the canyon of the Rio Santiago (figure 6.4; Weigand 1990a; Ohnersorgen and Varien 1996: Fig. 2). In both a mixture of group T and group G obsidian was used (see table 6.4). No workshop areas were identified at either site but waste was widespread at both, suggesting obsidian working at the household level. The presence of primary group T waste and the paucity of pecked-and-ground platforms on flake blades

(table 6.5) show that as with Ahualulco, group T material was not processed through the Guachimonton area before its arrival at Santa Quiteria and Las Pilas.

Although Santa Quiteria and Las Pilas are similar in several respects, they differ in some important ways. Las Pilas relied more on group T obsidian than did Santa Quiteria (table 6.4). Also, at Las Pilas there was more emphasis on core preparation techniques that produced multifacet platforms.

Sites in the area around the modern town of Amatitan include Protoclassic and Teuchitlan I components (figure 6.4; Ohnersorgen and Varien 1996: Fig. 2). They are treated here as a single unit, partially contemporaneous with the Teuchitlan habitation zone. Most of the obsidian used in these sites was group G material, although some group J obsidian was imported as unprocessed raw material. Group T obsidian is not present in the collected material (table 6.4).

The Magdalena area encompasses a number of sites within the Huitzilapa habitation zone and includes the area immediately to the west, along the east shore of the Laguna de Etzatlan (figure 6.4). They include both Protoclassic and Teuchitlan I components. Group J obsidian is dominant, apparently entering the sites in unprocessed form. Group G obsidian is secondary, and group T material is absent.

The San Juan de los Arcos site is located near the eastern end of the Laguna de Teuchitlan and has Protoclassic- and Classic-period occupations (figure 6.4; Ohnersorgen and Varien 1996: Fig. 2). No group T or J material appears in the collections (table 6.4). They consist of group G obsidian from unknown sources, perhaps including the source found by Weigand to the south of the zone. There is also a small collection from Tala Mill, a Teuchitlan I and II site just north of San Juan de los Arcos. It includes one group T waste piece, a group G flake blade worked bifacially, and a prismatic core of group G obsidian. Although the Classic-period material available at the time of analysis from the easternmost part of the region was very limited, it indicates that the area was largely beyond the distribution sphere of group T obsidian.

Obsidian source utilization in the Classic period

The La Mora-Teuchitlan source was heavily exploited in the Classic period, supplying the obsidian for a number of communities in the region. Foremost among these was the extensive Teuchitlan habitation zone. The elite of the Guachimonton precinct apparently dominated the exploitation, processing and circulation of this obsidian throughout the zone, with subordinate elites forming the secondary links in the distribution network. Despite their proximity to the source and the presence of attached specialists, however, the elite of Guachimonton did not exploit their advantage as fully as they might have. For one thing, the inhabitants of the other sectors of the Teuchitlan habitation zone had access, albeit usually on a lesser scale, to other sources of obsidian. Also, the elite of Guachimonton may not have restricted access to the La Mora-Teuchitlan source by other habitation zones in the region, even though the easiest and most direct route to the source required passage through the Teuchitlan zone. These other zones either exploited the source directly, received macrocores from Teuchitlan, or exploited other sources in the region. They did not get material that had been processed through the feature 83 workshop. If Guachimonton dominated the rest of the region politically, itself an uncertain proposition (Ohnersorgen and Varien 1996:118–119), it did not do so through control over the processing and distribution of obsidian.

The group T obsidian did not circulate beyond the region in large quantities. Of 109 obsidian items collected from Carmelita, a Classic- and Postclassic-period site in the Sayula area of Jalisco (figure 6.1), visual examination indicates that only one waste piece and three projectile points are of group T obsidian. The three points are all Classic-period stemmed types, similar to others from Carmelita but different from the Teuchitlan types. At most, they indicate the importation of small amounts of group T raw material from the highland lake basins and its local working into artifact form. Chemical analyses based on the University of Missouri Research Reactor data base suggest a relatively broad but sparse distribution of group T obsidian. Some of this material has been identified in sites dating about AD 600–1450 in Juchipila Valley of southern Zacatecas, in the area around Las Ventanas (figure 6.1; Weigand et al. 1999). Another sample reported by Darling and Glascock (1998:355–356) includes four group T prismatic blades, three from the site of Teul (figure 6.1) in the Tlaltenango Valley and one from a site in the Chapalagana Valley. Group T obsidian also appears in the Banderas Valley of coastal Jalisco (Joseph Mountjoy, personal communication, September 1998) and at the large site dating to AD 200–700 in Comala, Colima (Jorge Ramos and Lorena López, personal communication, June 1998). Juan Rodrigo Esparza López (1999) also has identified it at sites in the *tierra caliente* of Michoacan, about 150 km southwest of Patzcuaro, where it is most strongly represented in the early Classic but also occurs in lesser amounts in the Postclassic. It thus seems that modest amounts of group T material, often in the form of blades made in feature 83, circulated beyond the highland lake basins region (Darling and Glascock 1998:355).

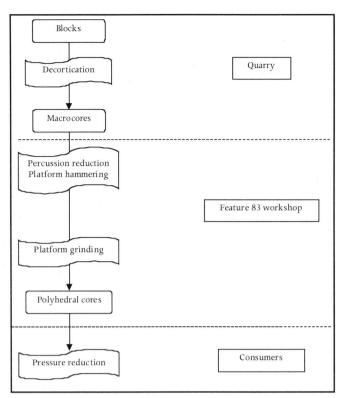

6.5 Core-blade reduction sequence for group T obsidian during the Classic period. *Illustration by Erick Rochette*

Some foreign obsidians appear in the highland lake basins, but the quantities are small. A fine blade of Pachuca source obsidian was collected from the Capilla precinct of the Teuchitlan habitation zone, not far from Guachimonton. This blade, and some Thin Orange sherds from Ahualulco, suggest limited contact with Teotihuacan (Weigand 1990a:29; 1992). Only eight items of group B obsidian were found in the Teuchitlan habitation zone, and the Magdalena, Santa Quiteria, and Amatitan zones produced only one item each of B material.

Postclassic Period

After AD 900 the Teuchitlan habitation zone was partially abandoned and the population became somewhat more evenly distributed throughout the highland lake basins, with major concentrations in the Laguna de Etzatlan basin and at the east end of the Laguna de Teuchitlan (figure 6.6; Weigand 1990b, 1993b). Because many of the sites have components of both the Santa Cruz de Barcenas (AD 900–1250) and Etzatlan (AD 1250–Conquest) phases, it is often difficult to assign the surface collections unequivocally to one or the other phase. For the most part, then, the Postclassic will be discussed as a single unit.

One very large and intensive workshop is located in the Las Cuevas site, a large Postclassic community on an island

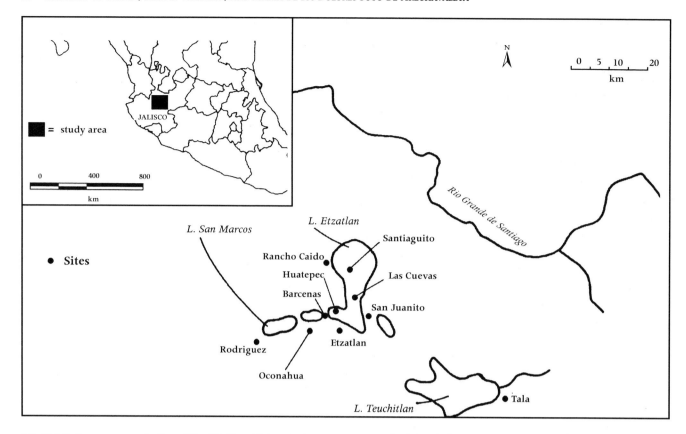

6.6 Habitation zones and sites of the highland lakes region, Jalisco, during the Postclassic period. *Illustration prepared by Michael Spence and Kate Dougherty based on an original by Phil Weigand*

near the east shore of the Laguna de Etzatlan (figure 6.6; Breton 1902:268; Weigand and Spence 1982; Weigand and García de Weigand 1994:12–13). Its size and intensity exceed feature 83. The size of the site as a whole and the public architecture, which includes a citadel-like structure on the ridge dominating the settlement, indicate a major Postclassic center. Etzatlan, another large Postclassic center on the south shore of the lake, claims to have conquered the area about AD 1500.

Obsidian workshop debris is distributed irregularly over some 15 ha of the Las Cuevas site (though this debris includes downslope wash). Much of the debris is related to core-blade production (figure 6.3e). Virtually all of the obsidian is of group J and had been transported there from the nearby La Joya quarry as macrocores (figure 6.2; Weigand and Spence 1982). The material from the densest part of the workshop area is primarily core-blade production detritus, but, toward the margins of the area, blades were being further processed into scrapers and projectile points. In some cases only the edges of the blades were retouched, while in others most or all of both faces were worked. The points are generally side notched or

unnotched (straight, concave, or convex base), although some stemmed specimens occur. Of the twenty-two unifaces manufactured from preform blanks, eighteen were made from flake blades and four were made from flakes (table 6.7). All of the twenty-one bifaces manufactured from preform blanks were made from blades: thirteen from flake blades and eight from fine blades.

Etzatlan, the Postclassic center on the south shore of the lake, had a population of about seventeen thousand (Weigand 1993b). Although much of the obsidian collected from the site dates to the Etzatlan phase, a few Santa Cruz de Barcenas collections from the area indicate that the local assemblages of both phases were similar. The obsidian is largely of group J.

The waste, not very common, consists generally of by-products of the later stages of core reduction. The bulk of the collection consists of blades (table 6.7). Cores are rare, and most points and scrapers were manufactured from blades. The only two cores from Etzatlan are both prismatic cores, producing fine (pressure derived) blades. The majority of the blades are fine blades (figure 6.3f), and the flake blades do not include many of the larger and less regular ones that characterize the earliest stages of core refinement. The mean width of the Las Cuevas flake blades, which include workshop material, is 37.9 mm (N=115, s.d.=13.3), while the mean width of the Etzatlan flake blades is 29.8 mm (N =153, s.d.=9.6).

Several features of the Etzatlan obsidian assemblage indicate that the inhabitants of Etzatlan received their obsidian from the Las Cuevas workshop, importing it as blades and as macrocores that had already been reduced to near the polyhedral stage. The smaller size (mean width) of the Etzatlan flake blades reflects their removal at an advanced stage of core reduction, and fine blades are more common than flake blades in the assemblage. Platform treatment at the two sites is very similar (tables 6.8, 6.9). Points and scrapers at both sites are generally the same forms, suggesting that some were imported as finished artifacts from Las Cuevas. The appearance of some forms at Etzatlan that are not found in the Las Cuevas assemblage, plus the presence at Etzatlan of unfinished specimens, indicate, however, that some of the Etzatlan bifaces and unifaces were manufactured locally from imported blades. Of the twenty-four unifaces manufactured from preform blanks, seventeen were made from blades (all flake blades) and seven were made from flakes. Of the thirty-four bifaces manufactured from preform blanks, eight were made from flake blades, twenty-four from fine blades (figure 6.3g-h), and two from flakes.

The high percentage of Etzatlan bifaces made from fine blades (75%) represents a marked shift, both from the previous Classic-period pattern and from the contemporary Las Cuevas workshop that supplied the material. A couple of factors may have contributed to this shift. For one, the manufacture of a point on a fine blade, frequently accomplished by limited retouching of the edges, requires little skill and time investment. The services of a specialist would not be necessary. Also, the points manufactured in this way tend to be narrower, thinner, and lighter in weight. It is therefore possible that this shift in technology was meant to accommodate a growing reliance on the bow and arrow.

The extensive use of Las Cuevas cores and blades was not limited to the Etzatlan area. Several other Postclassic sites to the west and northwest, here collectively designated as the Western area, also brought in quantities of group J material from Las Cuevas (table 6.7). One, Oconahua, was an important Postclassic center west of Etzatlan (figure 6.6). The Rodriguez site was a village at the western end of the region, while Barcenas was a village with some evidence of fortifications at the west end of the Laguna de Etzatlan (figure 6.6). Huatepec was a large village on an island near Barcenas. There are also a few other small Postclassic sites to the north of the Laguna de Palo Verde and Laguna de San Marcos, but these have not been included in the Western area category. These other sites used little or no group J material, relying almost exclusively on local G sources. Their small community size and more peripheral location, as well as the ready availability of group G obsidian, explain their lack of incorporation into the group J distribution sphere based on Las Cuevas.

Some of the Western area sites include earlier Protoclassic- and Classic-period components, raising the possibility that some of the obsidian (particularly of group G) collected from their surfaces might not be Postclassic. This is especially true for Oconahua, which had an extensive earlier occupation. It was consequently necessary to determine whether the group J obsidian there was Postclassic material or the reflection of an earlier procurement system. To this end four group J fine blades from Oconahua were submitted to Clement Meighan for obsidian hydration analysis at the UCLA Obsidian Hydration Laboratory. The band thicknesses are 2.3, 2.3, 2.7 and 3.0 microns (Clement Meighan and Glenn Russell, personal communication, 1979). Other hydration analyses of group J material from the region provide a framework for the interpretation of the Oconahua measurements. Several readings from Etzatlan, which is primarily Late Postclassic, fall largely in the 2.3 to 3.4 micron span, while those from an Early Postclassic site are mostly 2.8 to 3.6 microns, and a Las Cuevas series ranges from 1.8 to 6.5 microns (Meighan et al. 1974:150–151, 177–180; Meighan 1978:Table 3; Meighan and Vanderhoeven 1978:90; Spence 1974, 1978). The Oconahua blades, then, are certainly Postclassic, and probably Late Postclassic for the most part.

The very low group J waste counts, the absence of J cores, and the high proportions of J blades (with fine blades predominating) in Western area assemblages, as well as the platform preparation techniques, indicate that group J obsidian was imported primarily in blade form (tables 6.7–6.9). Much of the obsidian used in the Western area, however, came from the closer group G sources, which account for the great majority of the waste and most of the bifaces and unifaces. The projectile points made from group J blades are mostly of local forms, typologically distinct from the Las Cuevas and Etzatlan points but similar to Western area points of G material. A few group J forms are similar to those of Las Cuevas and Etzatlan and may have been imports, but these seem to have been the exceptions.

Two Postclassic collections from the southeastern part of the Laguna de Etzatlan basin, south of the La Joya source, are combined in the Southeast basin category (tables 6.7–6.9). There are high proportions of J waste and some group J cores were collected (figure 6.3d; table 6.7). Probably these Southeast basin communities brought obsidian in directly from the La Joya source as macrocores, rather than obtaining it through Las Cuevas in polyhedral core or blade

Table 6.7 Postclassic period artifacts by area and source

	Las Cuevas		Etzatlan		Western area		Southeast basin		North basin	
	J	Other	J	Other	J	Other	J	Other	J	Other
Waste	73	24	92	91	9	224	27	3	253	27
Cores	51	1	2			2	2		3	
Flake blades	115	3	187	9	50	37	9	1	63	4
Fine blades	57		243	6	84	9			24	
Bifaces	31	19	43	16	6	41	3		15	14
Unifaces	26		25	9	6	21	4	1	33	3
Bifaces on blades	21	2	32	1	3	5	3		9	2
Bifaces on flakes			2	4		7			3	4
Unifaces on blades	18		17	16	2	4	5	1		4
Unifaces on flakes	4		7	5	2	15	3		29	3
Total	396	49	650	157	162	365	56	6	432	61

Table 6.8 Postclassic period core-blade technology by area and source

	Las Cuevas		Etzatlan		Western area		Southeast basin		North basin	
	J	Other	J	Other	J	Other	J	Other	J	Other
CORE PLATFORMS										
Cortex										
Single facets	1					1			1	
Multiple facets	2								1	
Hammered	2									
Ground	28									
FLAKE BLADE PLATFORMS										
Cortex			1			3			2	
Single facets	9		2	3	5	11	1		14	
Multiple facets	2		3			1			4	
Hammered	28		36		8			3		
Ground	13		20		4				4	
FINE BLADE PLATFORMS										
Cortex			1							
Single facets										
Multiple facets	1									
Hammered	3		6	1	3					
Ground	10		42		15	2			3	

Table 6.9 Postclassic period platform overhang treatment

	Las Cuevas	Etzatlan	Western area	Southeast basin	North basin
J FLAKE BLADES					
Battered	25	27	7	1	12
Unaltered	3	1		1	5
Abraded	12	11	7	2	4
J FINE BLADES					
Battered		3			
Unaltered	1	9	1		
Abraded	5	34	14		1

form. This is not unexpected in view of their proximity to the La Joya source. The platform treatment (tables 6.8, 6.9) and the biface forms, however, are similar to those of Las Cuevas and Etzatlan, indicating a close cultural affiliation among these sites.

The North basin category (tables 6.7–6.9) includes a number of sites along the northwest edge of the Laguna de Etzatlan basin and on a nearby island: Santiaguito, Rancho Caido, and others (figure 6.6). The majority of the obsidian on these sites is group J, most of which is waste from the earlier stages of the reduction sequence. Twenty-eight percent of the waste fragments included cortex; and in a majority of these, the cortex covered half or more of one face. Cores are present and blades, particularly flake blades, are common (table 6.7). All of the group J unifaces were manufactured from flakes rather than blades. These data suggest that the North basin inhabitants obtained obsidian as largely unaltered raw material rather than importing it from Las Cuevas. They would have been able to reach the La Joya source without having to pass through Las Cuevas.

Blade manufacture in the North basin sites seems to have been more casual than it was in other areas (tables 6.8, 6.9). Fine blades are less common than flake blades, and most of the flake blades have single-facet platforms. Platform overhangs were usually left either unaltered or were removed by relatively forceful techniques rather than controlled abrasion. These differences in core preparation are supported by differences in projectile point types, most North basin points being of local types rather than of types dominant in the southern part of the basin (see, however figure 6.3i).

Only the eastern end of the region did not rely on group J obsidian. The Tala site, an independent and powerful Postclassic center at the time of the Conquest, lies at the east end of the Laguna de Teuchitlan (figure 6.6). The small collection from the site includes no group J obsidian. The waste consists of two group T and ten group G pieces, and the blades of one T and six G flake blades. All four bifaces are made of group G obsidian. Like the Classic period, the inhabitants of this area focussed primarily on local sources rather than depending on imports from the west.

In sum, a major distribution sphere was centered on the large Las Cuevas workshop. Etzatlan and other Postclassic communities south of the Laguna de Etzatlan relied heavily on cores and blades of group J obsidian imported from Las Cuevas. A number of Western area sites were also importing Las Cuevas blades but were able to temper their reliance on Las Cuevas to some degree by also exploiting the closer group G sources. The location of Las Cuevas was a major factor contributing to its role in obsidian processing and

trade in these areas. On an island near the La Joya source, it would have dominated access to this obsidian from the west and southwest and would also have been in an excellent position to participate in canoe trade on the lake. Its dominant role, however, was not because of location alone. Another important factor in such trade networks is the presence of artisans with the skill and experience to consistently produce superior products. The development of these skills depends in part on relatively unrestricted access to high-quality raw material that can be used to learn them (chapter 1; Darling 1993:251). Such artisans were clearly present at Las Cuevas.

Obsidian source utilization in the Postclassic period

The dispersed Postclassic settlements of the Southeast basin area were close enough to La Joya to exploit it directly, although their technological and typological similarities to Etzatlan and Las Cuevas show that they were not a distinct unit. The North basin communities not only obtained their J obsidian directly from the source but also had somewhat different core preparation procedures and a number of distinct point types. They probably formed a unit apart from, and perhaps even opposed to, the one centered on Las Cuevas and Etzatlan.

The distribution of artifacts, primarily fine blades, of group J obsidian extends well beyond the highland lakes region. Although much of what follows is based largely on visual identifications, samples tested by neutron activation analysis from the Carmelita site and from Chalchihuites and Loma San Gabriel sites in Durango have confirmed their reliability (Jane Pires-Ferreira, personal communication, December 1971). Ten of the 109 items from the Carmelita site are of J obsidian: two waste pieces, two flake blades, two fine blades, three points, and one endscraper. These, however, may include both Classic and Postclassic artifacts. Thirteen of twenty-one fine blades from the Schroeder site and eight of eleven fine blades from Navacoyan (figure 6.1) are of J material (Spence 1971:23–24), indicating a high proportion of J material among the imported fine blades of the Guadiana branch of the Chalchihuites culture (Las Joyas through Calera phases, AD 850–1350; Foster 2000). Three of five fine blades from Loma San Gabriel sites are of group J obsidian: one from Hervideros, one from La Manga (only 2 km from Schroeder), and one from Santa Ana, near the Chihuahua border (figure 6.1). All of the observable platforms on these Chalchihuites and Loma San Gabriel specimens were ground.

Group J fine blades are relatively common in material excavated by Stuart Scott from Postclassic sites in the Marismas Nacionales of coastal southern Sinaloa and northern Nayarit (figure 6.1). There is no group J waste from these sites. Also, slightly over half of the fine blades but none of the obsidian waste recovered by Joseph Mountjoy from a Late Postclassic component in the San Blas area of Nayarit (site 43), are made of group J obsidian. This obsidian was imported as fine blades, rather than as cores or unprocessed raw material (Mountjoy 1978:137). Eight of eighteen artifacts from a middle Cerritos phase context of the Amapa site were assigned by trace element analysis to group J, as was one blade from a late context of the Morett site in Colima (Ericson and Berger 1976; Ericson and Kimberlin 1977: Table 2). Finally, six fine blades of J obsidian were observed in Ana María Alvarez's material from Higuera de Abuya, a Postclassic site near Culiacan, in northern Sinaloa (figure 6.1).

The Las Cuevas site was apparently contributing fine blades to a widespread Postclassic exchange network, the Aztatlan sphere (Kelley 1986, 2000). Other materials circulating in this sphere included turquoise, marine shell, copper, polychrome ceramics, and other kinds of obsidian. Among the latter was the group B material, the high-quality green obsidian believed to come from an unidentified source somewhere in northwestern Jalisco or eastern Nayarit. Again, our visual identifications of group B material have been confirmed by trace element analyses of Chalchihuites culture (Jane Pires-Ferreira, personal communication, December 1971) and San Blas area collections (Fred Stross and Frank Asaro, personal communication, January 1976). Group B material at the Schroeder site includes two blades, two waste pieces, a point, and an expanded base drill (Spence 1971). In site 43 of the San Blas area most of the waste and slightly under half of the blades are of group B obsidian. It has also been identified in primarily Postclassic contexts at Ixtlan del Rio, Nayarit (Stross et al. 1976:253-254) and is common in both waste and blades in the Marismas Nacionales sites. It is not common, however, in the highland lake basin region of Jalisco, except for Las Cuevas. There it forms 13% of the waste and 12% of the bifaces and probably entered the site through its links with the Aztatlan network. There are a number of reciprocal trade goods present at Las Cuevas including turquoise, marine shell, and polychrome pottery from various regions of west Mexico (Weigand and Spence 1982:186).

Conclusions

By the Protoclassic period there is evidence of a low level of specialization in the production of obsidian artifacts in the region, probably consisting of only a few part-time artisans attached to elite households. Nevertheless, the fundamental techniques for a highly effective core-blade production system were already in evidence. Cores were reduced by percussion and then by pressure, the platforms pecked and ground to facilitate blade removal. We cannot say whether the technique of grinding was first applied to ritual/ornamental items of obsidian and later to cores or whether it developed first as a core production technique and was then applied to the ritual/ornamental goods. It seems likely that the same artisans were involved in both sorts of production, but even this cannot be established with the available data.

We are equally unsure about the structure of the craft at this time. The evidence from the tombs indicates that elites were appropriating at least some of the output of the artisans. However, we do not yet know if they also passed some on through exchange relationships to more distant elites or if they controlled its wider distribution within their own communities. Either would have implications, though not the same ones, for the further development of the craft.

By the Classic period, things are clearer. A much more well-defined and intensive workshop was present in the Teuchitlan zone, closely associated with the monumental civic-ceremonial architecture of the Guachimonton precinct, apparently the administrative and ritual center for the zone. Products from the workshop, in the form of macrocores, polyhedral cores, and blades of a variety of sizes were distributed throughout the zone via a network of lesser elites. Core platforms had been prepared in the feature 83 workshop by pecking and then grinding to facilitate their further reduction by less practiced knappers, though even in feature 83 some inter-artisan variability in this respect is apparent. This sort of variability may indicate that specialization was less than full-time (chapter 1).

Some of the lesser elites in the other Teuchitlan precincts apparently also had attached artisans, but these secondary production loci do not seem to have been very intensive. It is not clear whether these artisans were processing the obsidian for the use of their elite patrons, for distribution to residents in the rest of that particular sector of the zone, or whether in fact they were largely consumers of obsidian tools used in other production tasks.

The expanded population of the region offered a larger number of obsidian tool consumers for obsidian products. It can be seen that this increase in demand was not met by any radical changes in the organization of production, but rather by an intensification of the pattern of attached specialists that had already existed since at least the Protoclassic period. Also, most of the inhabitants of the Teuchitlan zone seem to have been capable of doing some obsidian working of their own and had access to material from alternative sources, to judge by the wide distribution in the zone of group G obsidian.

Furthermore, other extensive habitation zones in the region did not rely at all on the feature 83 workshop but apparently took their obsidian directly from the source. The elite of the Guachimonton precinct would have been able to control access to the La Mora-Teuchitlan source but do not seem to have exploited this advantage to its fullest extent. It is not clear whether this potential for monopolistic control was even sociopolitically possible for this non-capitalist society. It may be that the regional populations viewed the obsidian as a communal resource, open to all, or that the Guachimonton elite saw their greatest political advantage in an open-handed largesse. Torrence (1986:40–42) has shown that monopolistic control of a source can be a difficult and costly strategy. It would be helpful if we knew the identities and allegiances of the miners at the source, those who quarried the obsidian and did the initial processing. At present we cannot say whether they were simply temporary visitors from a variety of communities who obtained materials for their own use (for example, Torrence 1986:214–216); local inhabitants who processed obsidian for trade to other communities; or agents of the Guachimonton elite, ensuring that the elite received some benefit from the quarrying and exchange of the obsidian. We can say, however, that the Guachimonton elite did not take the further step of requiring that outgoing materials be processed through their workshop.

Finally, there is evidence that some group T obsidian, often in the form of blades, moved beyond the region. Some of this material was probably processed through the feature 83 workshop and distributed through the Guachimonton elite (Darling and Glascock 1998:355). The quantities, however, were modest. The long distance exchange of group T artifacts does not seem to have been a major factor in the structuring of the Classic-period production system.

The Postclassic period presents a rather different situation. A large workshop (considerably larger than feature 83) developed at Las Cuevas, a major Postclassic community that had some degree of control over the nearby La Joya obsidian source. The absence of residential architecture in the quarry area indicates that the source was exploited directly from Las Cuevas (Weigand and Spence 1982). Charlton (1984) notes that a center can achieve its maximum economic potential when it dominates all aspects of the production sequence—mining, processing, and distribution. Las Cuevas was in this position with respect to a number of other communities to the south and west, which depended on it for obsidian products, particularly cores and blades. The blades were then locally worked

further to form points, scrapers, and other articles.

The Las Cuevas artisans had a well-established set of procedures for core and blade production. The initial reduction to the macrocore stage was done at the quarry area. These macrocores were then further refined in the workshop, their platforms pecked and then ground to facilitate blade removal, probably in anticipation that further refinement would often be done by less skilled knappers who would appreciate this advantage. Evidence from other sites in and beyond the region shows that the workshop output was circulated in the form of both cores (at or near the polyhedral stage) and blades. In fact, some of the more distant sites, like the Schroeder site of Durango (figure 6.1), received only blades. This may simply be because, without local sources physically suitable for blade manufacture, artisans there could not develop the skills necessary for the effective reduction of cores (Darling 1993:251).

Las Cuevas played an important role in the trade network, which covered a much larger area and involved a much greater flow of materials than did the trade networks of the Classic period. The La Mora-Teuchitlan obsidian in the Classic period circulated in modest amounts, and even some of this may not have involved finished products or the participation of the Guachimonton elite. Also, people in these areas usually had access to other sources of obsidian, in some cases of equivalent quality. La Joya source material, on the other hand, appears frequently in Nayarit, Sinaloa, and Durango, even as far north as the Sonora and Chihuahua borders. The extent of the Aztatlan network, and the major role of Las Cuevas, is also revealed in the reciprocal goods that appear at Las Cuevas, where they are more common than in other Postclassic sites in the highland lakes region: turquoise from New Mexico (Harbottle and Weigand 1992), glazed and polychrome ceramics from New Mexico (Weigand 1977, 1979, 1993a:227–235), group B obsidian, marine shell, Iguanas-Roblitos polychrome pottery from the Nayarit coast, polychrome wares from the Lake Chapala area of Michoacan and the Autlan area of Jalisco, and some polychrome pottery that is probably from Sinaloa (Weigand and Spence 1982). Many of these areas had no adequate obsidian sources of their own and so must have relied on this trade for the finished obsidian products they desired. In some of these sites the quantities of imported blades were small enough that we believe they probably served some special function, like elite display, which would not have generated a large flow of material (Spence 1971:24). In others, like the San Blas and Marismas Nacionales areas (figure 6.1), however, the imported blades seemed to have been used in daily utilitarian tasks, which would have created a considerable and constant demand.

The prominent role of Las Cuevas as a major terminal point in the Aztatlan network, then, would have created a more consistent and predictable demand for products of La Joya obsidian. Furthermore, this demand would often have been for finished prismatic blades in the absence of local artisans skilled enough to reduce cores themselves. When this was added to the local demand from other Postclassic communities in the region, it was sufficient to support some highly skilled artisans at Las Cuevas who produced a consistent product (chapter 1). It appears, therefore, that the addition of considerable external demand to the preexisting local needs encouraged the development of a more intensive level of specialization at Las Cuevas than we saw in the earlier Guachimonton complex. Another factor was the stimulus offered by the wide range of exotic goods available through the Aztatlan network.

Comparison of this west Mexico sequence with the development of obsidian production in the Valley of Mexico, particularly Teotihuacan, highlights some important distinctions. Some of these, perhaps most of them, may be owing to the differences in scale of the two systems, the population in the Valley of Mexico being much larger and more urbanized. In the earliest stages of specialized obsidian production at Teotihuacan, in the Patlachique and Tzacualli phases, the artisans were not attached to the elite but rather worked in independent households to supply obsidian products to the population as a whole (Spence 1984). This offered a large consuming population for their output. It also directed their production toward goods for everyday utilitarian tasks, rather than for the display and exchange needs of the elite. This difference in the structure of demand between the systems of western Jalisco and Valley of Mexico clearly had important implications for the size and degree of specialization of the two industries (Hirth and Andrews, this volume).

Provisioning constraints, particularly the accessibility of obsidian sources and the degree of control over them, were also of fundamental importance (chapter 1). In the case of the highland lakes region of Jalisco the nearest obsidian sources were but a few kilometers from the major communities and provided obsidian well suited for core-blade production. For Teotihuacan, on the other hand, the nearest source was 16 km away, and the obsidian there was fine for biface and uniface production but not as well suited to core-blade manufacture. Material better suited for core-blade production came from the Pachuca source area, 50 km to the north, well beyond the easy access of most Teotihuacanos (Charlton and Spence 1982). These distances discouraged the development of a widespread,

unspecialized system of household production motivated by those who procured and worked obsidian on their own. Conversely, it encouraged the development of specialists who could establish procurement links with the source areas and who therefore had access to enough raw material to maintain their skills and train apprentices (chapter 1). By the Tlamimilolpa phase the Teotihuacan state had politically incorporated the Pachuca source area and set up a procurement system (Spence et al. 1984).

Even in the Postclassic period, Las Cuevas was, in contrast, unable or unwilling to fully control access to the nearby La Joya source. Northern basin and Southeast basin communities exploited it directly, similar to what a number of earlier Classic communities had done to the La Mora-Teuchitlan source. These differences in procurement were probably the result of both the distance from local communities to the sources, which would have affected direct exploitation by consumers, and the sizes of the consumer populations, which would have affected the degree to which artisans could have committed their time and resources to building procurement networks and manufacturing artifacts.

There is also the role of external trade to consider in these two regional systems. Although Teotihuacan carried on an extensive trade with other parts of Mesoamerica, that trade played little or no role in the structure of the Teotihuacan obsidian production system, which was aimed primarily at provisioning the large population in central Mexico under Teotihuacan rule (Spence 1996). In contrast, we are suggesting that the development of the Las Cuevas system was based in part on its role in extraregional exchange. Obsidian specialists had worked under the aegis of elite households since the Protoclassic period; so, when long distance trade was elaborated among the elites of west Mexico, these artisans were inevitably drawn into it.

Finally, grinding core platforms had developed by the Protoclassic period in west Mexico but not in the Valley of Mexico until the Postclassic. Despite the scale of production in Teotihuacan and the circulation of cores from the workshops to consumers who may have had relatively limited skills, cores were never ground in the Teotihuacan workshops. It seems likely, though, that Teotihuacan specialists would have been aware of the technique. Teotihuacan had contacts with the Gulf Coast, where platforms were ground at that time. That it was not done in Teotihuacan may simply reflect some sort of local conservatism, adherence to a well-established technological tradition (Sackett 1990:33) or one of those regional idiosyncrasies mentioned by Hirth and Andrews (chapter 1). It certainly was not because of any impeding physical property of the Pachuca obsidian, which later Aztec artisans always ground (Spence 1985).

ACKNOWLEDGMENTS

Weigand and Soto de Arechavaleta's work in the region was supported by the Mesoamerican Cooperative Research Fund of Southern Illinois University Museum, the State University of New York Research Foundation, and the Instituto de Investigaciones Antropológicas of the Universidad Nacional Autónoma de México. Spence's research was conducted on a Canada Council Leave Fellowship. We are grateful to Ana María Alvarez, the late Clement Meighan, Joseph Mountjoy, Otto Schondube Baumbach, and Stuart Scott for their help with various aspects of this work. A particular debt is owed to Celia García de Weigand for her constant and valuable participation in the fieldwork; it was she who first identified and brought to our attention the important feature 83.

CHAPTER SEVEN

Provisioning Constraints and the Production of Obsidian Prismatic Blades at Xochicalco, Mexico

KENNETH HIRTH

STUDYING OBSIDIAN ARTIFACTS and their process of manufacture is a valuable approach for creating a better model and understanding of economic and political interaction during prehistory in Mesoamerica. This chapter attempts to first broaden our understanding of Mesoamerican core-blade technology by examining the production of obsidian prismatic blades at the site of Xochicalco, Morelos, Mexico (figure 7.1). Once this is accomplished, it will identify what I believe are the most important variables creating variation in Xochicalco's obsidian core-blade technology. The obsidian sample used in this study was recovered from stratigraphic excavations in five craft workshops operating during the Epiclassic period (AD 650–900) when the site underwent a major cultural florescence and grew to become one of the prominent influential city-states and conquest polities in central Mexico (Hirth 2000). Uncommonly good conditions of preservation made it possible to recover production residues in craft workshops from both activity surfaces and midden contexts; it is this material that is used in the analysis presented here.

In a technological study the analysis of flaked stone tools is based on the morphological attributes of the finished artifacts and the waste residues and other debitage produced during their manufacture and use. Since flaked stone tools are primarily fashioned using a reductive technology, archaeologists have at their disposal an approach that is not only a highly sensitive and reliable means of reconstructing past behavior, but also an approach that can be applied and independently replicated by investigators interested in the same problems. The lithic technology approach permits an accurate reconstruction of the types of artifacts produced, the types of materials with which they are made, and the sequence of production steps or behaviors used to produce

them. When technological features are examined from a sequential perspective they permit the investigator to reconstruct the stages of production through which an artifact has passed.

While reconstructions of ancient technologies are important in their own right, they also provide important information about the socioeconomic conditions of prehistoric societies. Study of the morphology and variation in flaked stone artifacts supplies valuable insights about the causes, constraints, and socioeconomic conditions that produced stone tools. A variety of conditions shaped the production of prismatic blades in Mesoamerica including the local availability of obsidian, the demand for craft goods, and the economic and political processes structuring the procurement and distribution of obsidian. Identifying the linkage between technology and these broader conditions provides the archaeologist with a means of investigating the political and economic forces that supported it. Technological studies have excellent potential for clarifying and differentiating between political and commercial forms of resource procurement, production, and trade.

While the potential of technological studies is great, the range of issues that can be discussed in any individual chapter are limited. Here I examine the small core prismatic blade production strategy found at Xochicalco and discuss its implications for an understanding of obsidian craft activity in central Mexico. Manufacturing activities at Xochicalco reflect that of a *distant source* production locale. Provisioning constraints seem to be particularly important in shaping Xochicalco's obsidian industry during the Epiclassic period. Obsidian was obtained from a restricted number of source locales at a significant distance from the site. Artisans in Xochicalco's workshops appear to have had limited access to obsidian and the production sequence

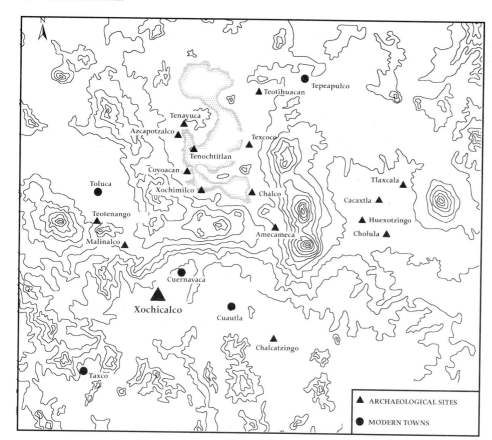

7.1 Location of Xochicalco and other important sites in central Mexico. *All illustrations prepared by the author*

used to produce prismatic blades was strongly shaped by the form and frequency with which obsidian entered the site. These two factors, the relative scarcity and form that obsidian entered the site also affected the type of training craftsmen received. The result is a distinctly regional production sequence at Xochicalco that emphasized: 1) the production of prismatic blades from small used and re-worked prismatic cores rather than large polyhedral cores and 2) the probable use of a small core, hand-held pressure technology for making prismatic blades (Flenniken and Hirth ND).

Xochicalco and its Obsidian Craft Industry

Xochicalco (figure 7.1) is a hilltop urban center located in the arid upland valleys of western Morelos 60 km southwest of Mexico City. Xochicalco grew to prominence between AD 650 and 900 when it conquered and integrated much of western Morelos into a centralized tribute paying domain. Epiclassic Xochicalco can be classified as a midsize urban center with a resident population of between ten and fifteen thousand persons. This population was concentrated on the slopes below and surrounding a hilltop administrative zone on the summit of Cerro Xochicalco. The impressive ceremonial architecture within this zone reflects Xochicalco's role as a regional political capital and influen-

tial religious center. Its intricate architectural plan and elaborate program of carved monumental art reflects a high degree of warfare and political competition during the Epiclassic (Hirth 1989, 1995a; Smith 2000a, 2000b). Archaeological excavations and the recovery of de facto artifact inventories on the floors of houses and temples throughout the site (Hirth 1995b) indicate that it was conquered, burned, and abandoned sometime during the middle to the late tenth century AD.

In 1993 stratigraphic excavations were conducted in five obsidian workshops within the Xochicalco urban core. Craft production at Xochicalco during the Epiclassic was organized primarily as domestic workshops with output intended for sale in the city's central urban market and in other towns and markets in the surrounding region. Some additional production also took place within the context of Xochicalco's central marketplace but the extent of production and whether this was carried out by some of the same individuals working in domestic contexts remains unclear.

Because obsidian does not outcrop naturally in Morelos, all the raw material worked in Xochicalco's workshops had to be imported from one of central Mexico's several source areas. Instrumental neutron activation analysis (INAA) was used to identify the obsidian sources employed to produce prismatic blades in Xochicalco's Epiclassic workshops.

These analyses indicate that the two major sources of grey obsidian imported to the site were Ucareo, Michoacan (64.7%), and Zacualtipan, Hidalgo (21.1%). Green obsidian from the Pachuca source was also used in prismatic blade production at Xochicalco (10.9%), as was grey obsidian from Otumba (1.2%) and another from an unknown minor source (2.1%). What is interesting in terms of source utilization is that sociopolitical conditions along trade routes rather than simple economic or energetic principles appear to have played an important role in determining the type and frequency of material used. Simple energetics would predict that the closest usable source of high-quality obsidian would be the most widely used. This, however, was not the case. Ucareo and Zacualtipan obsidian, which constituted 86% of the material utilized at Xochicalco, traveled 30 to 50% farther to reach the site (200–210 km) than would have been the situation if the Xochicalco craftsmen relied on closer sources such as Otumba (110 km) or Pachuca (155 km) to procure the bulk of their raw material.

Two hundred km can be used as an average provisioning distance for obsidian entering Xochicalco. This is a long distance under conditions of pre-Hispanic transportation technology (Hassig 1985; Sanders and Santley 1983) especially for something as heavy and bulky as natural stone. It is not surprising, therefore, to find that the lithic technology of Xochicalco's obsidian craft industry was governed by the quantity and form of obsidian that moved along trade routes entering western Morelos. The type of remains recovered in workshop production contexts suggests that Xochicalco craftsmen did not have direct access to the sources they relied upon but instead were dependent on obsidian reaching them as already shaped cores ready for the production of prismatic blades. In short, the production sequence at Xochicalco was strongly shaped by the obsidian entering the site as prefashioned cores. What developed at Xochicalco was a uniquely local production technology that emphasized: production of prismatic blades from small used and reworked prismatic blade cores rather than large polyhedral or macrocores, and the probable employment of a small core, handheld blade removal technology facilitating the production of small and narrow prismatic blades.

Summary of Xochicalco Prismatic Blade Production

The manufacture of an obsidian prismatic blade is part of a continual process beginning with the preparation of the core and ending with the removal of the finished blade. Although the lithic products and by-products produced along the way are all linked in a single sequential process, changes in production behavior produce morpho-

Table 7.1 Technological categories from prismatic blade production at Xochicalco, Morelos, Mexico

PERCUSSION TECHNIQUES: CORE SHAPING	
Macroflakes	0
Macroblades	0
Small percussion blades	15
PRESSURE TECHNIQUES: BLADE PRODUCTION	
First-series (1s) blades	17
Third-series (3s) blades	
Complete blades	11
Proximal segments	30,758
Medial segments	114,780
Distal segments	11,461
Plunging segments	1,758
Bidirectional blade segments	1,149
Third-series blade production by-products	
Overhang removal flakes	91
Languette flakes	469
Blade artifacts	
Hafted points	321
Eccentric blades	813
Notched blades	5,786
Pointed blades	3,507
Miscellaneous other blade artifacts	575
Blade artifact production by-products	
Snapped blade segments	1,454
Pressure and notch flakes	1,657
PERCUSSION AND BIPOLAR REJUVENATION DEBITAGE	
Faceted core-top fragments	2,273
Pecked and ground core-top fragments	1,742
Platform preparation debitage	53,126
Distal orientation flakes	3,879
Artifacts produced from rejuvenation debitage	260
BLADE CORES AND BLADE-CORE FRAGMENTS	
Exhausted prismatic blade cores	49
Bidirectional blade cores	5
Blade-core fragments	473
Total	236,429

logical divisions that make it convenient for analytical purposes to divide the process into stages of production. The major change that occurs during the reduction sequence is the shift from percussion techniques used in shaping the core to pressure techniques involved in removing prismatic blades (Hirth et al. 2000). Although a variety of models have been proposed for how reduction sequences are organized (Sheets 1975; Santley et al. 1986; Clark and Bryant 1997), all authors agree that the production by-products of percussion and pressure reduction are easily separable; macroflakes, decortication debitage, platform flakes, and macroblades are characteristic of percussion reduction, whereas irregular and regular prismatic blades reflect pressure techniques.

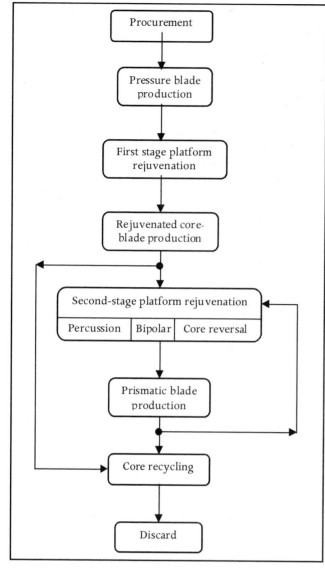

7.2 Model of pressure core reduction at Xochicalco

form where finished pressure blades can be removed. These are the dominant features of the assemblage:

- Third-series blade segments and the production by-products associated with their manufacture
- Blade artifacts made from prismatic blade segments and their associated production debitage
- Rejuvenation debitage associated with preparing a new platform on cores near exhaustion or to correct production errors
- Exhausted cores and core fragments

It appears that virtually all of the prismatic blades produced at Xochicalco were removed from already shaped prismatic blade cores. Obsidian apparently did not enter Xochicalco as either nodules or partially formed macrocores. Instead, obsidian was imported into Xochicalco as well-formed prismatic blade cores from which pressure blades had already been removed. These pressure cores entered the site with single-facet platforms and were rejuvenated as necessary to produce prismatic blades. Besides having the obsidian entering the site in a restrictive form, the fact that all the pressure cores were used *before* they reached Xochicalco suggests that they were procuring their obsidian from intermediaries who also may have been craftsmen rather than transport specialists coming directly from the source.

Figure 7.2 presents a model of pressure core reduction and rejuvenation at Xochicalco during the Epiclassic period. Three things are particularly striking about the prismatic blade reduction sequence at Xochicalco. First, all obsidian cores entering the site were used until they were completely exhausted, broken (figure 7.3), or recycled. Second, blade cores often underwent multiple platform rejuvenations to produce sets of distinctive debitage during the production process. Third, platforms on cores were primarily rejuvenated using pecking and grinding techniques that make it possible to distinguish the blades that were removed from imported cores with single-facet platforms from blades which were removed after rejuvenation. All three of these practices are compatible with an economizing production strategy designed to maximize the usage of a scarce commodity. Pecking and grinding for example, while being a labor-intensive practice is the most conservative and controlled means of rejuvenating core platforms. What is unusual about the Xochicalco reduction sequence is that prismatic blade cores were rejuvenated two to three times before disposal, which is a higher frequency than is found in other sites in Mesoamerica (Andrews 1999) or appears to be necessary from experimental replication (Clark 1988). Per-

The production sequence can be reconstructed at any place in time by comparing the ratios of artifacts and production debitage recovered in archaeological excavations to the expected ratios of artifacts from the complete production sequence beginning with core preparation and ending with prismatic blade production and core disposal. Table 7.1 summarizes the data on 236,429 pieces of analyzed obsidian that reflect the prismatic blade production sequence at Xochicalco. What is very apparent from this table is that two types of activities are clearly missing from the Xochicalco reduction sequence. First, virtually no percussion debris was identified indicating that cores were not being shaped on site. Second, and perhaps more interestingly, there is very little first series pressure debitage usually associated with transforming a shaped polyhedral core into a

cussion rejuvenation used to relocate the platform consistently reduced the mass of the core each time it was performed, which means that if not done carefully, multiple rejuvenations could decrease rather than increase the use life of cores, reduce their overall blade yield, and/or reduce the length of cutting edge available.

Several lines of evidence indicate that obsidian entered Xochicalco as prismatic blade cores with single-facet platforms shaped at the quarry locales where cores were manufactured. First, blade-to-core-top ratios for artifacts with single-facet platforms is 1:3 compared to a blade-to-core-top ratio of 35:1 for artifacts with pecked-and-ground platforms. This suggests that on the average fewer than one prismatic blade was removed from cores with single-facet platforms once these cores entered the site. Second, if a macrocore was completely reduced at Xochicalco the ratio of faceted to pecked-and-ground platforms on prismatic blades should vary somewhere between 1:1 or 2:1 with faceted platforms predominating because of the greater volume of the core that can normally be reduced before the Xochicalco craftsmen typically rejuvenated their platforms with pecked-and-ground surfaces. Ratios of faceted to pecked-and-ground platforms less than 1:1 would suggest that smaller partially reduced prismatic cores were entering the site rather than macrocores or polyhedral cores. The actual ratio of single-facet to pecked-and-ground platforms on prismatic blades is 1:80 reflecting the importation of already reduced prismatic cores that quickly underwent platform rejuvenation at Xochicalco.

Metric data collected by measuring core segments indicate that most cores with single-facet platforms entered the site with diameters between 3.0 and 4.6 cm (X=3.8 cm, SD=.836). Only one complete blade with a single-facet platform has been recovered at Xochicalco by the Proyecto Especial Xochicalco under the direction of Norberto González (Garza Tarazona and González Crespo 1995) from a cache in the upper ceremonial zone. This blade is 17 cm in length indicating that some of these cores were quite large. As a rule *single-facet cores* have slightly obtuse platform angles ranging from a low of 89 degrees to a high of 107.5 degrees (X=94.9, SD=4.56). Interestingly, but not surprisingly, *blades* removed from cores with single-facet platforms have platform angles that range from acute (74 degrees) to obtuse (102 degrees). The unmistakable conclusion drawn from both the blade ratio and platform angle data is that many of the cores with single-facet platforms were heavily used before they reached the site, some of which were nearing exhaustion and required rejuvenation before they could be further reduced.

One intriguing aspect of the Xochicalco assemblage is

2 cm

7.3 Two complete and exhausted cores from Xochicalco

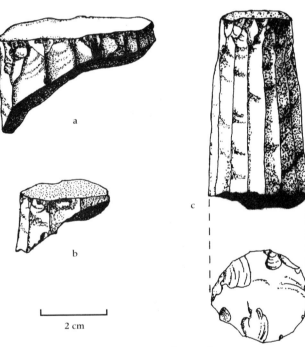

a

b

c

2 cm

7.4 Three production rejuvenation by-products:
a, single-facet core top removed by percussion rejuvenation; *b*, pecked-and-ground core top removed by percussion rejuvenation, *c*, pecked-and-ground core top removed by bipolar rejuvenation. *Illustration prepared by Bradford Andrews*

that prismatic blade cores underwent a large number of platform rejuvenations during their normal use life (figure 7.2). Many cores were rejuvenated two to three times before being discarded: once to remove the single-facet platform (figure 7.4a) and at least one more time to remove a pecked-and-ground platform (figures 7.4b-c, 7.5) . The sequence of multiple rejuvenations of blade cores at

2 cm

7.5 Pecked-and-ground core top removed by bipolar rejuvenation

2 cm

7.6 Example of a bowling-pin–shaped core nearing rejuvenation. Core is not from Xochicalco

Xochicalco stand in sharp contrast to what has been reported for assemblages elsewhere in central Mexico (see chapter 4). The question that needs to be answered is why were cores rejuvenated so many times at Xochicalco and what does this imply about the differences in Xochicalco's prismatic blade technology in comparison to other areas of Mesoamerica?

There are four possible reasons for why cores with single-facet platforms were rejuvenated shortly after entering Xochicalco. The first is that pecked-and-ground platforms were simply preferred by local craftsmen and cores were rejuvenated immediately to provide this type of platform. There are two technological advantages of working with a pecked-and-ground platform instead of a faceted one (see also chapter 3). The first is that a pecked-and-ground platform has a textured surface that provides a good seating or grip for the pressure tool (Crabtree 1968). The second is that the extensive fracturing caused by pecking the platform surface facilitated crack initiation to remove prismatic blades. Despite these technological benefits I believe that preference for this type of platform would by itself be insufficient to warrant rejuvenation because of the large amount of mass that was removed by percussion from the tops of single-facet cores during their initial rejuvenation. On average I estimate that between 1 and 4 cm of length was removed from the proximal ends of cores each time they were rejuvenated using percussion techniques. If rejuvenation was simply intended to created a pecked-and-ground platform as the preferred working surface, then why would any mass be removed from cores? The pecked-and-ground platform could be prepared without the removal of mass from the core.

A second reason for why cores were rejuvenated so often at Xochicalco may have been that craftsmen were less skilled than craftsmen elsewhere in central Mexico either owing to limited training or less practice because obsidian was not readily available. While training may have been different at Xochicalco than it was at sites where obsidian was locally and readily available, the data suggest that Xochicalco craftsmen were by no means unskilled. Cores at Xochicalco had on average 1.7 hinge fractures per core face, which is higher than the average of 1.0 hinge fractures per core characteristic of the specialized workshops at Teotihuacan (Andrews 1999). Nevertheless, examination of blade error data indicates that the majority of hinge fractures, which are the cause of most terminal errors in the manufacture of prismatic blades, were corrected at Xochicalco by standard lateral blade removal techniques. Although the Teotihuacan specialists appear highly skilled, an analysis of seven skill attributes reflected in the assemblages at Teotihuacan and Xochicalco revealed comparable aptitude at both sites. Finally, there is no indication from household consumption data that users were in any way undersupplied. Obsidian was apparently available to meet existing demand and workshop craftsmen at Xochicalco practiced their trade at a level commensurate with the level of obsidian consumption at the site.

A third possibility is that cores were rejuvenated immediately upon their arrival at the site because their shape impeded further removal of prismatic blades. This perspective assumes that most were imported as bowling-pin–shaped cores (figure 7.6) with obtuse platform angles and were unsuitable for continued blade removal until the platform was repositioned at the widest portion of the core where a platform angle of 90 degrees or less could be obtained. While this possibility is supported by some of the platform angle measurements on single-facet cores, it is contradicted by the results of some replication experiments, which show that it is possible with prior core maintenance to reduce an entire core without needing to rejuvenate its platform (Clark 1988). The interpretive problem here is that most replication studies (Crabtree 1968; Clark 1988), with the exception of the work of Gene Titmus, have used relatively short cores between 8 and 10 cm in length. While these lengths approximate the size of cores being used in Aztec-period workshops (see chapter 4), they are considerably smaller than the cores circulating during earlier periods. Cores entering Xochicalco were probably twice this length and until experimental studies are conducted on cores that fully approximate the range of pre-Columbian cores in both diameter and length it will be unclear how accurate the models of core maintenance and rejuvenation are based on replication alone.

A fourth and final explanation for repeated core rejuvenation at Xochicalco is that a slightly different reduction technology was employed favoring the production of multiple short cores. In 1982 John Clark published an important paper drawing upon ethnohistoric descriptions of prismatic blade production demonstrating that prismatic blades in ancient Mesoamerica were produced from a seated position with the core held between the feet (Clark 1982, 1989). While I fully agree with Clark that the Aztec foot-held technique was widely utilized across Mesoamerica at the time of the Conquest, a point is reached in small core-blade production where cores cannot be effectively held with the feet. At this point there are two options, discard the core or continue blade removal using an alternative technique. At Xochicalco, where obsidian was scarce, prismatic blade production apparently continued using an alternative handheld technique (Flenniken and Hirth 1997).[2] The cores

that were reduced using a handheld technique were those with lengths of 8 cm and less (Flenniken and Hirth ND).

Four lines of evidence support the possibility that a handheld technique was utilized to remove prismatic blades from short cores at Xochicalco. First, as mentioned above, as cores decrease in size they become difficult to hold in the feet without some supplemental way of anchoring or stabilizing them. Second, replication experiments by Jeffrey Flenniken have shown that it is possible to produce prismatic blades from short cores that are identical to those found at Xochicalco. Flenniken has consistently been able to produce blades between 2 and 6 mm in width and up to 8 cm in length from small cores with single-facet platforms using handheld techniques (Flenniken and Hirth ND). Third, the handheld technique not only would have required the production of short cores but it also would have favored the use of pecking and grinding to prepare platform surfaces since this technique would have helped brake the surface tension of the obsidian allowing for the easier removal of long blades (Crabtree 1968). It is possible that blades even longer than 8 cm were manufactured at Xochicalco using handheld techniques since most small cores here had pecked-and-ground platforms that would have made blade removal easier. Fourth and finally, while I have been able to remove blades from cores as small as 2 cm in diameter using a modified foot-held technique, there are some cores in our collection that have diameters of 0.5 to 1.0 cm, which I believe would have been impossible to reduce using anything other than a handheld technique (Flenniken and Hirth ND). The smallest core top in our collection had a platform only 2.8 mm wide and a core diameter of only 3.1 mm; there is every indication that blades continued to be removed after the core top was removed and a new platform was established lower on this core (figure 7.7).

Discussion

The data at hand suggest that provisioning constraints played an important role in structuring the form and composition of prismatic blade production at Xochicalco. Compositional analysis has shown that the bulk of the obsidian used at Xochicalco came from sources 200 or more km from the site. Distance increases the scarcity of obsidian and can place it outside the direct procurement of individual households. Instead, obsidian was an exchange commodity with much of the material used to produce prismatic blades entering craft workshops instead of being fabricated at the level of individual households.

Technological information indicates obsidian was moving in a relatively consistent and restricted form as used

2 mm

7.7 Smallest pecked-and-ground core top removed by percussion rejuvenation in the Xochicalco collection

prismatic blade cores from which a large number of prismatic blades had previously been removed. This is very different than what has been found at other sites in central Mexico, particularly the Valley of Mexico, during earlier and later points in time when macrocores, unused polyhedral cores, and even block obsidian were widely circulated. The provisioning of obsidian in the form of used prismatic cores instead of large unused polyhedral cores almost certainly was the result of restricted supply and access to this material.

Because obsidian was moving primarily as used prismatic cores, obsidian may have been procured through a network of itinerant craftsmen, who themselves produced blades for sale as they traveled throughout central Mexico. This explanation would reveal why cores are always used and significantly reduced in mass. If itinerant craftsmen were the source of both prismatic blades and cores for sites like Xochicalco that were located considerable distances from sources, then it created a controlled market where it was in the merchants' best interest to keep supply limited.

If these merchants had supplied Xochicalco with large unused cores, it would have placed them in direct competition with local craftsmen for large blades at the regional level. By supplying Xochicalco craftsmen with used cores they could have provided themselves with a means of avoiding time-consuming core rejuvenation at the same time they converted the residual mass of exhausted obsidian cores into alternative usable products. Since technological analysis indicates that platforms on cores were transformed from single-facet to pecked-and-ground almost immediately after the cores entered the site, it seems reasonably certain that the suppliers, in this case itinerant craftsmen, were not producing large numbers of blades from cores with single-facet platforms for distribution at Xochicalco.

Provisioning and production are closely interrelated activities and at Xochicalco the form and quantity of obsidian entering the site appears to have a direct affect on the technology used to produce prismatic blades. The production technology at Xochicalco is characterized by two important features: the production and use of small, short cores and the multiple rejuvenation of cores during their normal use lives from procurement to discard. There are two, and at this point equally valid, ways of interpreting why the production technology is structured in this way: a general scarcity of obsidian in western Morelos or the form of cores entering Xochicalco.

The idea that the production technology found at Xochicalco was the product of raw material scarcity relies on indications that many cores underwent multiple rejuvenations during their normal uselife. Some cores were rejuvenated anywhere from two to three or more times resulting in the production of small blades from increasingly smaller cores. One interpretation is that the scarcity of obsidian in western Morelos forced craftsmen to repeatedly rework cores to make sure that every gram of usable material was utilized. There are many small blades and core fragments in the assemblages to indicate that a large number of cores were used well into the production of small microblades of 2 to 3 mm in width. Nevertheless, the problem that Xochicalco craftsmen faced was that percussion rejuvenation produced waste and shortened the length of cores, thereby reducing the amount of blade length that could be removed from them. While bipolar rejuvenation minimizes waste and frequently is found in the collections, the regular use of percussion techniques suggests a considerable amount of mass was lost when cores were rejuvenated more than once using this technique.

Another possibility is that the production technology found at Xochicalco was a local innovation that was a function of developing an effective way of producing prismatic blades from the used prismatic blade cores with small diameters entering the site. From this perspective the first rejuvenation might have been intended to produce one or more small, short cores that could be easily worked using a handheld blade removal technology (Flenniken and Hirth ND). The use of pecking and grinding to produce rejuvenated platforms made it easier to detach blades using either a foot-held or handheld technology and provided an effective way for craftsmen with lesser degrees of skill to rejuvenate cores with less risk of core damage or destruction than is the case when percussion techniques are used alone. This technology would have been well adapted to the use of incoming cores that already had small diameters and obtuse platforms. What is interesting about initial rejuvenation of cores at Xochicalco is that a number of the incoming cores with single-facet platforms had platform angles and undamaged faces that were still usable for the production of prismatic blades. The fact that these cores were quickly rejuvenated after they entered the site indicates that there is a clear preference for cores with pecked-and-ground platforms, which made blade removal easier.

The two interpretations are not incompatible explanations for Xochicalco's unique rejuvenation-oriented technology. It is more likely that Xochicalco's technology is a combination of both provisioning constraints and idiosyncratic production behavior, skill, and artisan preference. Clearly the lack of access to large unused polyhedral cores had a strong effect on the structure of blade production; artisans were limited in what they could do as they worked exclusively with small diameter, used prismatic cores. Whether a handheld technology developed at Xochicalco as a specific response to these conditions or as a result of artisanal preferences or abilities remains unclear. What is clear is that the size and form of the cores that entered the site was an important variable in every subsequent step in the production process.

I have not discussed sociopolitical variables that may have affected provisioning or production. These are difficult to identify with site-based data like that available for Xochicalco. Nevertheless, by comparison with other data it is possible to identify that sociopolitical variables affected provisioning although it is difficult to specify exactly what they were. For example, it is known that obsidian from the Pachuca source reached Xochicalco during the Epiclassic period, although in a much lower frequency than it did during the previous Late Classic (Hirth and Angulo 1981; Hirth 2000). The dominate frequency of the distant Ucareo and Zacualtipan obsidian material over the closer and already circulating Pachuca obsidian indicates a sharp change in exchange and exploitation patterns from the Classic to the Epiclassic. A sharp difference can also be found in ceramic spheres within central Mexico during the Epiclassic period. The highly decorated Coyotlatelco B tradition found throughout the Valley of Mexico (Dumond and Muller 1972) is not distributed throughout western Morelos during this same period (Cyphers 2000; Hirth 2000). Since the Coyotlatelco B ceramic complex is the main decorated ceramic tradition in the Valley of Mexico during the Epiclassic, its absence in western Morelos, together with different architectural and artistic traditions, strongly suggests the existence of some sociopolitical boundary between these regions. Whether this division was based on ethnic, political, economic, or a combination of factors is a question that awaits future resolution. It appears, however, that sociopolitical variables did affect the movement of merchandise and interregional interaction between western Morelos and adjacent areas of the Valley of Mexico.

Conclusion

Xochicalco is over 200 km from the most frequently used obsidian source supplying its Epiclassic-period workshops. The data indicate that the craftsmen at Xochicalco had access to obsidian that arrived as already shaped and used prismatic blade cores. Missing from the lithic debitage are remains associated with the shaping of percussion cores and irregular or first-series pressure blades involved in the early stages of pressure blade reduction. The result was a prismatic blade production sequence that differs in three important respects from that reported elsewhere in central Mexico during this and previous time periods. First, prismatic blades were produced at the site from small diameter prismatic cores that underwent multiple rejuvenations from the time they entered the site until they were finally discarded; the goal of these multiple rejuvenations was to extract all usable blade edge from the available obsidian. Second, cores at Xochicalco were rejuvenated using pecking and grinding techniques, which makes it possible to distinguish blades produced from cores with single-facet platforms detached prior to rejuvenation from those detached after platforms were rejuvenated with pecked-and-ground surfaces. Third and finally, evidence for multiple rejuvenations at Xochicalco may be related to the practice of removing blades using both foot-held and handheld techniques. The handheld technique would have favored the production of multiple short cores during core rejuvenation. Evidence from the collections suggests that when possible, long cores often were divided in half using bipolar percussion to produce two short cores suitable for handheld blade removal.

The technological sequence recovered at Xochicalco represents one distinct pathway to prismatic blade production in central Mexico. Provisioning constraints had a major effect on shaping prismatic blade production at this site. It is likely that other technologies and constraints will be identified at other sites in the highlands as investigators turn their efforts to identifying and understanding regional variation in Mesoamerican lithic technology.

ACKNOWLEDGMENTS

Funding for the excavations at Xochicalco, Mexico, and the laboratory analysis of the material recovered was generously provided by the National Science Foundation.

NOTES

1. Percentages of obsidian sources reported here refer to the material used in prismatic blade production only. This constitutes 99% of the obsidian recovered in workshop contexts. It does not include the material used in bifacial or unifacial production, which appears to have utilized material from additional sources.
2. The idea of the handheld technique was first suggested by J. Jeffrey Flenniken after examining the Xochicalco collections. His ongoing experimental work with the handheld technique is clarifying how it was employed at Xochicalco.

CHAPTER EIGHT

Lithic Technology, Assemblage Variation, and the Organization of Production and Use of Obsidian on the South Gulf Coast of Veracruz, Mexico

ROBERT S. SANTLEY AND THOMAS P. BARRETT

THE SUITABILITY OF STONE TOOL MATERIAL for providing information about the organization of past economies is a product of the reductive technology involved in making such tools and the wear patterns created by their use. Information on economic organization can be retrieved from raw material sources, tool production sites, and tool consumption locations and used as a basis for reconstructing different elements of past economies. Evidence of modes of exchange also can be obtained, but this interpretive activity is more difficult, because the physical exchange process leaves few material remains.

In the highlands of Mesoamerica and in the adjacent Gulf Coast lowlands, obsidian was the primary material used to produce flaked stone tools throughout the pre-Columbian period. Few other suitable raw materials were available for use. Even when present, chert, quartzite, and chalcedony were not used to the same extent as obsidian. In this chapter we examine the variation among obsidian assemblages from two regions of southern Veracruz, Mexico: the Tuxtla Mountains and the Hueyapan region (figure 8.1). Obsidian does not outcrop naturally in either of these two areas. Instead, the sites correspond to the *distant source* areas discussed in chapter one, where knowledge of obsidian source deposits and the groups that controlled them would have been indirect. Surveys in these regions involved the surface reconnaissance of a large area, which was augmented in the Tuxtla region with intensive resurveys at select sites and a large number of excavations. These surveys and excavations have sampled archaeological deposits that span the Formative and Classic periods and indicate variation in the acquisition of source material, the principal products traded, and the reduction technology. This study demonstrates that there were several distinct distribution patterns for the manufacture and use of obsidian at production and consumption loci throughout southern Veracruz.

Study Regions

The Tuxtla mountains consist of an isolated field of volcanoes situated about 150 km southeast of the modern city of Veracruz. This region covers an area of 400 km², including one corridor of settlement stretching from the ar-

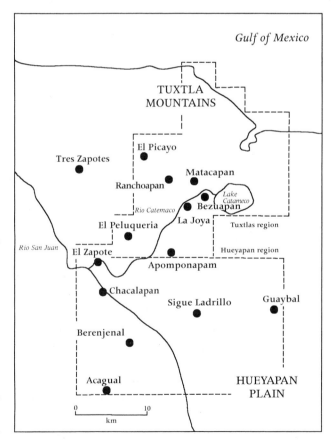

8.1 Map of the south Gulf Coast showing major archaeological sites. Dotted lines represent the boundaries of the Tuxtla and Hueyapan survey areas. *Illustration prepared by the authors*

chaeological site of Matacapan to the Gulf of Mexico and another following the course of the Rio Catemaco southwest until Chuniapan de Abajo. The Hueyapan region covers an area of 200 km² and is situated in the flatlands and nearby piedmont and mountains about 5 km southeast of the southern terminus of the Tuxtla survey. The scale of this reconnaissance provides a large sample of material that is representative of the variation in the settlement types and time periods in both regions.

Lithics were collected from all sites encountered during the surveys. A number of these sites were then excavated. These assemblages contain more than 28,000 obsidian artifacts. Most of this material represents the remains of a prismatic blade industry, which predominates at sites dating to the Classic and Postclassic periods. Prismatic blades are present in the assemblages as well as material associated with various stages in blade-core reduction (see Santley et al. 1986 and Santley et al. 1995 for a more extended discussion). The Matacapan material primarily comes from securely dated excavation contexts, whereas the assemblages from all other sites discussed below derive from surface survey. Recent excavations at La Joya and Bezuapan, two sites located directly to the south of Matacapan (figure 8.1), have also produced a large number of obsidian artifacts (Arnold et al. 1996; Pool 1997). These materials are not included in this study, although preliminary work on their assemblage closely agrees with the findings presented here.

Both regions were extensively surveyed and one or more surface samples were obtained from each site using the grab collection method. In the Tuxtla region the extensive survey was followed by an intensive survey at seventeen sites. Here the survey employed systematic transect sampling; transects were laid out every 50 to 75 m across each site, and controlled collections were retrieved from 3 x 3 m units every 13 m along each transect following the removal of surface vegetation. In addition, sets of excavations were conducted at eight different locations at Matacapan and at three areas of suburban occupation around its main center: Comoapan, Bezuapan, and La Joya (Arnold et al. 1993; Pool 1990, 1997; Santley et al. 1987, 1989). A more complete description of these methods of data retrieval is presented in Santley and Arnold (1996) and Santley et al. (1997).

Present work in the Tuxtla and Hueyapan regions indicates ten phases of archaeological occupation spanning the Formative, Classic, and Postclassic periods (table 8.1). All of these phases are present in the Tuxtla region (Santley and Arnold 1996), but in the Hueyapan region the Early Classic and Postclassic are either poorly represented or not present at all (Santley 1998). To facilitate interregional comparison,

these phases have been combined into two periods: Formative and Classic.

All obsidian was analyzed based on raw material type, technology of reduction, and type of tool forms produced. The type or sources of raw material were identified by appraising the color and quality of the obsidian artifacts (Barrett ND). These types were grouped into three categories, black, clear, and green, whose integrity was later confirmed by INAA (Santley, Barrett, Glascock, and Neff ND), when combined with information on raw material quality (see below). A technological classification was developed to identify the kinds of debitage produced during different stages in blade-core reduction because most of the material consists of prismatic blades (Healan et al. 1983; Santley et al. 1986). This typology supplied information on the kinds of reduction activities that took place at specific sites and across the landscape. Finally, a large number of formal tools were present in the assemblages, most of which were prismatic blades. Other formal tools included flaked items such as bifaces, unifaces, and implements produced from prismatic blades and their reduction debitage. Information on the amount and type of edge wear was also collected from these tools (Barrett ND).

Obsidian Source Reliance

More than 28,000 lithic artifacts were recovered during the survey and excavations in the Tuxtla and Hueyapan regions, of which approximately 97% were made of obsidian. Obsidian does not naturally occur in the southern Gulf lowlands, even though the Tuxtla region is of recent volcanic origin (Santley, Nelson, Reinhardt, Pool, and Arnold ND). Consequently, obsidian had to be imported long distances. To establish which sources were imported, two hundred pieces of obsidian from securely dated contexts in the Tuxtla region were subjected to INAA (Santley, Barrett, Glascock, and Neff ND). An INAA study of the obsidians from the Hueyapan region has yet to be conducted. Thus, the following discussion relies largely on color comparisons between the two areas, anchored with the INAA study from the Tuxtla mountains and our findings of their raw material quality.

INAA indicates that Guadalupe Victoria was the major source used during the Early and Middle Formative in the Tuxtla region (57.9–66.7%). This source declined dramatically in frequency in the Late Formative (10%), rose once more during the Early Early Classic (56%), only to fall off yet again in the Late Early Classic (5.3%). This Classic period decline was offset by an increase in the amount of obsidian imported from Zaragoza (85–100%). Obsidian from Guadalupe Victoria is generally clear with internal banding

Table 8.1 Chronological periods and phases

Years	Column 1	Column 2	Column 3	Column 4
1500 AD	Postclassic	Period V		Postclassic
1400			Aztec	
1300				
1200			Mazapan	
1100				Terminal Classic
1000	Late Late Classic	Period IV	Coyotlatelco	
900				
800	Early Late Classic			Late Classic
700	Late Middle Classic	Period IIIB	Metepec	
600	Early Middle Classic		Xolalpan	Middle Classic
500				
400	Late Early Classic	Period IIIA	Tlamimilolpa	Early Classic
300				
200	Early Early Classic		Miccaotli	Protoclassic
100 AD		Period II	Tzacualli	
0	Late Formative			Late Preclassic
100 BC			Patlachique	
200				
300		Period Late I	Ticoman III	
400		Period Early I	Ticoman II	
500		Rosario	Ticoman I	
600	Middle Formative	Guadalupe	Cuautepec	Middle Preclassic
700			La Pastora	
800				
900		San Jose	El Arbolillo	
1000				
1100	Early Formative		Bomba	
1200			Manantial	
1300		Tierras Largas	Ayotla	
1400			Coapexco	
1500 BC				

Source: Blanton et al. 1982; Coe 1966; Sanders et al. 1979; and Santley and Arnold 1996

Table 8.2 Obsidian procurement by quality of raw material and color

QUALITY OF RAW MATERIAL (by %)

	Excellent	Good	Poor	N
Guadalupe Victoria		60.4	39.6	48
Zaragoza	55.9	41.7	2.4	127
Pico de Orizaba	84.6	15.4		13
Sierra de Pachuca	100.0			8
Paredon	100.0			2
San Martin		100.0		2

COLOR (by %)

	Black	Green	Clear	N
Guadalupe Victoria	18.8		81.3	48
Zaragoza	95.2		4.8	125
Pico de Orizaba	15.4		84.6	13
Sierra de Pachuca		100.0		8
Paredon	50.0		50.0	2
San Martin	50.0		50.0	2

and internal inclusions, while Zaragoza is black with only some evidence of banding. Obsidian from Pico de Orizaba occurs in the earlier half of the sequence but is most frequent during the Middle Formative (16.7%). Although never very common, all of the material from Pachuca dates to the Classic period, with a peak in Early and Middle Classic times (10–10.5%). Obsidian from Paredon and San Martin Jilotepeque is also present and dates exclusively to the Formative period.

The quality of raw material varies by source (table 8.2). Guadalupe Victoria obsidian is generally good to poor in quality (60.4–39.6%). It contains internal inclusions and fracture planes and hence was not used to make prismatic blades. Obsidian from Zaragoza, in contrast, is excellent to good in quality (55.9–41.7%) and was used to a much greater extent when prismatic blades were the primary product used in the Tuxtla region. Pico de Orizaba obsidian also is excellent to good in quality (84.6–15.4%). Although never very common except during the Middle Formative, material from Pico de Orizaba was used to produce both small percussion flakes and blades as well as prismatic blades removed by pressure flaking. Material from the Pachuca source is always of high quality.

Overall, the work in the Tuxtla region suggests that color and raw material quality are good indicators of obsidian source utilization. Most of the obsidian in the assemblages from Guadalupe Victoria (81.3%) and Pico de Orizaba (84.6%) is clear with the remainder in these samples being black (table 8.2). In contrast, the majority of the Zaragoza material is black (95.2%) with just a small percentage of clear. All the obsidian from Pachuca is green and the few specimens from Paredon and San Martin

Jilotepeque range from clear to black. This patterning corresponds with data on raw material quality. Generally, material of good to poor quality was utilized during the Formative period for all types of tools, with most of it coming from Guadalupe Victoria, whereas excellent to good obsidian from Zaragoza was the primary material imported during the Classic period.

These trends in color, raw material quality, and source reliance make it possible to extend the results of the INAA study to the much larger sample of material from the entire survey and excavations. Black obsidian makes up most of the obsidian imported throughout the sequence; although it is less common in the Early and Late Formative (56.4–60%) than it is during the Classic period (82.8–92.8%). Clear obsidian, on the other hand, is very common in the Early and Late Formative (33.3–41.8%), but its frequency drops greatly in Classic times (1.9–12.1%). Green obsidian is never very common, but its frequency increases steadily throughout the sequence, reaching a peak in the Late Middle Classic (13.4%).

The material from the Hueyapan region has not been studied using INAA. Information on color, however, was recorded. Only a few collections with obsidian date to the Early Formative, and sample size is very small (N=6). Black and clear obsidian each account for one-half of the obsidian sample. During the succeeding Middle Formative period, the incidence of obsidian increases, with black obsidian accounting for 63.2% of the assemblage. Clear obsidian makes up 36.8% of the Middle Formative assemblage. The same pattern of obsidian procurement continues into the Late Formative period. For the first time, black obsidian is not the most common color represented in the Late Formative assemblage but not by an appreciable margin (48.8%). These distributions begin to change during the Middle Classic. No Early Classic contexts were reported, but these most likely are loci that contain Middle Classic material based on Santley's past experience in the Tuxtla mountains. Black obsidian continues as the most common color in the assemblage during the Middle Classic (81.5% of all material), with clear obsidian accounting for 17.9% and green obsidian only 0.5%. The Late Classic represents the final occupation in the Hueyapan region for which there is archaeological evidence. Like the Middle Classic, black obsidian predominates (85.3%), with clear (13.7%) and green (1.0%) material accounting for the remainder of all obsidian.

To summarize, we believe that much of the obsidian imported into the Tuxtla and Hueyapan regions during the Formative period came from Guadalupe Victoria, with Zaragoza being an important secondary source. Zaragoza became the predominant source during the succeeding Classic

Table 8.3 Classic-period obsidian assemblages from center and small sites (%)

	Decortifaction material	Macro debitage	Macrocore reduction	Prismatic blades	Pressure core reduction errors	Pressure cores	Percussion blades/flakes	Flake cores	Total
TUXTLAS CENTERS									
Black	0.01	0.0	1.9	76.6	4.1	1.8	9.7	1.8	14,581
Clear	1.00	0.1	4.9	53.1	4.1	0.3	21.4	3.1	714
Green	0.10	0.1	0.4	90.3	1.7	0.1	4.1	0.4	990
TUXTLAS SMALL SITES									
Black	0.10	0.0	1.9	65.6	10.7	0.9	6.6	2.9	3,253
Clear	0.60		0.6	15.0	18.5	0.4	21.8	8.6	513
Green			2.1	69.1	4.3	1.1	2.1	1.1	94
HUEYAPAN CENTERS									
Black	0.30	4.2	4.2	73.6	6.3	2.3	23.7	1.9	1,226
Clear		3.9	2.0	36.0			55.3	0.5	203
Green				94.7			5.3		19
HUEYAPAN SMALL SITES									
Black		2.4	3.2	76.6	0.9	0.7	14.3	0.4	1,633
Clear		0.8	1.0	35.1			59.2	1.8	387
Green			15.8	68.4	10.5		5.3	5.3	19

period. We suspect that a similar dependence on Zaragoza obsidian occurred during the Postclassic, although more work needs to be done to confirm this suspicion.

Exchange from the Source Deposits

Several industries are present in the obsidian assemblages. The most common industry consists of material from pressure core reduction and the use of fine prismatic blades (table 8.3). The core-blade industry dominates samples from the Classic period, although it is also a major component during the Formative period. Much of this material probably came from Zaragoza, but obsidian from Pico de Orizaba, Guadalupe Victoria, and Pachuca is also present. The second industry involves the production of small simple blades and flakes. This material is common during Formative times and also occurs during the Classic period. Guadalupe Victoria appears to be the major source used in this industry although Zaragoza is also present. The third industry was devoted to the production of unifaces and bifaces. This material is primarily black in color, suggesting that the Zaragoza was the principal source relied on for this obsidian.

All of the obsidian sources studied to date contain substantial quantities of heavy percussion debris (Michels 1975; Spence and Parsons 1972; Cobean et al. 1991; Santley et al. 1986). Although materials from most of these deposits have not been adequately analyzed (for example, the sources that ring Pico de Orizaba: Zaragoza, Guadalupe Victoria, and Cerro de las Minas), a few general comments can be made. Obsidian deposits in Mesoamerica consist of vein deposits and nodules, both of which can be present at the same source. Vein deposits occur in the form of large subterranean flows of obsidian that occasionally outcrop on the surface. These flows were generally obtained by tunnel mining, with vertical shafts descending from the surface until the vein was encountered, at which point it was followed horizontally until exhaustion (chapter 2). At these sites vast amounts of heavy percussion material are present, including obsidian blocks, primary reduction by-products with cortex, flaw-ridden macrocores, and other kinds of heavy percussive material such as decortication flakes, large percussion flakes, and crested ridge blades. In contrast, nodules occur in various sizes and are deposited in the soil as ejecta in and around volcanic cones. According to Spence (1981:776), this type of material was collected at Otumba from stream courses, although strip mining of the banks of arroyos is another possibility. The presence of heavy decortication and percussion flakes suggests that nodules were tested for inclusions and the presence of internal fracture planes before removal from the quarry. The macrocore appears to have been the primary item obtained from vein deposits, whereas the nodules that were acquired appear to have been partially processed prior to transport.

The assemblages from the Tuxtla and Hueyapan regions contain only a limited amount of black obsidian macro debitage from block and nodule reduction, indicating that most of this obsidian was imported in already processed form (table 8.3). Black obsidian reduction debitage is present in both regions, but it is somewhat more common in the Hueyapan region. This variation suggests that the Tuxtla area received more refined black obsidian than the Hueyapan region and that some second stage processing occurred at sites located between the sources and the southern Gulf lowlands. We suspect that a segment of the black obsidian assemblage was also exchanged as finished tools.

Clear obsidian macrocores and prismatic pressure cores were also distributed to the southern Gulf lowlands in the Classic period. In the two regions there is debitage indicative of both macrocore and pressure core reduction. Macrocore reduction debitage is less common in the Hueyapan region, suggesting that more clear obsidian prismatic cores ready for blade removal were obtained in this area than in the Tuxtla region (table 8.3). It must be pointed out, however, that exhausted clear obsidian prismatic cores are generally less common than those of black obsidian in both the Tuxtla and Hueyapan regions. This may indicate that compared to black obsidian, a larger share of all Classic-period clear obsidian was exchanged as finished prismatic blades. The same may be true for assemblages from Formative-period sites. Much of this second stage processing of clear obsidian probably also occurred at sites situated between the quarries and the southern Gulf lowlands.

Green obsidian is also present in many samples, albeit in nominal amounts (table 8.3). Virtually all of this material consists of fine prismatic blades from the Classic period. A few green obsidian prismatic cores and debitage from their reduction are also present, but these are confined largely to the Tuxtla region. Interestingly, many of the platforms on green obsidian artifacts from the Tuxtla mountains are ground, but platform grinding is an attribute rarely found on blades at Teotihuacan, which was probably the main processing point for Pachuca obsidian from central Mexico during the Classic period (Spence 1981, 1987). This finding indicates that some intermediate point between Teotihuacan and the southern Gulf lowlands was involved in the grinding of prismatic core platforms and the subsequent production of prismatic blades before being sent to the Tuxtla and Hueyapan regions.

The preceding summary of the core-blade industry indicates variability in the kinds of products circulated from different source deposits to different parts of the southern Gulf lowlands. The macrocore was the major object made of black obsidian that was sent to the Tuxtla and Hueyapan regions, but the Tuxtla Mountains apparently received a greater number of prismatic cores ready for prismatic blade production. In contrast, more clear obsidian macrocores were sent to the Tuxtla Mountains than the Hueyapan region. Green obsidian was imported to both regions mainly

as fine prismatic blades. A few green prismatic cores were also imported, but they occurred mainly in the Tuxtla region. Other sites situated between the sources of green and clear obsidian and the southern Gulf lowlands probably processed macrocores into prismatic cores and/or prismatic blades prior to sending them to the Tuxtla and Hueyapan regions.

Specialization at Consumer Sites

Specialization is a means of livelihood in which producers of a good or providers of a service gain some, most, or all of their subsistence from its fabrication, use, or distribution. Three general classes of specialization could be related to prismatic blades. First, the blades themselves may have been produced at specialized production sites. Deposits at these sites should contain production by-products such as macro debitage and material produced as the result of prismatic core reduction, and most prismatic blades found in such contexts should exhibit little evidence of use. Second, some sites may have been involved in the specialized use of obsidian in butchering or some other cutting activity that required obsidian prismatic blades. In such contexts little reduction debitage should be present, and the assemblage should predominantly consist of prismatic blades that exhibit worn edges. Third, specialized sites may contain evidence of both specialized production and use. Assemblages formed as a result of these three specialized activities also should contain larger quantities of obsidian than that present in normal domestic or unspecialized contexts. Finally, it is expected that specialists should make fewer errors during macrocore and prismatic core reduction since intuitively one would expect them to be more skilled than knappers processing only limited amounts of material in unspecialized domestic household settings.

To monitor aspects of this variation, we introduce two simple statistics. The first is the ratio of expected-to-observed blade fragments, and it measures the degree to which there are missing pressure blades. The expected frequency is the number expected given the number of prismatic cores found in archaeological contexts, assumed to be one hundred blades per core, which break into three fragments: one proximal, one medial, and one distal. A ratio approaching 1 indicates that most of the observed blades can be accounted by the number of cores present. A ratio of less than 1 means that the site received more finished blades than can be accounted for given the number of cores, while ratios greater than 1 show that a large proportion of the blades produced were deposited in off-site contexts. This value was derived by taking the average weight of an unreduced prismatic core minus the average weight of

Table 8.4 Classic-period assemblages by obsidian type: ratio statistics for centers and small sites

	Observed prismatic blades	Pressure cores	Reduction debitage	Expected prismatic blades	Expected/Observed blades	Errors/Core
TUXTLAS REGION						
Centers						
Black	11,175	261	598	78,300	7.0	2.3
Clear	379	2	29	600	1.6	14.5
Green	894	1	17	300	0.3	17.0
Small sites						
Black	2,114	29	348	8,700	4.1	12.0
Clear	77	2	95	600	7.8	47.5
Green	65	1	4	300	4.6	4.0
HUEYAPAN REGION						
Centers						
Black	902	28	77	8,400	9.3	2.8
Clear	26					
Green	18					
Small sites						
Black	1,251	11	15	3,300	2.7	1.4
Clear	136					
Green	13		2			

an exhausted prismatic core and dividing this by the average weight of a complete pressure blade. The resultant statistic was 108 blades per core, which was reduced to 100 to account for errors incurred during blade removal. These values were obtained from unreduced prismatic cores accompanying burials and exhausted prismatic cores and complete blades recovered from a variety of contexts at Matacapan.

The second statistic monitors the skill involved in removing blades from prismatic cores. This measure is based on the number of errors incurred during pressure blade removal per exhausted core. An error refers to the presence of hinge recoveries, ridge blades, plunging blades, manufacturing error flakes, and proximal core truncations in the assemblage (see Santley et al. 1986 for a description of these errors and their recoveries). Given the same type of raw material, we assume that knappers who are more skilled make fewer errors during the process of prismatic blade removal than producers who were less skilled. Consequently, values approaching 0 indicate that knappers were highly skilled, while higher ratios indicate progressively greater levels of wastage and hence a lower level of knapping efficiency. Black obsidian from Zaragoza is suitable for prismatic blade manufacture, while clear obsidian from Guadalupe is not because it often contains inclusions and internal fracture planes. Both materials were manufactured into prismatic blades, however, indicating extreme care in testing the internal structure of the clear obsidian before its export from

the source deposit. Since both types of obsidian entered the Tuxtla and Hueyapan regions as macrocores, the frequency of errors was probably not a function of material quality or core size.

Summary information on the composition of Classic-period obsidian assemblages composition from the Tuxtla and Hueyapan regions is presented in table 8.3. The artifacts recovered include: decortication flakes and blades, subsequent macro debitage produced during block and nodule reduction, material produced during macrocore reduction, prismatic blades, reduction errors incurred during prismatic blade removal, exhausted prismatic cores, and small flakes and flake cores, especially of black obsidian. The Tuxtla centers and small sites mainly received black obsidian macrocores, although a few blocks and nodules also were imported. Table 8.4 shows that the number of expected black obsidian blade fragments recovered from survey and excavation at centers exceeds the number of prismatic blades found (7.0 and 9.3), indicating that many black obsidian prismatic blades were exported for use off-site. The black obsidian ratios for small sites are much less (2.7 and 4.1). The expected/observed ratio for clear and green obsidian fall into the same range (1.6 and 7.8) as those for black obsidian, indicating a similar focus on export for use off-site. The ratios for green obsidian are the lowest of the three color classes (0.3 and 4.6) and suggests that green obsidian may have been primarily imported as prismatic blades. Knappers at centers made fewer mistakes in the re-

Table 8.5 Classic-period obsidian assemblages: content for specialized production sites

	Decoration material	Macro debitage	Macrocore reduction	Prismatic blades	Pressure core reduction errors	Pressure cores	Percussion blades/ flakes	Flake cores	Total
BLACK OBSIDIAN (%)									
Matacapan	0.2	0.0	1.9	77.7	3.7	10.2	10.2	0.3	13,366
Ranchoapan	0.4		2.3	76.7	0.6	2.5	6.0	6.0	485
El Peluqueria	0.2			33.7	17.4	1.5	42.4		406
Apomponapam	0.5			85.0		1.5		3.0	200
Guayabal			2.2	87.5	1.5	8.8			136
Sigue Ladrillo		1.4	0.1	30.0	0.1		67.1		140
Acagual		1.7	1.7	77.7	2.5		15.7		121
Berenjenal		6.9	2.8	70.1		1.7	17.7	0.3	361
El Zapote		10.9	7.0	62.5		0.8	18.8		128
CLEAR OBSIDIAN (%)									
Matacapan	0.2		6.0	57.3	0.6	2.1	25.2	2.4	497
Ranchoapan				66.7	33.3				3
El Peluqueria									
Apomponapam				13.3	0.9			0.9	15
Guayabal				62.5			31.3		3
Sigue Ladrillo				18.8	8.3		72.9		48
Acagual				14.9			85.1		74
Berenjenal				48.0		0.6	40.0		50
El Zapote			2.0	80.0			20.0		5

duction of black obsidian prismatic cores (2.3 and 2.8) compared to the lithic workers at small sites (1.4 and 12.0). Although the ratios are much higher, the pattern for clear obsidian is similar (14.5 at centers and 47.7 at small sites). Obsidian workers processing green obsidian, in contrast, apparently made more mistakes per core at centers (17.0) than at small sites (4.0). The ratios for green obsidian are generally lower than those for the other types of obsidian, a finding that also can be explained if most of this material entered the southern Gulf lowlands as finished prismatic blades.

In the Tuxtla region only Matacapan, Ranchoapan, La Joya, El Peluqueria, and Apomponapam qualify as specialized sites based on the regional surveys and excavations (figure 8.1). These sites produced the largest obsidian assemblages and the highest obsidian densities. La Joya is the only village-level site of the five. Most of the obsidian from La Joya dates to the Early and Late Formative periods. Small blades and flakes removed from cores by direct percussion dominate the assemblage. These objects probably were the result of production, as the assemblage contains very few unifaces and bifaces. We believe these small blades and flakes were imported since few exhausted cores have been found from which they could have been struck. Philip Arnold's subsequent excavations at La Joya show the same pattern (1977). At La Joya the density of obsidian is much higher than that for any other Formative site in the Tuxtla region (1.38–2.24 vs. 0.11–0.47 pieces per collection). At certain locations within the site obsidian densities exceed ten fragments per collection. The higher density of obsidian, in addition to its presence in dumps containing ceramics and other artifacts, suggest that obsidian small blade and flake use was specialized but that this specialization occurred on the household level. It is difficult to determine exactly what this specialization involved. Santley et al. (1997) have suggested that these obsidian tools may have been used as bits in manioc graters. Because obsidian is very brittle and not well suited to such a task, this interpretation is unlikely.

The other four samples date to the Classic period. Three come from centers: Matacapan, Ranchoapan, and Apomponapam; the fourth from a hamlet: El Peluqueria (table 8.5). Ranchoapan has the largest concentration and highest density of obsidian and is situated 5 km west of Matacapan. Ranchoapan covers 225 ha and is the second largest Classic period site in the Tuxtla region. Most of the obsidian from Ranchoapan consists of material produced from the reduction of black macrocores and pressure blade cores. More than 76% of the assemblage consists of irregular and fine prismatic blades, many of which have very worn edges suggesting they were produced for heavy-duty use on site (table 8.5). The samples with the greatest obsidian densities (2–12 pieces per collection unit) come from a single 5-ha area located in the northern part of the site.

This area also produced most of the ceramics from Ranchoapan. The pottery assemblage includes all of the utility and service ceramics in common usage during Middle and Late Classic periods as well as most of the figurines and ground stone found at the site, implying that the obsidian recovered was reduced in domestic contexts. The number of reduction errors per prismatic core is 0.3, one of the lowest values of this index for specialized production-use sites, indicating a comparatively high level of knapping skill (table 8.6). The ratio of expected-to-observed blade fragments is 9.7, which suggests that most of the prismatic blades produced are missing, once again consistent with off-site use. The density of material at Ranchoapan was on a scale at least one order of magnitude less than that recorded for major Mesoamerican production sites such as Teotihuacan (Spence 1981), Tula (Healan 1986; Healan et al. 1983), and Colha (King and Potter 1994; Shafer and Hester 1991). This suggests that Ranchoapan's specialized production nucleus was probably part time and likely occurred in household contexts.

The assemblage from Apomponapam is very similar to that from Ranchoapan. The Classic-period center is located about 12 km south-southwest of Matacapan. Most of this assemblage consists of black obsidian (table 8.5). Black prismatic blades dominate the assemblage, but there is little evidence (other than exhausted prismatic cores and blade shatter) to suggest that they were produced there (table 8.6). The number of expected prismatic blades greatly exceeds the number found, suggesting that many blades were produced for off-site use (table 8.6). There are also major differences in assemblage size between different collection units at Apomponapam. Of the 215 pieces of obsidian collected, 177 come from a single collection unit, the remainder from 8 others (tables 8.5, 8.6). The assemblage also contains a relatively large number of formal bifaces and percussion material from their manufacture.

At Matacapan the pattern of specialized production and use was quite different. Downtown Matacapan consists of a large group of mounds arranged around a central plaza. These mounds are of two types: conical temple mounds and large rectangular platform mounds that supported elite residences. Most of the black obsidian recovered from surface contexts occurs near platform mounds. Here densities as high as 50 to 60 pieces per collection unit are not uncommon, the greatest recorded for any context at any site in the Tuxtla region. Interestingly, a large number of Teotihuacan-style ceramics were recovered near mound 18 and it is here that more than 40% of the obsidian recovered is green. Almost all of this material consists of prismatic blades, which exhibit only limited evidence of use, although debitage as-

sociated with macrocore and pressure core reduction is also present. The expected-observed ratio of prismatic blades is 4.3, indicating again production for use in a non-houselot context, perhaps off-site (table 8.6). Knappers reducing prismatic cores made about 3.5 errors per core, the greatest for any specialized site in the region, indicating a low level of skill. An alternative interpretation of this evidence is that these knappers had greater access to raw material and hence were less concerned with making errors during reduction because they were associated with Matacapan's elite. The location of these dumps near high-status residences and the fact that prismatic blades were not extensively utilized suggest that obsidian was used for a series of elite related cutting activities such as auto sacrifice, ritual cannibalism, or butchering meat. These localized high-density obsidian scatters may be specialized discard contexts because they are not associated with any ceramics or other household trash. The remaining high-density obsidian areas occur in areas of Matacapan devoted to ceramic production, the principal specialized industry at the site (Santley et al. 1989). Macro debitage and reduction errors are more common in these areas. Just what the blades were used for is difficult to determine, although many were utilized until exhaustion. The incising and sculpting of Matacapan's finely decorated service wares is one possibility. The preparation of kindling for kiln firing is another.

El Peluqueria is situated 16 km southwest of Matacapan. The site is unusual because it is the only small hamlet discussed here with a large sample of obsidian (406 pieces). It is also remarkable because most of the black prismatic blades are microblades. Many of these very small, delicate blades exhibited only limited evidence of use and appear to have been either intentionally snapped or broken during some activity that left behind little to no edge wear. The presence of platform-faceting flakes, first-series blades, ridge blades, manufacturing error flakes, blade core shatter, and exhausted prismatic blade cores indicates that prismatic cores were imported and reduced on site. The expected-to-observed ratio of prismatic blades is 13.1, suggesting that almost all of the blades removed from prismatic cores were destined for use off-site (table 8.6). The number of reduction errors per prismatic core is 1.3, a value that falls midway in the skill index. The assemblage contains an even greater number of small percussion flakes and blades similar to those obtained from La Joya and other Formative-period sites in the Tuxtla region. Like other materials from El Peluqueria, these flakes and blades were produced in black rather than clear obsidian, suggesting that they are contemporary with the pressure blades and do not date to the Formative period. We currently do not know how this obsidian was used but some fine-grain engraving, incising, or cutting activity such as tattooing or shaving is a good possibility.

During the Classic period, the Hueyapan region received the same kinds of material as the Tuxtla mountains. Most of the evidence for the importation of primary material (represented by block and nodule reduction, macrocore reduction, and pressure core reduction) comes from centers, not small sites (table 8.3). The expected/observed ratios for blade fragments at both centers and small sites greatly exceed 1.0, again indicating production for use off-site (table 8.4). In contrast to the Tuxtla region, the Hueyapan knappers made fewer errors during pressure blade removal, especially at small sites. This suggests that the small-site knappers were more skilled and had to conserve their raw material to a greater degree than lithic workers at centers. In the Hueyapan region the five Classic-period centers of Guayabal, Sigue Ladrillo, Acagual, Berenjenal, and El Zapote were prominent importers, processors, and consumers of obsidian (table 8.5). These sites occur on the alluvial plain, in the adjacent piedmont and in the Tuxtla mountains (figure 8.1).

Guayabal, the only one of five sites situated in the mountains, relied on black obsidian, primarily imported in macrocore form. The incidence of reduction errors in black obsidian (1.5 per core) was less than that at major centers processing obsidian in the Tuxtla region (table 8.5). In addition, the expected/observed ratio of prismatic blades (30.3) indicates that a significant amount of the obsidian processed here was destined for use off-site (table 8.6). Most of the black obsidian assemblage consists of prismatic blades (87.5%) with highly damaged cutting edges indicating a final stage of use in some heavy-duty cutting task. Clear obsidian is also present at Guayabal, but only as prismatic blades.

Sigue Ladrillo, located in the neighboring piedmont also received a substantial amount of its Classic-period black obsidian in macrocore form (table 8.5). Clear obsidian was imported to Sigue Ladrillo in the same form, although in much smaller amounts. The black obsidian assemblage from the site is unusual because it is dominated by small flakes and blades struck off cores by direct percussion. The same is true for the clear obsidian assemblage. These findings make the assemblages from Sigue Ladrillo look very much like those from Formative sites in both regions.

Acagual, Berenjenal, and El Zapote are all located on the alluvial plain, that part of the Hueyapan region which had the longest history of pre-Hispanic occupation. Like Guayabal, black obsidian predominates, with prismatic blades composing most of the assemblages at all three sites

(table 8.5). Macro debitage and macrocore reduction debitage is present, sometimes in comparatively great amounts. Errors incurred during pressure core reduction, however, are not very common, suggesting that the knappers processing prismatic blades in black obsidian were highly skilled. Many of these blades were produced for off-site use, as the number of expected blades greatly exceeds the number retrieved from survey contexts (table 8.6).

The preceding description of specialized production sites during the Classic period indicates a complicated production-distribution structure at sites in both the Tuxtla and Hueyapan regions. Although black obsidian macrocores were the primary object entering centers and select smaller sites, blocks, nodules, prismatic cores, and prismatic blades were also traded to the southern Gulf lowlands. In addition, clear obsidian was distributed to the southern Gulf Coast mainly in macrocore form, but there is some evidence that a few sites received this obsidian as prismatic cores and finished prismatic blades. Green obsidian was imported largely as prismatic blades, although there are sites that occasionally received macrocores and pressure cores. Small flakes and blades (and the cores discarded after reduction) were also imported in black and clear obsidian during the Classic period but to a much lesser extent than during the preceding Formative period.

Furthermore, most of the obsidian prismatic blades being produced at both centers and small sites were intended for off-site use. This finding was unanticipated. Standard central place models of production-distribution structure indicate that centers generally provide goods for smaller sites situated around them. Thus, high ratios at centers should have been made up for by much lower ratios at small sites, with the average for all sites approaching 1.0. This was definitely not the case on the southern Gulf Coast. Much of the prismatic blade assemblage produced therefore appears to be missing, which can only be explained if obsidian was disposed of outside of residential contexts.

Finally, skill in reducing pressure cores varies in an intriguing manner between the two regions. On the one hand, knappers at small sites in the Tuxtla mountains generally made more errors reducing black obsidian prismatic cores than workers at centers (table 8.3). This kind of production behavior makes sense if skill is a function of production intensity, with specialists residing at centers and less specialized knappers living at rural sites. In the Hueyapan region, on the other hand, more pressure core reduction errors were committed by obsidian workers processing black obsidian at centers, not at small sites (table 8.3). Reduction behavior of this sort is unusual. Perhaps

Table 8.6 Classic-period ratio statistics for specialized production sites

	Observed prismatics	Pressure cores	Reduction debitage	Expected prismatics	Expected/Observed prismatics	Errors/Core
BLACK OBSIDIAN						
Matacapan	10,385	143	496	42,900	4.3	3.5
Ranchoapan	372	12	3	3,600	9.7	0.3
El Peluqueria	137	6	8	1,800	13.1	1.3
Apomponapam	170	3		900	5.3	0.2
Guayabal	119	12	2	3,600	30.3	
Sigue Ladrillo	42	1				
Acagual	94		3			
Berenjenal	253	6		1,800	7.1	
El Zapote	80	1		300	3.8	
CLEAR OBSIDIAN						
Matacapan	285	3	3	900	3.2	1.0
Ranchoapan	2	1	1	300	150.0	1.0
El Peluqueria						
Apomponapam	2	1	1	300	150.0	
Guayabal	20					
Sigue Ladrillo	4					
Acagual	11					
Berenjenal	24					
El Zapote	4					

knappers at centers in the Hueyapan region had greater access to obsidian and for that reason were more casual in prismatic core reduction. If this was the case, then knappers in the Hueyapan countryside may have had comparatively less access to obsidian and thus had to conserve material to a greater degree. It should be pointed out that knappers in the Tuxtla region generally made about the same or more errors than lithic workers in the Hueyapan region. This observation suggests that sites in the Tuxtla mountains had greater access to black obsidian than the Hueyapan region. This may be because Teotihuacan merchants and their descendants, who were the likely traders of obsidian to the southern Gulf Coast during Middle and Late Classic times, lived at Matacapan and in its immediate territory (Santley et al. 1987). This hypothesis is supported by the fact that green obsidian from Pachuca, the principal source traded by Teotihuacan from central Mexico during the Middle Classic, is always more common in the Tuxtla than the Hueyapan region.

Patterning at Unspecialized Consumer Sites

A large number of sites processed obsidian in only nominal amounts or were the recipients of prismatic blades only. Some of the material consumed by these unspecialized sites was processed for use on-site, but much of it was also destined for use off-site, as discussed above. Just what these tasks were is impossible to define at present, but cutting activities associated with the processing of maize during and after harvesting and the butchering of game encountered in and around agricultural fields are good possibilities for off-site activities.

Consumers using obsidian blades received a remarkably standardized product. Metric characteristics of a series of black obsidian blades from excavated contexts at Matacapan and the Tuxtla regional survey is presented in table 8.7. Included in the table are blade averages as well as their standard deviations. As is readily apparent, the means show little variation, and their standard deviations indicate a high degree of clustering about the mean. The average black obsidian percussion blade from Matacapan was 4.3 cm long, 1.6 cm wide, 0.36 cm thick, and had a platform angle of 91 degrees. In contrast, percussion blades from the survey were somewhat shorter (3.8 cm) but slightly wider (2.2 cm) and thicker (0.6 cm) and had a platform angle that was not as steep (80 degrees). Irregular prismatic blades in black obsidian from both Matacapan and the survey were generally shorter and somewhat thinner than black percussion blades; their platform angles averaging 90 to 91 degrees. The fine black obsidian prismatic blades produced are very similar to irregular prismatic blades, although they appear to have been somewhat longer (5.5–6.8 cm). The measurements for clear and green obsidian blades are very similar to those for black obsidian blades. Many of the platforms on black irregular and fine

Table 8.7 Classic-period blade characteristics from the Tuxla region (by blade type)

	Length (cm)	SD	Width (cm)	SD	Thickness (cm)	SD	Platform angle	SD
Matacapan Black								
Percussion blades	4.3	1.4	1.6	0.5	0.36	0.19	91	6.0
Irregular pressure	2.9	0.9	1.2	0.3	0.24	0.08	91	5.8
Fine pressure	6.8	1.7	1.0	0.2	0.24	0.07	92	5.3
Matacapan Clear								
Percussion blades	3.1	1.7	1.0	0.2	0.37	0.12	92	4.8
Irregular pressure			1.2	0.3	0.24	0.07	93	2.8
Fine pressure	7.9	0.0	1.0	0.2	0.22	0.05	92	3.5
Matacapan Green								
Percussion blades								
Irregular pressure	2.5	0.0	1.1	0.3	0.28	0.11	93	4.7
Fine pressure			1.0	0.2	0.23	0.05	94	5.2
Tuxtlas Survey Black								
Percussion blades	3.8	1.5	2.2	0.3	0.60	0.20	80	12.0
Irregular pressure	3.5	1.3	1.1	0.3	0.30	0.10	90	7.3
Fine pressure	5.5	0.0	1.1	0.3	0.30	0.08	91	5.8
Tuxtlas Survey Clear								
Percussion blades			2.5	0.0	1.90	0.0		
Irregular pressure			1.2	0.2	0.30	0.10	86	8.1
Fine pressure			1.1	0.3	0.30	0.05	77	28.0
Tuxtlas Survey Green								
Percussion blades			1.5	0.0	0.40	0.00	90	0.0
Irregular pressure			0.9	0.0	0.20	0.00	89	0.0
Fine pressure			1.1	0.2	0.20	0.06		

prismatic blades are ground. Platform grinding is a very labor intensive technique of platform preparation, which, we suspect, improves the probability of successful prismatic blade removal (see chapters 3, 6, and 7). The shorter length of black irregular prismatic blades in comparison to fine blades suggests that they were removed from pressure cores before the removal of fine prismatic blades. No companion statistics are available for the Hueyapan region, although visual inspection of the blades implies very similar patterning.

Analysis of the materials from Matacapan and the Tuxtla survey indicates three levels of use intensity: 1) edge damage visible only under a small hand lens, 2) moderate damage in some heavier duty cutting activity, and 3) extensive wear. Classes of edge wear among these three modes are much rarer in the assemblages. Some material was used for limited fine cutting and then immediately discarded. Other material was likely used for the same purpose and then cycled into activities that produced moderate edge wear, some of which was later cycled to other activities that produced the heaviest damage. This suggests that some of the prismatic blades recovered were discarded after they were no longer useful as fine cutting tools, while others were

rendered unusable only after more use and/or recycling events. This patterning, we suspect, is closely associated with the variability in obsidian accessibility. Sites with blades exhibiting all three modes of use wear come from time periods when obsidian was comparatively more accessible. On the other hand, sites with collections exhibiting greater amounts of moderate and heavy edge damage may come from time periods when obsidian was less accessible. During these time periods there appears to have been a greater need to recycle tools into more heavy-duty tasks after the prismatic blades could no longer be used for fine cutting.

The southern Gulf lowlands primarily received macrocores and prismatic cores from which pressure blades were removed. Measurements of both irregular and fine prismatic blades indicate that producers were very much concerned with producing a highly standardized product. The prismatic blades used in this area exhibit several levels of use intensity ranging from activities that produced minimal amounts of edge damage to others that resulted in much heavier wear. This variation suggests that there were changes in short-term accessibility to obsidian, with consumers recycling blades to other tasks depending on the availability of suitable material either as cores or as finished tools.

Summary and Concluding Remarks

In this chapter, we have argued that the organization of past economy can be reconstructed using information on obsidian assemblages from raw material sources, tool production sites, and tool use locations. Integrating evidence from all of these sources provides a more complete picture of system structure than any one of the three does by itself. Because obsidian reduction is a subtractive technology, the kinds of products circulating throughout the economic landscape can be determined in some detail. The weak link in our consideration of obsidian assemblage variability from the southern Gulf lowlands concerns how obsidian blades were used. Research on this topic will require experimental studies of various activities, the kinds of wear produced, and comparisons of types of damage present with those evident on archaeological samples (Burleson 1999; Lewenstein 1987).

Nonetheless, a number of summary and concluding remarks can be made. Most of the raw material imported to the Tuxtla and Hueyapan regions during the Formative period was clear obsidian, which the INAA study suggests probably came from Guadalupe Victoria. This material was imported to the southern Gulf Coast both as flake cores from which small blades and flakes were removed and as finished blades/flakes. This obsidian was of good to poor quality, based on surface texture, the amount of visible inclusions, and the number of fracture planes present. How these blades and flakes were used cannot be securely established at present, although their utilization as bits in manioc graters is a possibility.

The Classic period coincides with an increased reliance on black obsidian, which came primarily from the Zaragoza source. This shift in source utilization corresponds temporally with a dramatic increase in prismatic blade utilization in both of our regions. In general this material is of excellent quality suitable for the manufacture of all kinds of tools, especially prismatic blades (see Santley, Barrett, Glascock, and Neff ND for a more extended discussion). Trace-element analysis has established that material from Zaragoza was the primary source relied on by a number of regions of the southern Gulf lowlands during the Classic period (Cobean et al. 1971, 1991; Hester, Heizer, and Jack 1971; Hester, Jack, and Heizer 1971; Knight 1999; Stark et al. 1992).

Most of the information on product import, local cycling, and artifact use comes from assemblages that date to the Classic period. Generally, it appears that the black obsidian macrocore was the primary object imported to the Tuxtla and Hueyapan regions (compared to blades/flakes and flake cores during the Formative period), although some blocks and nodules, prismatic cores, and prismatic blades were also exchanged to the southern Gulf lowlands during the Classic period. This increasing focus on the same source, with sites manufacturing the same products, suggests the development of a more widespread production-distribution system focused on high-quality material suitable for successful prismatic blade removal. Clear obsidian from Guadalupe Victoria and green obsidian from Pachuca were also imported, the latter normally as fine prismatic blades.

After arriving on the southern Gulf Coast, macrocores were reduced to prismatic cores from which prismatic blades were removed. Many of these cores arrived at centers that used blades in specialized tasks. Other cores entered villages and hamlets. Thus, small communities often were not dependent on tools produced at centers. Specialists frequently made errors during prismatic blade removal, but these generally were less common at centers, especially in the Tuxtla region. These specialists most likely worked obsidian in household contexts, not in workshops or larger scale manufactories. The number of cores found at most sites cannot account for the number of blades present, usually by a very significant margin. This indicates that most prismatic blade production was for use off-site, probably for activities associated with subsistence. The product made by knappers in most settings in the Tuxtla region was quite uniform in size and shape, implying a great degree of standardization. Although we lack metric data, the same appears to be the case in the Hueyapan region. The amount of use evident on blades varies greatly; some blades exhibit virtually no edge damage, while others were worn to exhaustion. This patterning suggests variation in accessibility to obsidian products through time and across space.

The degree to which the patterning we have observed on the southern Gulf Coast of Mexico is present in other parts of Mesoamerica is undetermined. The production-distribution-consumption approach to obsidian economy we have employed in this chapter is a fruitful way to view the structure of a prehistoric economic system. Future research will, we hope, improve on this research perspective, yielding more information about past obsidian economy.

ACKNOWLEDGMENTS

The fieldwork described here was generously supported by grants from the National Science Foundation, the Heinz Trust, the University of New Mexico, and several anonymous sources. Various individuals facilitated this research throughout the years. In particular, we thank Thomas W. Killion and Javier Urcid for access to the obsidian collections from the Hueyapan region and for comments on an earlier draft.

CHAPTER NINE

Early Classic Obsidian Core-Blade Production

An Example From the Site of Dos Hombres, Belize

RISSA M. TRACHMAN

A S POINTED OUT IN CHAPTER 1, archaeologists lack an extensive knowledge of the variation in obsidian core-blade production and its causes through time and over space. This chapter will be primarily concerned with provisioning constraints and, to a lesser extent, production constraints. The provisioning constraints dealt with here apply to supplying a site with obsidian. Similarly the production constraints considered here apply to the ways in which production is effectively carried out at the site itself.

Recently a collection of production debris was excavated from an Early Classic tomb in the B-4 group (operation 8) at the site of Dos Hombres, Belize. As discussed in chapter 1, the site of Dos Hombres corresponds to a distant source location in relation to the obsidian it relied upon. Not surprisingly, the production activities identified here reflect the general scarcity of obsidian used in core-blade production. In examining this collection, it became clear that an additional, previously undocumented technique of platform creation and rejuvenation had been taking place (Trachman 1999a). This chapter presents the evidence for production at the site, documents the evidence for this additional technique, and attempts to explain the technique in terms of the broader goals of this volume. That is to say, the technique will be placed into perspective socially, politically, and economically. The people of the B-4 group will be addressed from two perspectives, as the probable consumers of the raw material and as the possible producers of finished prismatic blades. Dos Hombres presents a unique opportunity to examine these issues at a small consumer-end site in the southern Maya lowlands, a perspective that is largely unexplored.

Archaeological Context

During the 1997 field season of the Programme for Belize Archaeological Project (PfBAP), a large collection of obsidian artifacts was excavated from the B-4 group at the site of Dos Hombres. The PfBAP is a long-term research effort in northwestern Belize (figure 9.1). It endeavors to record and identify archaeological remains of the ancient Maya in the Rio Bravo Conservation and Management area, which encompasses more than 250,000 acres of land in northwestern Belize (Valdez 1998). The goals of the PfBAP are to define the political, economic, and social structures that gave rise to and supported the ancient cities of the Three Rivers region, with attention focused on middle-sized and small-sized sites (Valdez and Adams 1995).

Sites investigated in the Three Rivers region include Rio Azul (Adams 1987, 1989; Adams et al. 1984), La Milpa (Hammond and Tourtellot 1993), Las Abejas (Sullivan 1997), Dos Hombres (Brown 1995; Durst 1998; Houk 1995, 1996; Lohse 1997, 1998, 1999), Blue Creek (Guderjan and Driver 1995), and Kinal (Adams 1991). Mapping projects have been undertaken at Gran Cacao (Lohse 1995) and at Ma'ax Na (Shaw and King 1997; Shaw et al. 1999). Investigations have also begun at Chan Chich (Houk 1998) and a mapping project is currently being designed for the site of Great Savannah (Fred Valdez, personal communication).

Dos Hombres (figure 9.2) is situated approximately 1.5 km east of the foot of the Rio Bravo Escarpment in the Rio Bravo Embayment, which includes the Rio Bravo floodplain (Brokaw and Mallory 1993). The architecture in the Dos Hombres site center is organized into four groups, A through D (Houk 1996).

Investigations of the B-4 group (figure 9.3) began in the 1997 field season, which was led by Jeff Durst. Excavations of structure B-16 (operation 8) in the B-4 group, buried in the Early Classic, revealed a red plaster floor that had been patched to cover a previous opening (Durst 1998). The bulk of the obsidian deposit discussed in this chapter was found

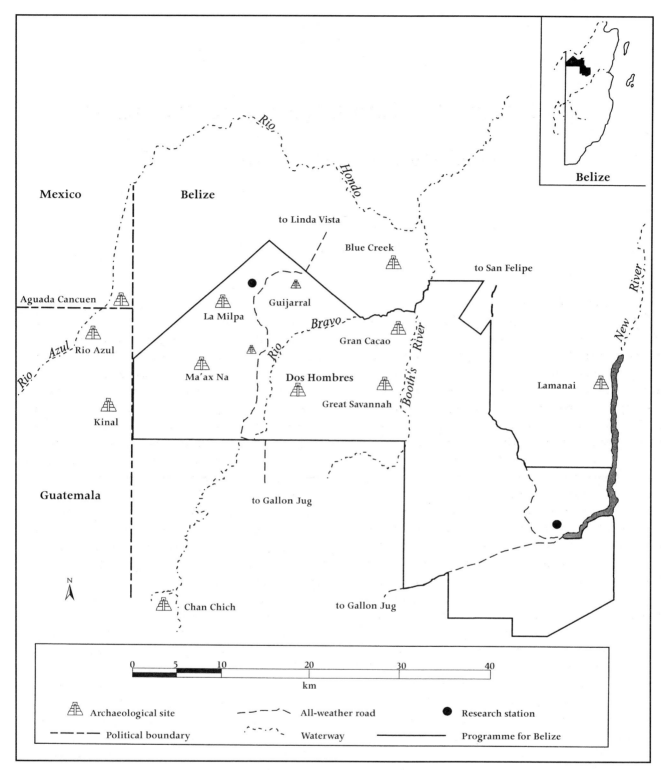

9.1 Map of the Programme for Belize Archaeological Project area.
Illustration prepared by Jon Lohse

beneath this plaster patch, in the fill overlying an Early Classic tomb (figure 9.4). Structure B-16 is the only fully excavated structure in the B-4 group to date.

Technological Evidence

As Payson Sheets (1975) noted, a technological analysis is essential to determining the procedures implemented in manufacturing a desired end product. Sheets was able to derive stages of production, or a production sequence, for his Chalchuapa collection. A production sequence refers to a hierarchy of procedures used in the method of production of a given item (Sheets 1975:372). Establishing a sequence of production can direct us to a better understanding of the organization of production, in addition to aiding in the identification of artifacts that occur in specific stages of production.

Clark and Bryant (1997) continue the emphasis on technology and production sequences, while adding artifact morphology to this perspective. They note that Sheets' behavioral analysis is helpful in differentiating between the percussion and pressure techniques used to produce prismatic blades but lacks the ability to identify different types of blades produced by the same technique (Clark and Bryant 1997). The typology resulting from the Ojo de Agua study is a more encompassing one, providing the ability to distinguish finer stages of production by considering technology and morphology.

It should be noted that the analysis of the obsidian collection from operation 8 is ongoing. Initially the data were classified according to the technological schemes set forth in earlier studies by Clark and Lee (1979), Crabtree (1968), Hester (1972; 1975), and Sheets (1972). During the process of the analysis (see Trachman 1999b), it became clear that some of the finer distinctions presented by Clark and Bryant (1997) would also prove useful and are used here.

TECHNOLOGICAL DEFINITIONS

It is important to define the terms that are used in the analysis of the collection presented in this chapter. A *blade* is a flake with parallel edges that is at least twice as long as it is wide (Crabtree 1972; Hester et al. 1971; Owen 1988). A blade can be produced by either pressure or percussion techniques (Sheets 1975; Clark and Bryant 1997). A *prismatic blade* is a blade with one or more dorsal ridges, removed from a specially prepared core (Crabtree 1968; Hester 1975), and is trapezoidal or triangular in cross section (Crabtree 1972). The process of preparing a core for the removal of pressure blades or prismatic blades generates debitage or production debris. Production debris was

sorted into four categories: 1) *flakes*, a chip or spall removed when force is applied to a nodule or core (Shafer 1969), which possesses a bulb of force and a remnant platform (Valdez 1986); 2) *flake fragments*, flakes that do not possess a bulb of force or platform (Shafer 1969) and are mostly shatter from the manufacture of blades, removal of flakes, or the breakage of flakes not associated with production; 3) *chunks*, small fragments with acute angles that do not exhibit platforms or bulbs of force; and 4) *utilized flakes*, flakes showing evidence of use, often in the form of minute flake removals on the distal or lateral edges (Valdez 1994).

A *platform* is the surface on a core from which flakes or blades are removed by either percussion or pressure (Shafer 1969). A remnant of the platform is usually visible on the flake or blade removed. Platforms may be treated in order to aid the stoneworker in removing the blades. For the purposes of this analysis, platform surfaces have been classified in the following four ways: 1) the *single-facet* or *simple* platform, prepared by creating a single-facet or smooth, flat surface (Hester 1975; Hester et al. 1971; Shafer 1969); 2) the *multifacet* platform, prepared with two or more facets (Shafer 1969) usually by the removal of two or more flakes to prepare or rejuvenate the platform; 3) the *ground* platform consisting of a pecked-and-ground platform surface; and 4) the *crushed* (or shattered) platform, consisting of an undetectable platform on a blade or flake that was obliterated during the removal process (Hester et al. 1971). While core platforms in the operation 8 collection exhibit evidence of minimal platform *abrasion*, they should not be confused with the pecked-and-ground platforms typically associated with the Terminal Classic and Postclassic periods. Definitions of the pressure blade types presented here include first-series (1s), second-series (2s), and third-series (3s) blades, as well as small percussion blades and flakes, plunging blades, proximal and distal rejuvenation flakes, and platform rejuvenation flakes (see chapter 1; Clark and Bryant 1997).

SAMPLE

The operation 8 collection contains 23,074 obsidian artifacts. Of these, 21,730 were located in the fill directly above the tomb and below the patch in the floor (see figure 9.4), all of which were designated suboperation 36 (see Trachman 1998, for suboperation descriptions). A 25% sample of the artifacts (N=5,711) was chosen for analysis and all of these artifacts were categorized according to the definitions outlined above. Metric data were collected on 19% of that group (N=1,067) for future statistical analysis. Where metric data were recorded, platform types were also

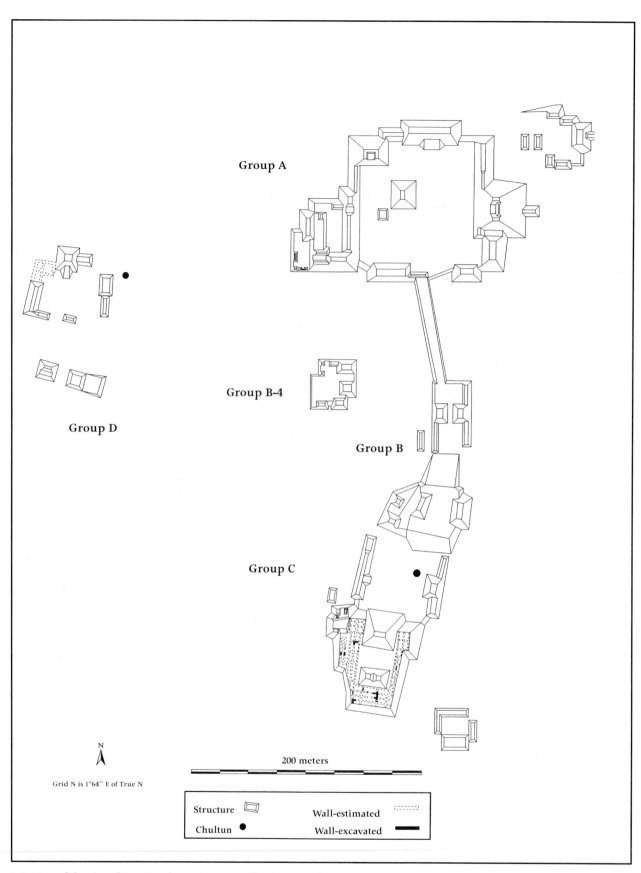

Group A

Group B-4

Group D

Group B

Group C

N

Grid N is 1°64″ E of True N

200 meters

Structure

Chultun ●

Wall-estimated

Wall-excavated

9.2 Map of the site of Dos Hombres, Orange Walk District, Belize, Central America.
Illustration prepared by Jon Lohse. Adapted from Lohse 1999:Fig. 3 and Houk 1996:Fig. 1.4

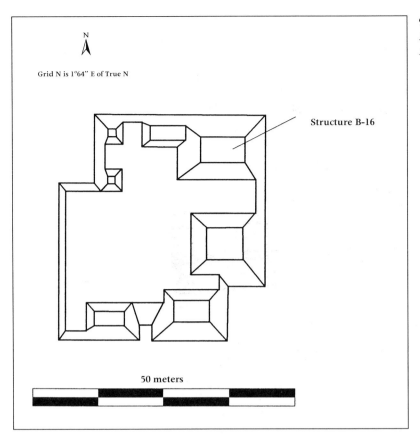

9.3 Map of the B-4 group with structure B-16.
Illustration prepared by Jon Lohse. Adapted from Houk 1996:Fig. 1.4

noted. The technological analysis is summarized in table 9.1.

There are two potential biases in the sampling strategy. First, artifacts from only two excavation levels were fine-screened (⅛ inch), while the remainder of the fill was screened with ¼-inch screen. Neither fine-screened lot has yet been analyzed. This could account for the low number of distal fragments (table 9.1). Second, most if not all of the cores and core fragments were counted and categorized. This accounts for the seemingly high percentage of cores in the sampled group.

In addition to the types of debitage listed in table 9.1, small percussion flakes, proximal, lateral, and distal rejuvenation flakes, and platform rejuvenation flakes (from both proximal and distal ends) have been observed. The blade category includes mostly pressure and at least a few percussion blades (figure 9.5). First- and third-series blades (figure 9.6) are readily identifiable in the collection, while second-series blades (figure 9.7) are more difficult to identify. Metric data were gathered on 923 blades and fragments, indicating that 449 of those are microblades. Microblades, as described by Hester et al. (1971), are those blades that measure 10 mm or less in width. The majority of platforms identified on blade artifacts (74%) were single-facet (Trachman 1999b).

One hundred of the 723 polyhedral cores and fragments (figure 9.8) were analyzed for metric data and platform type.

Sixty-nine percent have single-facet platforms (Trachman 1999b). There are at least four whole polyhedral cores that are in the percussion stage, three of which still exhibit cortical material (figure 9.9). Of the 723 cores and core fragments, at least 14% have some cortex on them.

Crabtree noted that prismatic blade cores commonly have blades removed from "one or more faces of the preformed core but not around the entire perimeter" (1968:455). Many of the operation 8 cores have both remnant percussion scars and pressure blade scars. When both are present on a single core, the pressure blade scars, overlay or intrude into the remnant percussion scars, indicating that pressure blades were not removed around the entire perimeter. I refer to these as *asymmetrical polyhedral* cores.

PECKED/SCORED ATTRIBUTE

A pecked or scored attribute has been noted on fifty-four polyhedral cores and core fragments that reflects a technique of core platform creation and rejuvenation technology that was used at Dos Hombres. This attribute occurs around the circumference of these cores and at the edges of their platforms, following a line generally perpendicular to their long axis (figure 9.10). Data recorded on forty-two of these cores and core fragments are presented in table 9.2. There are an additional twelve pieces in which the attribute

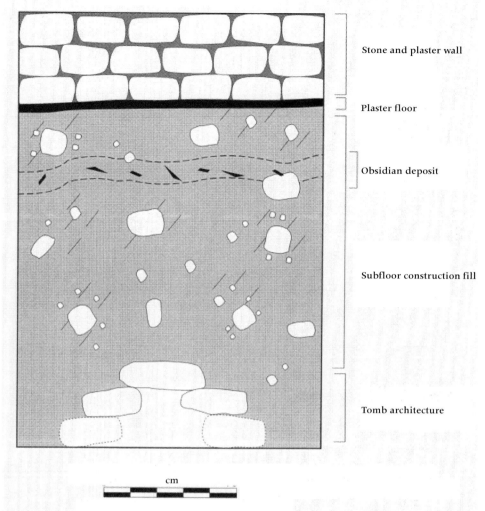

Stone and plaster wall

Plaster floor

Obsidian deposit

Subfloor construction fill

Tomb architecture

cm

9.4 Tomb excavation, west wall profile. Schematic profile of the operation 8 tomb excavation indicating the approximate location of the obsidian deposit. *Illustration prepared by the author*

was observed but are not discussed here because their fragmentary condition precluded the accurate measurement of their platform dimensions.

Data recorded in table 9.2 were gathered in order to document the pecked and scored lines. General measurements of length, width, and thickness were taken. Since the pecked or scored line appears only on proximal or whole fragments, the additional measurement of platform circumference was recorded. Length and width of the remnant pecked or scored line on each core was measured. These measurements are useful for comparison or identification only, as will be explained below. The rejuvenation fragment column in table 9.2 is, admittedly, interpretational. The data in this column are gathered from assessing the presence or absence of percussion scars and the positioning of the attribute.

The forty-two cores in the sample were separated into categories on the basis of whether they had a pecked line or

a scored line. The difference is related to the morphology of the line. A pecked line refers to pecking the core in such a way to form a line evidenced by minute cones, whereas a scored line refers to scratching or dragging a line on the core. There are some differences in the cores and fragments on which the two attributes appear. The scored line appears only on proximal fragments. All but two of the proximal fragments with scored lines exhibit only pressure blade scars. In addition the scored lines appear on the distal end of these proximal fragments. Where the scored or pecked line reflects rejuvenation in this manner, the circumference of the old platform will not be the same as the circumference of the rejuvenated platform. In such cases, the circumference of the distal end of these proximal fragments was measured (table 9.2). Two proximal fragments (marked with an asterisk in table 9.2) deviate from this pattern. These specimens exhibit no extant percussion facets, yet the pecked line is positioned, like the non-rejuvenation pieces,

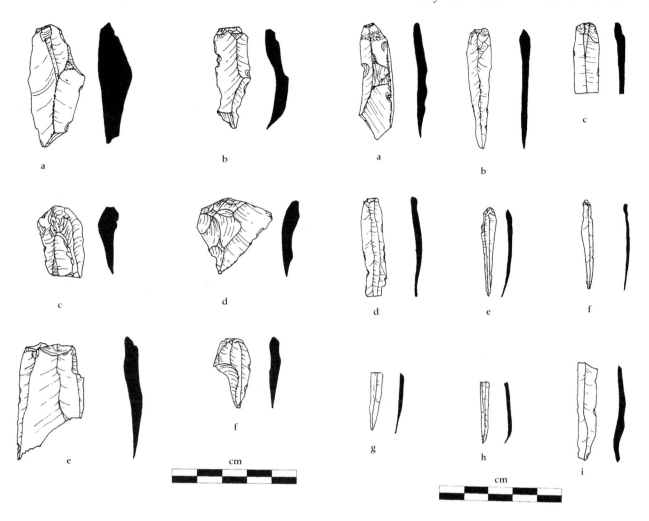

9.5 Percussion blades: *a-d,* **percussion flakes;** *e,* **macroflake;** *f,* **distal rejuvenation flake.** *Illustration prepared by Ashlyn Madden*

9.6 Obsidian blades: *a,* **first-series blade;** *b-i,* **third-series blades.** *Illustration prepared by Ashlyn Madden*

at the platform edge.

One percussion core (specimen 8-36A-2NS-22; see table 9.2) stands out from the rest. The pecked line is clear on a portion of the core, however, the platform is oriented at an extreme angle (figure 9.11). In other words, it has the same pecked line perpendicular to its long axis, but the platform itself does not follow the pecked line like it does for the other specimens in the collection. Two extremely fragmentary specimens not recorded in table 9.2 also exhibit characteristics that are similar to this specimen.

Three important findings are apparent from the analysis and observation of these data. First, asymmetrical polyhedral cores predominately exhibit pecked lines (figures 9.12, 9.13). In these cases, the pecked line is observed on the percussion facets only. The pressure blade scars crosscut the pecked line. It is therefore likely that when pressure blades were removed from the core, so too were portions of the pecked line indicating that the full length of the pecked

line originally encompassed a percussion core with a much larger circumference.

Second, percussion stage cores reflect the most abundant evidence of pecked lines. Since pressure blades were not removed from them, segments of the pecked line were not obliterated. (Note that the pecked line is still somewhat incomplete but not because of blade removal, a point that is addressed below.) In addition, although the platform surfaces of the five percussion cores are very flat and smooth, a distinctive breakage pattern is apparent. These five platform surfaces each reveal two opposing points of possible pressure or contact (no cone of force). The compression rings, however, emanate from only one of these two points. These compression rings are very diffuse and in some cases almost nonexistent.

Patterns on the platform surface provide further evidence that the pecked line was produced before the break was initiated. When comparing the platform surfaces of the

Table 9.1 Summary of technological analysis results

	Qty	%
Debitage		
Flakes	1,333	61.1
Flake fragments	602	27.6
Utilized flakes	99	4.5
Chunks	148	6.8
Total	2,182	100.00
Blades/fragments		
Proximal	1,371	48.9
Medial	1,171	41.7
Distal	188	6.7
Whole	75	2.7
Total	2,805	100.00
Polyhedral Cores/fragments		
Proximal	255	35.3
Medial	190	26.3
Distal	236	32.6
Whole	42	5.8
Total	723	

percussion cores with those of the pressure cores, it becomes evident that blade detachment had removed some of the original rejuvenation breakage pattern. Also, if the pecking had been done after the break, small flake scars would litter the surfaces of the platforms; this is not the case. Furthermore, several first-series blades in the collection have the pecked line near their platforms (figure 9.14), indicating that they were removed after the pecking was performed.

Third, it appears that the differentiation between the pecked line and the scored line may be a function of the general thickness of the core body, that is, the area being pecked or scored. As previously stated, the scored lines only appear on proximal rejuvenation fragments produced during platform rejuvenation. The circumference of the fragments at the scored line (the distal end of the proximal fragment) are significantly smaller than the original estimated circumference of the percussion cores with pecked lines in the collection.

PECKED AND SCORED INITIATION

The presence of asymmetrical polyhedral cores indicates an additional step in platform creation and rejuvenation technology utilized by the ancient craftsperson at the site of Dos Hombres. A discussion of this technology based on the data presented above is essential in order to place it into a production sequence.

Approximately 77% of all cores and core fragments analyzed (tables 9.1, 9.2) have single-facet platforms. One of the forty-two specimens without a single-facet platform (8-36A-2NS-22 in table 9.2) may reflect a different situation and is

discussed below. Single-facet platforms are common for polyhedral cores in Mesoamerica. These surfaces are described as flat and smooth, often so smooth that grinding or abrading of the platform surface was required to prevent crushing of the platform and slippage of the pressure tool during blade removal (see Crabtree 1968; Dreiss 1988; Hester 1972; Sheets 1975; chapters 3 and 7). In the Maya region, platform surface abrading appears as early as the Late Preclassic (Sheets 1972). The physical properties of obsidian (that is, conchoidal fracture) can make these flat, smooth platforms difficult to generate through percussion techniques alone.

PROPOSED TECHNOLOGY

Based on the evidence from the Dos Hombres, operation 8 collection, I have proposed (Trachman 1999a) that the pecked and scored lines were produced by the prehistoric obsidian worker to create the plane of weakness that obsidian lacks. A modern glass cutter follows the same procedure today. First, a line must be ground or scored in the desired area with a specific tool. Next, bending pressure or force in the form of a tap is applied resulting in a break along the scored line (Clow and Clow 1976; Duncan 1975; Greene 1984; Isenberg and Isenberg 1972; Lips 1973). It has been demonstrated that scoring a glass rod around its circumference will produce a simpler break (Greene 1984; Rawson 1980; Stanworth 1950). As Rawson explains, "If the rod is heavily abraded before it is broken, a simple transverse break is observed originating from the rod surface....In fracture of an unabraded rod, the fracture usually forks and the rod breaks into at least three pieces" (1980:149). Stanworth further states, "Glass...will break in the zone of maximum tension only if a suitable flaw exists in this zone. If no such suitable flaw exists, then the fracture will commence at a flaw in a zone of smaller tension" (1950:67).

I suggest the pecked and scored lines reflect the techniques used to create and rejuvenate obsidian polyhedral core platforms at Dos Hombres. This technique resembles the procedure used to break glass rods, only on a larger scale. Accordingly, Gene Titmus and I have begun an experimental investigation in order to assess the feasibility of such a technique and attempt to replicate both the pecked and scored attributes and the distinctive breakage pattern noted on the platform surfaces of the percussion cores in the operation 8 collection.

Initial attempts at replication entailed pecking a line around the circumference of a polyhedral core about 7 to 10 mm below its platform using a chert biface. We then used bipolar percussion to remove a small tabular flake. The resulting platform surface was very concave, not flat like

Table 9.2 Analysis of core specimens with pecking or scoring attribute, RB-2, Op8

Lot	Spec.	Category	Length	Width	Thickness	Weight	Line length	Line width	Platform circumf.	Scar type	Rejuv. frag.	Pecked/ scored	Cortex
8-36A-2, NS	18	Proximal	29.03	41.99	36.25	47.16	72.55	132-6.65	130.20	Percussion	n	p	y
8-36A-2, N	201	Whole	45.22	47.54	34.97	80.57	14.39	3.06-4.82	131.40	Percussion	n	p	y
8-36A-2, NS	44	Whole	43.93	41.12	36.74	66.60	38.48	1.58-4.33	109.36	Percussion	n	p	y
8-36A-2, NS	22	Whole	67.09	46.23	30.47	63.94	64.95	1.64-6.15	137.79	Percussion	n	p	y
8-36-2	11	Whole	49.10	44.07	32.28	65.64	52.76	1.56-5.09	112.94	Percussion	n	p	y
8-36A-2, NS	31	Whole	46.82	25.10	12.89	19.81	15.44	2.63-4.86	58.03	Both	n	p	n
8-36-4	148	Whole	43.71	32.46	18.36	30.79	30.21	2.82-6.15	77.84	Both	n	p	n
8-36-4	134	Whole	48.09	27.66	12.67	21.82	23.11	2.91-5.08	62.77	Both	n	p	n
8-36A-2, N	204	Whole	43.89	18.35	15.98	13.02	8.40	1.57-2.68	46.47	Both	n	p	n
8-36-2	14	Whole	48.97	22.40	12.32	13.74	13.57	1.50-2.92	57.78	Both	n	p	n
8-36-2	9	Whole	54.54	29.19	16.13	26.44	17.68	1.10-3.06	66.05	Both	n	p	n
8-36A-2, N	37	Whole	65.07	27.26	13.27	25.68	10.79	1.40-2.48	56.75	Both	n	p	n
8-36A-1	78	Proximal	34.74	24.57	11.53	13.55	14.76	2.78-4.73	47.36	Both	n	p	n
8-36A-2, NS	247	Proximal	32.77	22.84	10.49	12.12	23.44	2.98-3.61	49.40	Both	n	p	n
8-36A-2, NS	248	Proximal	21.16	20.55	13.47	8.24	17.75	3.09-5.27	50.48	Both	n	p	n
8-36A-2, NS	32	Proximal	22.81	22.74	14.49	9.70	21.07	1.87-3.14	50.83	Both	n	p	n
8-36A-2, NS	33	Proximal	20.35	16.06	9.69	3.95	11.59	1.15-2.88	30.38	Both	n	p	n
8-36A-2, N	207	Proximal	29.15	23.21	9.53	7.12	15.07	2.54-3.74	50.86	Both	n	p	n
8-36A-2, N	216	Proximal	23.19	24.70	17.48	11.15	33.65	1.89-3.28	67.05	Both	n	p	n
8-36-5	56	Proximal	39.78	18.76	12.37	13.55	16.37	1.36-3.13	41.21	Both	n	p	n
8-36-5	63	Proximal	32.85	21.22	17.05	12.96	15.80	1.44-5.55	61.15	Both	n	p	n
8-36-5	84	Proximal	35.25	22.67	13.89	13.08	11.15	1.78-2.22	47.76	Both	n	p	n
8-36-5	126	Proximal	40.80	25.69	16.65	20.71	16.50	1.97-4.08	53.28	Both	n	p	n
8-36-2	05	Proximal	20.75	20.81	11.26	6.52	18.57	1.10-3.13	48.18	Both	n	p	n
8-36-2	17	Proximal	35.86	21.01	12.41	14.38	9.71	2.88-3.89	46.90	Both	n	p	n
8-36-2	43	Proximal	18.58	18.13	18.65	6.81	11.08	1.47-2.37	50.18	Both	n	p	n
8-36-2	39	Proximal	19.98	26.55	10.86	8.09	8.46	2.25-3.60	51.87	Both	n	p	n
8-36-2	57	Proximal	39.73	27.18	20.49	18.96	14.75	1.46-4.81	59.92	Both	n	p	n
8-36-1	27	Proximal	20.26	26.86	16.91	10.21	16.89	2.04-3.46	66.84	Both	n	p	n
8-36-4	153	Proximal	20.33	20.94	11.51	6.30	31.52	<1	40.00/51.94	Both	y	Scored	n
8-36-4	159	Proximal	15.61	16.98	12.14	3.93	29.06	<1	36.44/42.25	Pressure	y	Scored	n
8-36-2	91	Proximal	16.14	16.92	13.10	3.73	18.09	<1	36.18/49.09	Both	y	Scored	n
8-36-2	94	Proximal	21.99	16.68	11.06	5.15	26.31	<1	31.37/47.08	Pressure	y	Scored	n
8-36-2	100	Proximal	24.20	24.59	16.66	12.53	36.60	<1	49.31/68.48	Pressure	y	Scored	n
8-36-2	97	Proximal	27.64	22.77	15.16	12.41	12.95	1.68-3.95	50.59	Pressure*	y*	p	n
8-36-2	176	Proximal	15.36	17.58	10.78	3.89	33.15	2.08-5.25	46.01	Pressure*	y*	p	n
8-36-2	103	Proximal	11.98	17.17	13.58	3.67	37.83	1.18-2.41	42.93/50.16	Pressure	y	p	n
8-36-2	118	Proximal	11.51	21.32	18.25	5.51	38.45	1.14-3.15	60.57/62.17	Pressure	y	p	n
8-36-4	182	Proximal	18.89	24.66	14.94	7.83	58.16	1.17-3.03	43.99/58.16	Pressure	y	p	n
8-36-5	127	Proximal	21.35	17.76	14.57	6.91	52.18	1.11-2.34	34.66/52.18	Pressure	y	p	n
8-36A-2, NS	185	Proximal	14.73	18.20	11.65	4.53	23.77	1.33-2.35	36.94/51.27	Pressure	y	p	n
8-36A-2, NS	193	Proximal	25.77	25.93	20.07	18.38	25.44	1.39-4.43	56.54/77.30	Both	y	p	n .

* Core tablets produced during rejuvenation that have only pressure facets and a pecked line at preceding platform. Pecked initiation was used to rejuvenate the preceding platform but not to remove the tablet during the subsequent rejuvenation.

Note: All measurements in millimeters and maximum values; weight in grams

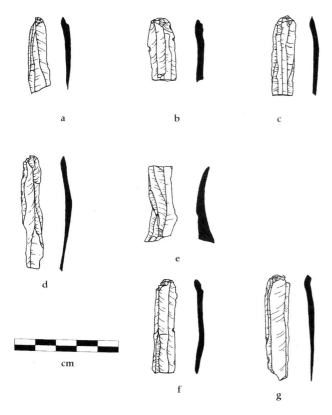

9.7 Obsidian blades: *a-e,* **possible second-series blades;** *f-g,* **third-series blades.** *Illustration prepared by Ashlyn Madden*

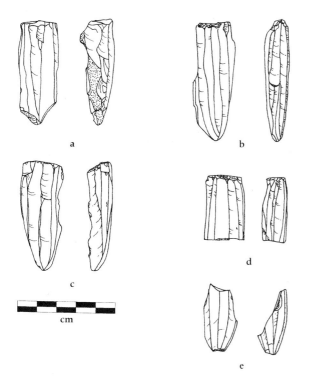

9.8 Obsidian artifacts: *a-c,* **exhausted pressure blade cores;** *d,* **pressure blade core;** *e,* **plunging blade fragment.** *Illustration prepared by Ashlyn Madden*

the surface of the operation 8 cores. After several unsuccessful attempts to replicate the prehistoric platform surfaces, a second set of experiments was performed using a different method.

Again a line was pecked with a chert biface only this time it was placed about halfway between the two ends of a polyhedral core. The break was then initiated by laying the specimen on a concave surface, as would be present on a metate, and applying indirect percussion to the pecked line. The concave surface and indirect percussion recreated the bending effect suggested above and produced a successful break along the pecked line. Thus, both the remnant pecked line and the breakage pattern on the surface of the operation 8 percussion cores was replicated. The bending break initiates from the pecked line on the core face adjacent to the concave metate surface. As in the operation 8 cores, this indicates the transmission of force opposite the core face where indirect percussion was applied. For the replicated specimens this is the point where the break initiates and the compression rings emanate. What I observed on the operation 8 cores as a second point of applied force (from which compression rings do not emanate) is the point at which the indirect percussor was placed in contact with the pecked line. The break produces two smaller cores each having a very smooth, flat platform with very diffuse compression rings and no cones of force, unlike the previous bipolar experiments. We refer to this rejuvenation technique of pecking or scoring followed by a bending break as the *pecked* or *scored initiation* method. It is clear that what is found in the Dos Hombres collection are percussion core segments that have already gone through this process. I have documented and referred to these percussion core segments as if they are whole (see table 9.2) based on their relative size to the whole exhausted asymmetrical specimens.

Another effect that the pecked or scored initiation method had on the replicated specimens is that remnants of the pecked line can be found on both of the resulting core products. As such, these measurements do not reflect the true length or width of the pecked line on any given artifact prior to the break initiation. Thus, the length and width measurements of the pecked or scored line of these artifacts (see table 9.2) can only be used to identify the use of this method. Given the evidence and the nature of the technology, it seems likely that the percussion core with an extreme platform angle (specimen 8-36A-2NS-22; see figure 9.11) and remnant pecked line may represent a production failure. In the process of our replication experiments, one attempt ended in failure. The experimental specimen did not sit properly on the metate during the break and produced a twisting fracture that replicated the break observed on specimen 8-36A-2NS-22.

Recreating the bending break may have some definite implications regarding core rejuvenation as evidenced from the operation 8 collection. One reason that the pecked initiation may work could be related to the position of the pecked line in reference to either end of the core. In other words, in the attempt at bipolar removal the pecked line was placed 7 to 10 mm below the previously utilized platform, but the circumference of this core at the pecked line is 158 mm. As observed in the artifacts (see table 9.2) that are interpreted as rejuvenation fragments or tablets, the circumferences are rather small and the distances from the previous platform to the pecked or scored lines (length measurement of the fragment) are short. The lengths, then, should be considered with the circumferences in order to provide a ratio. This type of ratio may indicate the distance from the end or previous platform necessary for successful removal to be a function of the circumference, as well as whether or not it may be scored versus pecked.

As is clear, there are still many questions to be answered with experimental investigation. The preliminary results, however, have greatly improved the prospects of placing the pecked and scored initiation techniques into a reduction sequence.

REDUCTION SEQUENCE

Sheets (1972, 1975), Clark (1988, 1997), and Clark and Bryant (1997) have presented a series of reduction sequences. In attempting to place pecked and scored initiations into perspective, I will focus on the sequence presented by Clark and Bryant (1997) because it designates finer distinctions within the stages of both the percussion and pressure procedures. A summary of this reduction sequence can be found in the introduction to this volume. Clark and Bryant state that "not every nodule necessarily passed through each of these stages; it depended on the nodule's size and whether or not it was rejuvenated" (1997:112). It is from this perspective that the technology proposed in this chapter will be placed into their typology.

The evidence from the Dos Hombres collection combined with experimental results has yielded important information regarding the placement of pecked and scored initiations within a reduction sequence (figure 9.15). Pecked initiations are likely to have occurred sometime between the macrocore II and polyhedral core stages. The evidence from the operation 8 collection reveals that the percussion cores still retain some cortex and the percussion scars have somewhat semiregular ridges. The presence of first-series blades bearing the pecked line, as well as the

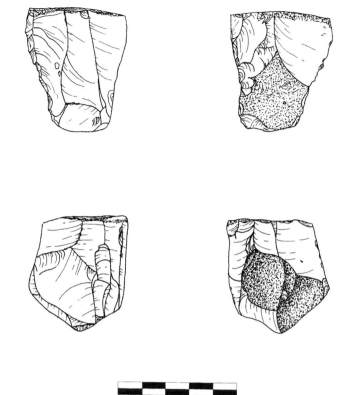

9.9 Percussion cores with cortex. *Illustration prepared by Ashlyn Madden*

cm

Left, **9.10 Percussion core with pecking at platform and cortex at distal end.** *Illustration prepared by the author*
Right, **9.11 Percussion core (specimen 8-36A-2NS-22) with pecking and an extreme platform angle.** *Illustration prepared by the author*

9.12 Polyhedral core specimens showing pressure blade scars, except for percussion core at far right. *Illustration prepared by the author*

9.13 Polyhedral core specimens showing percussion blade scars, except for right percussion core at far right. Note pecking at platforms. *Illustration prepared by the author*

9.14 First-series blade with remnant pecking. *Illustration prepared by the author*

asymmetrical polyhedral cores with corollary percussion scars and small amounts of cortex remaining on a portion of them, signifies that pressure blades could be removed directly after the percussion core was severed.

A macrocore II that has undergone a pecked initiation will produce a proximal and distal fragment. The percussion stage cores in the operation 8 collection reflect this transitional state. From the percussion perspective, these could be referred to as percussion stage II distal or proximal fragments and may have been immediately reduced with pressure into whole polyhedral cores. I have referred to these percussion stage pieces as if they are whole (cores) because of their potential for moving directly into the pressure stages.

Pecked initiations and scored initiations as a rejuvenation method are placed in the reduction sequence in the same fashion as any other rejuvenation strategy. At any point during the process of transformation from a prismatic core II to a prismatic core III, the necessity could arise to rejuvenate the platform, just as in the transformation from prismatic core III to an exhausted polyhedral core. Evidence from the Dos Hombres cores is consistent with the placement of this rejuvenation technology along this portion of the sequence. Proximal fragments were apparently removed from pressure cores for the purpose of rejuvenation. Rejuvenation is intended to lengthen the use life of the core either when its platform becomes too small to set the pressure tool or when errors accumulate during blade removal. It is important to note that the scored and pecked initiations for the purpose of rejuvenating the platform are but two of the rejuvenation strategies represented in the operation 8 collection. As reflected in the analysis above, there are several proximal and distal rejuvenation flakes present in the debitage. Therefore, at least three platform rejuvenation techniques were utilized by the producers of the operation 8 collection.

Interpretations

Similar deposits of obsidian, as well as chert, associated with tombs have been found at several Classic Maya sites (figure 9.16): Altar de Sacrificios (Smith 1972), Dos Pilas (Stiver 1994), Rio Azul (Hall 1986), Tikal (Moholy-Nagy 1991; 1997), Uaxactun, and Yaxchilan (Coe 1965). Although in ritual context, the tomb collection from operation 8 is primarily composed of production waste. If the deposit is to be considered in terms of production, it should be regarded as being in at least secondary context. Moholy-Nagy (1997) defines secondary context as material transported across an unknown distance from the locus of its production or use. Some deposits of workshop debris from the Maya lowlands that have been recognized (some in secondary contexts) are Ojo de Agua (Clark and Bryant 1997), Tikal (Moholy-Nagy 1979), Quirigua (Sheets 1983b), Yaxchilan (Clark 1997), El Pozito (Neivens and Libbey 1976), and El Pilar (Olson 1994).

Discard behavior may be an important factor in evaluating the context of these materials (Schiffer 1972; Hayden and Nelson 1981). It is possible that storage or accumulation of production waste may be intentional for the purpose of using it later in ritual interments (Moholy-Nagy 1997; Clark 1997). This may indicate that the operation 8 collection represents the ritual deposition of accumulated production waste from a workshop or dump that was stored in another location until it was deposited in the tomb. It is important to note here that even though it is in secondary context, collections like this can provide important information regarding craft production technology among the Classic Maya (Moholy-Nagy 1997; Stiver 1994).

Obviously, since the obsidian deposit is in secondary context, the original locale of the blade workshop is not known. It seems likely that the workshop was nearby, as no other contexts have yet been found with obsidian production waste at the site of Dos Hombres or in the PfBAP area. It is probable that the people of the B-4 group were involved in obsidian production in some way. If the actual blade producer or workshop was not located in the B-4 group, then the people living here might have financed or arranged the venture. In any case, someone at the site of Dos Hombres was producing prismatic blades somewhere near the site center.

As Hirth and Andrews have noted in the introduction to this volume, provisioning constraints are those factors where the movement and distribution of the raw material have direct influence on production technology. They conceptualize provisioning constraints as three important factors including the type and form of raw material, availability and distance from source, and sociopolitical conditions governing distribution.

The type and form of raw material coming in to the site of Dos Hombres is significant to any interpretation of the operation 8 collection. Since the pecked and scored initiations have not been reported before, it is my belief that the technique was being performed at the site of Dos Hombres rather than at the quarry. It is therefore likely that the blade producers were receiving the material in the form of percussion cores in a stage similar to Clark and Bryant's (1997) macrocore II. Clark (1987, 1988) has noted that the exchange of specialized commodities had to be coordinated. The obsidian workers at the quarry would have been required to preform macrocores,

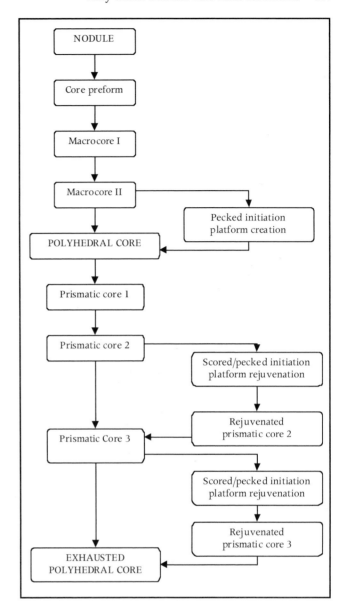

9.15 Idealized reduction sequence that includes scored and pecked initiations. *Illustration prepared by Erick Rochette*

whereas the blade producers at the receiving end would have needed the skill to work the macrocore into its polyhedral form and further reduce it using pressure to make prismatic blades (Clark 1988).

At Dos Hombres the macrocores (stage II) underwent pecked initiations before the removal of pressure blades. A pecked initiation performed at the macrocore II stage produces two usable cores. Pecked and scored initiations continued to be used to rejuvenate the polyhedral cores in various stages of pressure blade removal. It is likely that the Dos Hombres knappers wanted smaller cores. There are two possible explanations for this. First, it is possible that the final product (very small blades) was desired for some

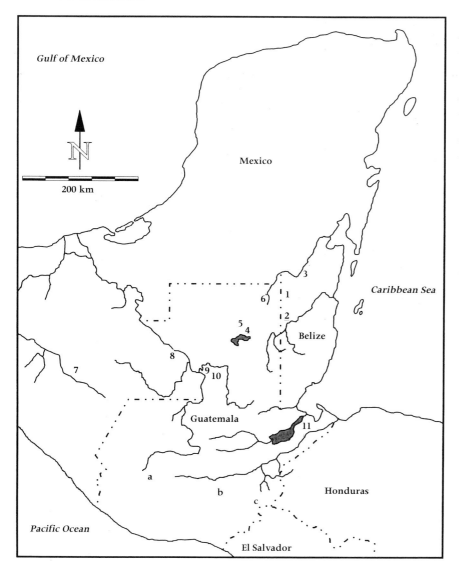

9.16 Map of Maya region showing three major obsidian sources in relation to Dos Hombres. Obsidian sources: *a,* San Martín Jilotepeque; *b,* El Chayal; *c,* Ixtepeque. Maya sites: *1,* Dos Hombres; *2,* El Pilar; *3,* El Pozito; *4,* Tikal; *5,* ; *6,* Río Azul; *7,* Ojo de Agua; *8,* Yaxchilan; *9,* Altar de Sacrificios; *10,* Dos Pilas; *11,* Quirigua. *Illustration prepared by Jon Lohse*

special purpose. Further investigation would be required to assess what this purpose may have been. Second, it is possible that the Dos Hombres knappers wanted to increase the distribution of this imported resource within the community. Obsidian was not a resource available in abundance at this site because of its distance from the source(s).

The closest sources to Dos Hombres are those located in southern Guatemala (see figure 9.16). San Martín Jilotepeque, El Chayal, and Ixtepeque, all in the Guatemalan highlands, are three of the major sources located at a distance of approximately 400 to 500 km from northern Belize (Dreiss and Brown 1989). Transporting obsidian nodules over this great distance would not be practical, especially when they could be reduced to some extent at the quarry.

Only three pieces of green obsidian have been excavated in association with the B-16 structure. The Pachuca green

obsidian likely indicates an indirect form of contact with central Mexico, specifically Teotihuacan in the Early Classic. The remainder of the tomb collection is expected to derive from one or more of the major sources in southern Guatemala. Neutron activation analysis data indicate El Chayal was the predominant source represented, though additional testing will be required to establish realistic percentages (Trachman 1998, 1999b).

Cores would also have been costly, with their value being related to the labor expended in their manufacture at the quarry and the transport costs figured in terms of their weights over distance (Clark 1987). It is these two factors, the expense of cores and necessary coordination between quarry sites and consumer sites that make it seem unlikely that blade producers at distant source locations would be unskilled. Importing communities or consumer sites would have a strong need for skilled knapping ability (Clark 1987).

In other words, the blade producers at these sites could not afford to lose significant amounts of obsidian as a result of manufacturing errors.

Distance may also have affected the size of the cores being transported. Smaller macrocores may have been easier to transport to more distant sites than larger cores or they may have facilitated distribution from quarries to consumer sites. It is conceivable that the blade producers within the site of Dos Hombres were using the pecked initiation in the late percussion stages to produce very flat, smooth platform surfaces. Since the technique produces no waste flake(s), it is also possible that it was used in order to conserve the raw material or increase distribution to consumers within the site.

Conclusion

In conclusion, there is sufficient evidence to indicate that the operation 8 collection from the site of Dos Hombres is the result of production activity. The analysis of the collection revealed previously unidentified attributes consisting of pecked and scored lines that broadens knowledge of the variation in obsidian core-blade technology. These served to control the initiation of breakage for successful platform creation and rejuvenation. Preliminary experiments have aided greatly in placing pecked and scored initiations into a localized reduction sequence. It was likely that the distance of the site from the obsidian source influenced the size of the macrocores, the need for conservation of the material, and therefore the variation in production technology seen in the Dos Hombres operation

8 collection. The pecked and scored initiation method is an example of a technological adaptation to the conditions of access to raw material and the range of form in which obsidian circulated during the Early Classic.

ACKNOWLEDGMENTS

I am truly grateful to Ken Hirth and Bradford Andrews for their forethought in designing the concepts for the volume and inviting me to submit this manuscript. I would especially like to thank Dr. Fred Valdez for giving me the opportunity to perform the analysis and guiding me during it. Dr. Thomas R. Hester's advice and comments have been truly invaluable. Gene Titmus also played an essential role in perceiving, performing, and guiding the experimental investigation. The research was supported by the Programme for Belize Archaeological Project under a permit from the Department of Archaeology, Belmopan, Belize; an undergraduate research fellowship sponsored by the University of Texas Office of the Vice President for Research; and a scholarship stipend from the UT Liberal Arts Scholarship fund with the aid of Assistant Dean Barbara M. Myers. I am truly indebted to Drs. Valdez and Hester, along with Payson Sheets, John E. Clark, Ken Hirth, Gene Titmus, James Woods, and Jon C. Lohse for their comments concerning the ideas presented here. Figures 9.1-9.14 are courtesy of the PfBAP. I also thank Jeff Durst for allowing me to participate in the operation 8 excavations. The illustrations represented in figures 9.5 through 9.9 were prepared by Ashlyn Madden.

CHAPTER TEN

Core-Blade Technology
in Mesoamerican Prehistory

KENNETH HIRTH AND J. JEFFREY FLENNIKEN

THIS VOLUME ADDRESSES two simple but important issues. The first was to identify whether variation existed in the technology used to manufacture Mesoamerican-style prismatic blades and, if so, to evaluate how extensive this variation might be over time and space. If variation was encountered, then the second question was whether it was possible to infer its causes. This second objective is more difficult because of the way that different variables can combine to produce variation in lithic technology. Nevertheless, it is this dimension of technological research that holds the most potential for interpreting the organization of pre-Hispanic socioeconomic systems; so, attempts along this line are worth the effort.

The results are fairly clear. A comparison of the contributions in this volume reveals significant variation in the range of production technology used in different areas of Mesoamerica. When we selected the contributors for this volume, we did so *with* the intent of *identifying* rather than *creating* a case for variability in production systems. In the process, we assembled a group of researchers who could reliably discuss the lithic technology in their respective regions. After all, one of the primary weaknesses in lithic analysis over the past twenty-five years has been the absence of detailed analysis of lithic assemblages from archaeological sites across Mesoamerica. We felt that if differences existed, solid analysis would reveal them. Even if differences were not found, we knew the volume contents would contribute to a better understanding of the parameters of core-blade production.

The results have been surprising. We anticipated that there would be considerable overlap and duplication in technology between different areas because of the similarity of prismatic blades found throughout Mesoamerica. The most remarkable aspect of this research, however, was that

none of the core-blade technologies discussed are exactly identical to one another. They all differ from each other in subtle ways, either in the variety of items produced (for example, macrocores, polyhedral cores, preforms, or prismatic blades) or the technology that was employed to produce them. As lithic assemblages are examined from additional regions and time periods in Mesoamerica, the range of variation in core-blade production systems will, we believe, only increase.

Variation in Mesoamerican
Core-Blade Technology

Technology as the term is used in this volume refers to the total set of techniques employed in the procurement, manufacture, and use of flaked stone tools. These techniques are the manifestation of behavior that produce quarry pits and result in the distribution of formed artifacts (for example, cores, prismatic blades, and tools), and related debitage across the physical landscape. The reduction techniques employed in manufacturing flaked stone tools were culturally determined and temporally specific. Debitage and to a lesser extent formed artifacts are what constitute the lithic assemblages found in many prehistoric sites in Mesoamerica. Therefore, an understanding of the lithic technological processes involved in creating the formed artifacts and associated debitage is essential for identifying and studying prehistoric reduction techniques in both time and space.

The contributors to this volume have identified that variation can be found, and indeed should be expected, in the way core-blade technology was practiced across Mesoamerica. There are really only two laws in lithic technology. The first law is, a knapper must have stone to manufacture stone tools. The second law is, the stone tool cannot be larger than the stone. Other than this, the various production pathways that flaked stone tools may follow are virtually infinite. The acquisition of stone, however, is the all-important first step in flaked stone tool manufacture, and Alejandro Pastrana's research documents the acquisition (mining) and use of obsidian at Sierra de la Navajas from ca. 2700 to 1500 BP. In chapter 2 Pastrana discusses the technology of obsidian mining and quarrying techniques and how the size, shape, and quality of the raw material related to the synchronic and diachronic intended end products of manufacture (cores, blades, unifaces, or bifaces). He identifies that considerable technological variation can be found in the types of products manufactured at the quarry, how they are linked to the kinds of obsidian available, and how demand affected exploitation at Sierra de las Navajas over time.

In chapter 3, Dan Healan discusses the technological variation found at both ends of a single core-blade continuum. He examines Ucareo obsidian and follows its exploitation beginning at the quarry and continuing through its use in prismatic blade production at Tula, Hidalgo. Ucareo was an important source area that supplied obsidian to Tula and many other central Mexican sites during the Epiclassic period (AD 650–900) (Garcia Chavez et al. 1990; Healan 1993; Hirth 2000). This discussion provides valuable information on core processing technology at the Ucareo quarry. Obsidian cores produced at Ucareo were quite long (22–23 cm) compared to those found at Tula (9 cm) and, in contrast to reduction sequences reported elsewhere in Mesoamerica, were produced directly from nodules without passing through an intermediate macrocore preparation stage (Clark and Bryant 1997). Cores at this source were prepared with single-facet platforms well into the Postclassic when faceting, pecking, and grinding techniques were eventually introduced to prepare core platforms.

At Tula, polyhedral cores were imported with single-facet platforms. Healan provides a detailed discussion of the prismatic blade reduction sequence at Tula, including the use of bidirectional polyhedral cores, ground platform preparation (both faceting as well as abrasion), pressure blade removal, and recycling techniques. Particularly important at Tula is the change in core morphology from single-facet to pecked-and-ground platforms. His discussion of basalt grinding slabs used in preparing pecked-and-ground platforms adds important information to this reduction sequence. This study together with reduction sequences presented by Andrews for Teotihuacan, Parry for Otumba, and Hirth for Xochicalco provide new comparative technological data on core-blade production

in large central Mexican urban centers.

In chapter 4, William Perry uses ethnohistoric and archaeological data to document the technological variation in core-blade production at Otumba, a late Aztec site in the Basin of Mexico. Obsidian entered the site in the form of macrocores. Core platforms were faceted, pecked, and ground after they reached the site at the same time that macroblades were removed to finish shaping them. These cores were formed so that the prismatic blades removed would have rectangular distal portions; pointed blades were deliberately avoided. Furthermore, Parry reports that at Otumba blades often were removed from one face of the core only. This additional dimension of variation in core-blade production highlights the errant assumption that Postclassic workshops in the Basin of Mexico normally engaged in the symmetrical removal of blades from all sides of a core. This demonstrates yet another dimension of the technological variation found in the preparation and use of cores that can be linked to behavioral choices.

Research presented by Bradford Andrews in chapter 5 provides evidence of another dimension of variation in core-blade technology, the implementation of what he calls a linked-sequence model for core-blade reduction in the San Martin workshop at Teotihuacan. Obsidian appears to have entered the workshops as either macrocores or macroblades. Pachuca and Otumba obsidian were treated differently within these workshops, the former being used for the entire range of tools while the latter was used mainly to make bifaces and unifaces. Macroblades of Otumba obsidian were imported and then reduced directly into bifaces. In contrast, most of the Pachuca obsidian was imported in the form of macrocores. The transformation of these imports into polyhedral cores yielded macroblades that were then used in biface reduction. This effectively linked both production processes. The linked-sequence model reveals another dimension of the variation in core-blade production found throughout central Mexico during the Classic period.

In chapter 6, Michael Spence, Phil Weigand, and Maria Soto de Arechavaleta describe useful technological information on a little-known area of western Mexico where sites are in relatively close proximity to obsidian sources. Their description of "hammered," pecked, and pecked-and-ground platforms exposes another element of variation in prehistoric Mesoamerican core-blade technology. From a diachronic perspective, the use of pecking during core platform preparation in western Mexico may be one of the earliest applications of this technique for prismatic blade production in Mesoamerica.

Kenneth Hirth's discussion of core-blade production at

Xochicalco in chapter 7 provides an example of how technology may change to compensate for the reduced availability of raw material. Obsidian entered the site as relatively small and nearly exhausted prismatic pressure cores with single-facet platforms that were quickly rejuvenated before additional prismatic blades were produced. Core preparation debitage was nonexistent in the recovered assemblage. Instead, incoming cores were rejuvenated by sectioning them and establishing pecked-and-ground platforms on these much smaller core sections. Technological data are presented to argue that blades were removed by handheld pressure from these small rejuvenated cores rather than by foot-held pressure as has been suggested for blade detachment elsewhere in Mesoamerica (Clark 1982; 1989b). The limited availability of obsidian at Xochicalco resulted in pushing the core-blade production sequence found throughout Mesoamerica to its absolute technological limit. It is interesting to note that the technological variation exhibited in the Xochicalco assemblage contains the same technological attributes found elsewhere in Mexico, just rearranged somewhat as a result of material constraints that necessitated adaptation within a single reduction technology.

Robert Santley and Thomas Barrett demonstrate in chapter 8 that surface-collected assemblages can contribute technological data useful for defining flaked stone reduction sequences at the regional level—in this case, near Veracruz. Like the preceding chapter on Xochicalco, these authors supply information on the types and quantities of obsidian and how these factors related to production over time in a geographic area located a considerable distance from any obsidian sources.

In chapter 9, Rissa Trachman adds extremely interesting perspective to understanding of Mesoamerican core-blade technology by examining core-processing techniques at the ancient Maya site of Dos Hombres, Belize. The scarcity of obsidian in the Maya lowlands resulted in the implementation of creative ways to segment cores and rejuvenate core platforms. At Dos Hombres a pecked and/or scored line was employed to dictate the direction of the percussion "rejuvenation" fracture to ensure successful results. While the attributes of pecking and scratching were widely employed in Mesoamerica for platform preparation and core-face rejuvenation, scoring for fracture control is another application of this technique that has previously gone unnoticed by archaeologists. In the course of the discussion, Trachman also provides useful technological data on the core-blade reduction for this area of the Maya lowlands.

Research is productive not only when it answers a specific inquiry posed by the investigator but also when the results pose a new set of questions that researchers had not previously considered. While the contributors to this volume have addressed the issue of whether variability existed in core-blade technology across Mesoamerica, the results have definitely presented a series of additional questions yet to be explored. In the remainder of this discussion we will consider three areas of productive research for future investigators: establishing the origins of Mesoamerican core-blade technology, reconstructing the nature of quarry and workshop specialization, and identifying the multifaceted character of Mesoamerican core-blade technology.

Origin of Mesoamerican Core-Blade Technology

As fascinated as archaeologists tend to be with the question of origins, it is curious that few investigators—with the exception of John Clark (1987) and William Parry (1994)—have taken up the question of the developmental history for obsidian prismatic blade production. The core-blade technology encountered by the Spanish was over three thousand years old and prismatic blades produced at its inception are nearly identical to those produced at the time of the Conquest. Some of the earliest prismatic blades in Mesoamerica are those recovered from the late Coxcatlan and Abejas phase deposits in the Tehuacan Valley, which date to as early as 3500 BC (MacNeish et al. 1967:18). From these early beginnings, core-blade technology spread over a wide area of Mesoamerica and by 700 to 1000 BC had largely replaced simple expedient flake and bipolar technologies. It is during this period that prismatic core-blade technology became the dominant industry in the Gulf Coast (Coe and Diehl 1980:247–249), the Valley of Mexico (Tolstoy et al. 1977:102), the Valley of Morelos (Grove 1974:33,48), the Valley of Oaxaca (Marcus and Flannery 1996; Pires-Ferreira 1975:Table 5), Chiapas (Clark and Lee 1984), and the Chalchuapa area of El Salvador (Sheets 1978:Tables 3 and 5).

William Parry has discussed the origin of core-blade technology in terms of its relationship to the development of early craft specialization in Mesoamerica. According to Parry (1994:94) all prismatic blades, even those found in the earliest deposits, were commodities produced by specialists for regional and interregional exchange. He feels that obsidian core-blade production represents a unique technology that must have involved craft specialists engaged in producing prismatic blades and other specialized commodities for exchange. He believes that prismatic blade manufacture, specialized craft production, and commodity exchange were inextricably linked. In his model it is the demand for, and trade of, finished prismatic blades that provided the stimuli for the emergence of craftsmen in areas close to obsidian source locales.

Taking a slightly different perspective, John Clark focused on the spread of core-blade technology throughout Mesoamerica. For Clark (1987), core-blade technology spread as a result of competitive elite behavior. His argument consists of four points. First, that expedient flake technology in obsidian and other materials preceded the adoption of obsidian prismatic blade technology throughout Mesoamerica and was functionally sufficient to meet the population's cutting needs; in short, there was no *technological* advantage for a shift from flake to blade technology. Second, that prismatic blade technology is difficult to learn and requires specialized training. Third, that the production of prismatic blades requires coordination over space between individuals producing cores at the source and those craftsmen at greater distances from the source who receive cores and produce blades from them. Fourth and finally, Clark feels that the requirements of core-blade production are sufficiently complex that they necessitate elite sponsorship to finance and coordinate resource procurement from the quarry to workshop. The adoption of prismatic blade technology in his view is specifically linked to the emergence of chiefdom societies without which it would not have spread throughout Mesoamerica (Clark 1987:274).

Even though Clark's arguments are both logical and compelling and there is much to suggest that elites were involved at some level in the spread of core-blade technology throughout Mesoamerica, we know from other areas of the world that prismatic blades were made from pressure cores in societies well below that of chiefdom societies. Examples include the large pressure blades of paleolithic Europe (Pelegrin 1997); the Neolithic pressure blades of southwestern Asia, the Levant (Inizan and Lechevallier 1994), north Africa (Tixier 1976), and the Indo-Pakistani subcontinent (Inizan and Lechevallier 1990); the Arctic microblade tradition (Andrefsky 1987; Bradley and Giria 1996); and the Dyuktai/Yubetsu pressure blades of paleolithic Siberia and Japan (Flenniken 1988; Kobayashi 1970). Raw material and social conditions differ in each of these situations. These examples represent both mobile and sedentary societies that produced prismatic blades out of a variety of materials including obsidian, flint, and chert.

What will be required to resolve the development of obsidian core-blade production in Mesoamerica is the location and careful exploration of early production areas. Both Parry (1994) and Clark (1987) are concerned with two fundamental questions: how were early core-blade production systems organized and how specialized were they?

Were early specialists independent producers meeting the demand of their respective populations or were they the clients of emerging elites who sought greater control over interregional trade by linking specialists to them through patron-client relations? Whatever the structure of early prismatic blade production, it is likely that specialists were involved. All of the current experimental work carried out to date (Clark 1982; 1988; Crabtree 1968) suggests that the manufacture of prismatic blades involved some special skill and training, which implies the existence of craft specialists in the societies that used them.

What is important to note is that the arguments of Clark and Parry are complementary rather than mutually exclusive. It is very possible that specialists producing prismatic blades appeared first in areas near quarry sources (Parry's argument) but did not spread throughout Mesoamerica until later, when preformed cores replaced raw material and finished blades as the primary commodity moving through interregional exchange (Clark's argument). Clearly nodular obsidian used in the production of expedient flakes preceded the manufacture and exchange of prismatic blades. While expedient flakes produced from obsidian may be as sharp and useful as prismatic blades (Clark 1987), this technology is somewhat inefficient when viewed from a transportation perspective. An exchange system based on the movement of unmodified raw material is a less efficient means of procuring and transporting cutting edge over long distances than is the case if standardized preforming is used. It is for this reason that raw material was shaped into bifacial cores by Clovis hunters in North America because cores were a more efficient way of moving usable stone across the landscape. One can envision a desire on the part of both the traders and the populations consuming obsidian to increase the cutting edge per unit of weight moving through interregional exchanges. The introduction of core-blade technology would certainly represent such an increase over bipolar and expedient flake technology. The extent to which this was a combination of market (bottom-up) forces and elite (top-down) initiatives requires further investigation.

The question of how obsidian craft specialization evolved will only be resolved by careful problem-oriented research. Theory abounds in the absence of data and, unfortunately, the data are not presently available to address these issues. What we do know, however, is that the large population centers of early chiefdoms were points of significant consumption. The Olmec center of San Lorenzo on the Gulf Coast had access to and was consuming steady supplies of obsidian in the form of prismatic blades by the San Lorenzo phase (1150–900 BC), although where these blades were manufactured remains unclear (Coe and Diehl 1980:248). Some of the earliest evidence for obsidian craft specialization in Mesoamerica comes from the highland site of Chalcatzingo, Morelos. Here workshop debris dating to the Cantera phase (500–700 BC) was identified on a residential terrace (terrace 37) on the northwest periphery of the site (Burton 1987). While the workshop is located in the region's most important elite center, it is not directly associated with an elite household like we see for patron-client production of shell and other ornamental items at Copan (Widmer ND). At Chalcatzingo obsidian craftsmen appear to have been independent specialists residing at the periphery rather than within the central confines of the ceremonial center. It will not be possible, however, to clarify the linkage and interdependence between elite and obsidian specialists until good excavation data are available that clarify the social contexts of obsidian production areas within Mesoamerican societies.

Although none of the volume contributors deal specifically with Formative period production systems, chapter 6 addresses issues of specialization among chiefdom societies in western Mexico during the Classic period. These societies are analogous in structure to the chiefdom societies that Clark (1987) suggests were involved in the control and spread of core-blade technology early in Mesoamerican prehistory. This chapter reports the appearance of a large specialized obsidian blade workshop in the Guachimonton precinct of the Teuchitlan site. Three things are important about the workshop. First, the level of production within this workshop is high, exceeding that found at other sites during this period. Second, the workshop's proximity to ceremonial architecture in the Guachimonton precinct suggests that craftsmen operated under the supervision of site elite. Third, craftsmen in this workshop were working obsidian from the Group T source, which was only 3 km from the workshop and which they were close enough to control.

Despite proximity to the source and the intensity of production at the Guachimonton workshop, there is no evidence that Teuchitlan ever monopolized control over regional production. Other sites throughout the region were accessing raw material directly from the Group T source instead of getting processed tools from the Guachimonton workshop. Furthermore, this workshop did not maintain exclusive distribution of its products to households even within the Teuchitlan site; obsidian from other sources was readily entering and being worked within domestic settings throughout the site. This indicates two things about the structure of obsidian craft production in chiefdoms of western Mexico. First, that even large-scale

production like we find at the Guachimonton workshop (Soto de Arechavaleta 1990) was not sufficient to supply all sites with the obsidian they required for daily cutting needs. Second and equally important, the Guachimonton elite were not capable of maintaining exclusive control over obsidian production even by sponsoring the production of high-quality prismatic blades.

What the Guachimonton example may suggest is that although patron-client production may be found in chiefdom societies, it was not sufficient to supply households with all the obsidian tools they normally consumed. Independent craft specialists also appear to have existed in other sites that were not under elite control. It also suggests that patron-client production may have been geared toward providing preferred or high-quality prismatic blades produced to meet elite consumption and distribution purposes. Sponsored production may have been intended to produce finished goods that were distributed to lineage or clan members under the elite's control or used as trade items in broader interregional exchange networks with other elites. The demand produced by interregional trade appears to have been the basis for obsidian craft specialization at the Postclassic site of Las Cuevas, which prompted a higher level of production than is found at Guachimonton.

Quarry and Workshop Specialization

A basic feature of Mesoamerican core-blade production is that it was a segmented reduction technology. Rarely in Mesoamerica do we find the complete core-blade reduction sequence, from core shaping through blade production and discard, located at a single site location. Instead production steps are segmented and located in different places across the landscape. In Mesoamerica this is a function of two conditions: the normal uselife of a flaked stone tool and the highly localized nature of obsidian sources.

All flaked stone artifacts are subjected to a culturally determined, long, nonlinear, often circuitous, multilocational uselife. In obsidian core-blade reduction, stone changes from cores to blades and blades may change from one tool to another before they are eventually discarded. Because tool stone and finished tools move dynamically throughout the environment, each flint-knapping activity associated with their modification within this trajectory may appear as an unrelated event representing different times in prehistory, or, at best, variation within one or more reduction technologies. To understand and identify a flaked stone reduction technology, it must be viewed as a complete system where the whole is greater than the sum of the parts. Production segmentation is expressed most strikingly in Mesoamerica by the differences in manufacturing activities found at quarry locales as opposed to workshop areas located away from quarries.

Three features structured the organization of lithic industries in Mesoamerica: the sedentary nature of its prehistoric societies, the high demand for and use of obsidian cutting tools, and the highly localized nature of obsidian source deposits. Obsidian is readily available in only a few areas of highland Mesoamerica. Most populations in this region were sedentary by 900 to 1000 BC, which meant that obsidian had to move to the consumer through indirect means rather than the consumer procuring it by direct visitation to source locales. Production activities were strongly influenced by the relative availability or scarcity of obsidian within a region. Two variables appear to have had a particularly important affect on the availability of obsidian throughout Mesoamerica, distance from source and the type of distribution system through which it moved. These conditions worked with other factors to structure the form of organization and the type of technology employed to create a diverse patchwork of related production strategies across Mesoamerica all oriented towards the production of obsidian prismatic blades.

In this volume distance from source was used as an practical device for organizing the regional presentations of core-blade reduction sequences. Three broad categories were used to group the variation in terms of distance from source. *At-source* production areas were those located directly at obsidian quarries while *proximate source* locations grouped together production areas and activities located withing a 10 to 100 km radius of source locations. *Distant source* areas were those situated beyond a 100 km radius of obsidian sources. Individual procurement behavior for tool stone was assumed to vary widely across all three of these categories. As a rule, however, we would predict ceteris paribus that obsidian availability should decrease in proportion with the distance from the source because of the energetic constraints and the social costs involved in moving raw material or finished artifacts over space. While this may be patently obvious to most investigators it is useful to clarify how distance from source can affect the level of specialization and the organization of production within these three broad zones of obsidian availability.

Distance from source can affect the structure of core-blade technology in several different ways. First and fundamentally as the contributions in this volume have demonstrated, distance from source can have an important effect on the technology employed in core-blade production. When obsidian was relatively scarce or available in restricted forms we see the use of production techniques oriented toward maximizing output from limited raw material. This was the case at both Xochicalco and Dos Hombres where innovative rejuvenation techniques were employed in small core production strategies.

Distance from obsidian sources can affect organization of production. First, increased distance from a source can result in a decrease in the quantity and constancy of obsidian reaching an area either because direct procurement becomes more difficult or intervening trade and distribution mechanisms do not provide a constant supply of raw material. Limiting the supply or predictability of obsidian reaching craftsmen has a direct effect on the level and structure of craft specialization. Full-time specialization can become untenable if craftsmen are unable to get enough obsidian to maintain continuous production necessary to support their families throughout the year. Under these circumstances, part-time craft production would be a more viable form of specialization because fluctuating or limited supplies of obsidian reaching craftsmen could be balanced by some level of agricultural production to support the domestic unit. While part-time production may be advantageous for individual craftsmen because it minimizes their subsistence risk, it means a lower level of output/craftsmen to meet the total regional demand for obsidian tools. Second, since regional consumer demand for obsidian can be considered to be a constant at any given time with respect to the output craftsmen are willing to produce, limited availability of obsidian may result in a proliferation of part-time craft specialists in workshops located at considerable distances from obsidian sources.

Finally, the availability of obsidian in any region where direct procurement is impossible will be directly related to the type and efficiency of the distribution system through which it moves. Access to a predictable supply of raw material is critical for any craftsman. What is important to recognize, however, is that in Mesoamerica interregional trading networks were largely dendritic in structure (Hirth 1978; Santley and Alexander 1992). In dendritic networks the volume of a resource moving through it will be inversely proportional to the distance over which it moves. More efficient distribution systems may develop to offset this problem which could include the development of trading partnerships, the emergence of professional merchants, and the appearance of regional marketplaces all in an effort to ensure a sufficient level of raw material. Where economic forces fail, societies can employ state-controlled forms of resource procurement or resort to the use of less desirable local resources like chert or other workable stone.

The combined effect of distance from source and the intervening provisioning network directly affected the nature of the flaked stone assemblages found in workshop locales. Workshops close to obsidian sources or supplied by efficient supply networks frequently will contain quantities of large debitage and artifacts of all sizes. In contrast, workshops at greater distances or supplied by less efficient provisioning mechanisms may have assemblages that are smaller in size and have smaller sized debitage. A challenge for future research is to recognize and differentiate between these two production conditions. Researchers must develop mechanisms for consistently identifying workshop assemblages at *distant source* locations where the size and quantity of debitage materials is correspondingly different from workshops located close to obsidian sources.

While we often think of core-blade production in synchronic, structural terms, it is clear that the segmental nature of production has considerable chronological depth. We see this most clearly in the way the relationship between quarry and workshop locales changed over time and it is to this question that we now turn. During the Formative and Classic periods, there is little evidence for the production of finished artifacts at quarry locales. Instead, quarry production is limited to mining raw material and shaping macrocores and other preforms for use elsewhere. Finished goods including final prismatic blades were prepared in specialized work areas within domestic settings away from quarry areas like we find at the early workshops at Chalcatzingo (Burton 1987) and Kaminaljuyu (Hay 1978; Hirth ND). This differs from *chert* and *chalcedony* production in the Maya region where finished goods were manufactured by craftsmen residing at the quarries or at nearby outcrop sites.[1] It is only during the Postclassic period, as both Pastrana and Healan point out in their contributions, that we begin to see an increase in the production of specialized items at obsidian quarries.

Although many quarry sources have not been intensively studied, it is clear that there was a change from low-level mining during the Formative period to heavier exploitation and more specialized use during the Classic and Postclassic periods. Intensive exploitation of the Sierra de las Navajas source begins during the Classic period with heavy use of this material by workshops at Teotihuacan. Furthermore, beginning during the Classic period there was increased selectivity in the sources available to and used by domestic workshops throughout the central Mexican highlands. Obsidian from Otumba and Paredon, which were used for prismatic blade production during the Formative period (Grove 1987; Charlton et al. 1978), are largely replaced by obsidian from Sierra de las Navajas during the Classic. Although Otumba obsidian continued to be exploited throughout the Classic, it was primarily used for the production of bifaces (chapter 5).

From the Classic period onward, we can detect increasing divergence in the production activities carried out by different specialists at quarry and workshop locales. This change was probably prompted by an increased demand for finished goods and their wider distribution through more efficient economic networks (Santley 1983, 1984). This would have meant that processing activities at the quarry were increasingly governed by the needs of craftsmen in non-quarry workshops. Andrews (chapter 5) identified some of these activities in his discussion of linked production sequences at Teotihuacan. Similarly, Santley and Barrett (chapter 8) note differences in the importation of macrocores and polyhedral cores in the Gulf Coast, which may relate to the demand for different types of products. It may be that increased demand for specialized products by workshop craftsmen during the Postclassic led to higher levels of specialized production activity at quarry sources as noted by Pastrana at Sierra de las Navajas.

From a diachronic perspective, shifts in obsidian exploitation patterns at the end of the Classic period may have more to do with changes in the structure of specialization and disruptions in the organization of production than it does any other factor. Most researchers have assumed that changes in obsidian frequencies at individual sites over time reflect changes in the control or direction of trade routes. If mining and quarry-based obsidian processing became a specialized activity during the Classic period, disruption in these operations would have led craftsmen in the outlying workshops where finished goods were prepared to acquire obsidian from alternative sources. A case in point may be the importation of obsidian from Ucareo, Michoacan at Tula (chapter 3) and other sites in the Valley of Mexico at the beginning of the Epiclassic (Garcia et al. 1990) rather than using locally available material from Sierra de las Navajas. The preference for a distant obsidian source over a closer, local source of similar quality does not make sense either in energetic terms or as a product of changing trade routes. It is more likely that the Sierra de las Navajas source was not heavily utilized during the Epiclassic period because quarry specialists were not producing the polyhedral and macrocores in demand by workshop craftsmen located throughout the Valley of Mexico.

The evidence from both Tula and Xochicalco show that obsidian exploitation during the Epiclassic is not a simple function of energetic costs. Workshops at these sites were not using obsidian from the closest available sources.

Craftsmen did not go directly to quarry sources during this period, but relied instead on specialists at quarry locations to preform cores that were transported to them by trade intermediaries. It is likely that a disruption in specialized mining activities at Sierra de las Navajas at the end of the Classic period forced craftsmen throughout the Valley of Mexico to rely more heavily on imported macrocores from more distant sources like Ucareo. At Tula, craftsmen only shifted back to using Sierra de las Navajas obsidian around AD 900 when, as Pastrana demonstrates, mining was again a large scale activity and cores were being preformed at the quarry.

Core-Blade Production as a Multifaceted Process

The contributions in this volume underscore the idea that the production of obsidian prismatic blades was a multifaceted process. There is no single production sequence that can be applied to all areas of Mesoamerica. There were actually multiple production sequences that vary from one another as a result of the technological, production, and provisioning constraints that pre-Hispanic craft specialists faced in different areas. Because of the limited research from actual production contexts, a single core reduction model has (Clark 1988:Fig 5; Clark and Bryant 1997) has unfortunately and inadvertently become the standard for discussing how prismatic blades were produced in all areas of Mesoamerica. The contributors to this volume have reversed this impression by summarizing the variation found in the technology and organization of production employed at both quarry and workshop locales in a few different areas of Mesoamerica.

Research at quarry locales indicates that cores were shaped by percussion following at least two different sequences. Where raw material occurs in irregularly shaped nodules, cores were worked from macrocores into polyhedral cores by the successive removal of percussion flakes and blades (Clark and Bryant 1997:Figs. 2, 3). Conversely, where raw material occurs in large blocky chunks like Healan reports from Ucareo, craftsmen have the opportunity to produce polyhedral cores by removing percussion blades without the cores passing through the form we refer to as macrocores. Although analysis is still underway, this direct shaping of polyhedral cores from blocky material is also found at the Early Classic obsidian workshops at Kaminaljuyu (Hirth ND). When we add to this the preparation of pecked-and-ground platforms on percussion cores beginning during the Postclassic (reported here from Sierra de las Navajas and Ucareo) and the production and use of asymmetrical cores like Parry reports from Otumba, the variation in production technology increases again.

Most of the variation found in the production of prismatic blades can be found in workshops outside of source areas. Much of the technological variation identified in this volume begins with the form that obsidian entered the workshops. Production sequences differ from one another depending on whether cores entered workshops as fully or partially shaped macrocores (chapters 4, 5, 8, and 9), symmetrical and asymmetrical polyhedral cores (chapter 3, 4), or already shaped prismatic blade cores (chapter 7). Production also varied depending on whether cores were intended for prismatic blades only or for both prismatic blades and bifacial flake blanks as Andrews reports for Teotihuacan. Variation was noted by both Spence et al. and Santley and Barrett in the form that obsidian moved within even relatively small regions. Finally, distance and scarcity can affect how craftsmen treat the obsidian once it entered the workshop. Both Xochicalco (chapter 7) and Dos Hombres (chapter 9) are located at considerable distances from sources, and although obsidian entered these sites in different forms (prismatic cores versus macrocores), craftsmen at both sites quickly rejuvenated cores into multiple smaller core segments.

The fundamental principle at work is that craftsmen sought to produce usable products from the obsidian to which they had access. In most instances these products were prismatic blades. Moreover, craftsmen were interested in producing blades as expeditiously as possible and would adopt as many shortcuts as they could to do so. If it would have been possible to produce finished prismatic pressure blades directly from a block of raw material we believe they would have done it. They were not bound by, or perhaps even thought in terms of, the analytical stages of core-blade production that researchers contrive to categorize archaeological materials. As a result we should expect to find variation in the core-blade production sequences employed across Mesoamerica as a function of the technological, provisioning, and production constraints that affected how obsidian tools were produced.

Variation is an unavoidable aspect of lithic reduction technologies. An example of how this variation can be represented within a single reduction sequence can be found in North America with Clovis flaked stone tool production. Excavations at the Anzick site recovered a complete Clovis reduction sequence that included large bifacial cores, flake blanks, bifacial blanks, preforms, and complete Clovis points (Wilke et al. 1991). In Clovis technology large bifaces were produced, which served as cores for the production of flake blanks that subsequently were transformed into bifacial blanks using direct freehand transverse percussion. These bifacial blanks were then pressure flaked into preforms, which in turn were manufactured into Clovis points. Flake tools such as knives, scrapers, or saws were also produced from these large bifacial cores. Broken cores were laterally cycled into Clovis points.

This well-designed and integrated technology provided a fail-proof reduction strategy with minimal loss of high-quality stone (Wilke et al. 1991:245). However, the flint-knapping activities involved in this reduction strategy rarely took place at one location on the landscape.

If sites where these different flint-knapping activities were analyzed and reported as individual, segregated flint-knapping events, the complete picture of Clovis reduction technology would be missed. Without reference to the Anzick cycle researchers could misidentify the variation inherent in Clovis technology and classify sequential production tasks as unrelated activities and/or variations within one or more biface reduction technologies.

Variation within Clovis technology certainly did occur. Some of the causes for this variation included limited lithic resources and the size, shape, and quality of available tool stone as well as variation in skill. Clovis technological variation is identifiable because researchers studying the Clovis production systems are aware of and expect to find technological adaption across the landscape. The same needs to be true for investigators studying variation in Mesoamerican core-blade technology. Researchers must identify, describe, and understand the technological features of their respective assemblages as a first step in characterizing the range of variation and its root causes within a single reduction technology like core-blade production.

There are some researchers who may not like the prospect that obsidian prismatic blade production was a multifaceted process that did not employ a single reduction sequence. To those individuals, we can only say take heart. Patterned variability is the lifeblood of archaeological interpretation and because of the reductive nature of flaked stone tool production, technological analyses provide investigators with a reliable approach to reconstruct prehistoric behavior. The greater the amount of variation found in lithic assemblages, the more information they probably contain about past production activities. The goal for future investigation is to identify the causes that produced variation in obsidian blade technology in different times and places throughout Mesoamerica. To reach this objective we must increase our understanding of the settings and conditions affecting core-blade production. Once we demonstrate how variation in lithic assemblages is linked to the many varied natural and socioeconomic variables that structure production we will be able to use technological analysis to develop a fuller understanding of the structure and development of prehistoric economic systems.

Notes

1. The pattern of exploitation in the chert-rich zone of northern Belize is for craftsmen to reside at outcrops, so that both mining and production takes place within a residential setting. Examples of sites with specialized lithic production in chert include Colha (Shafer 1982a; Shafer and Hester 1991), Kichpanha (Shafer 1982b), Kunahmul, and Maskal (Gibson 1982).

Bibliography

Acuña, René
1985   *Relaciones geográficas del siglo XVI: México, Vol. I.*
        Universidad Nacional Autonóma de México, Mexico
        City.

Adams, Richard E.W.
1987   The Rio Azul archaeological project, 1985 summary. In
        Rio Azul reports number 3, the 1985 season, edited by
        R.E.W. Adams, 1–27. University of Texas, San Antonio.
1989   The Rio Azul archaeological project, 1986 summary. In
        Rio Azul reports number 4, the 1986 season, edited by
        R.E.W. Adams, 1–23. University of Texas, San Antonio.
1991   The Maya lowlands archaeological project of the
        University of Texas at San Antonio. *Mexicon* 13:22–24.

Adams, Richard E.W., Grant D. Hall, Ian Graham, Fred Valdez,
Stephen Black, Daniel Potter, Douglas J. Cannell, and Barbara
Cannell
1984   Final report. In *Rio Azul project reports, number 1, final
        1983 report*, edited by R.E.W. Adams, 1–24. Center for
        Archaeological Research, San Antonio: University of
        Texas.

Adams, William, and Ernest Adams
1991   *Archaeological typology and practical reality.* Cambridge:
        Cambridge University Press.

Anderson, Douglas
1970   Microblade traditions in northeastern Alaska. *Arctic
        Anthropology* 7:2–16.

Andrefsky, William
1987   Diffusion and innovation from the perspective of wedge
        shaped cores in Alaska and Japan. In *The organization of
        core technology*, edited by J. Johnson and C. Morrow, 13–
        43. Boulder: Westview Press.

Andrews, Bradford
1997   Inferring craft labor intensity in Xochicalco's Epiclassic
        obsidian blade workshops. Paper presented at the 62nd
        Annual Meeting of the Society for American
        Archaeology,
        Nashville, Tennessee.
1999   Craftsman skill and specialization: Investigating the
        craft production of prehispanic obsidian blades at
        Xochicalco and Teotihuacan, *Mexico.* Ph.D. dissertation,
        Department of Anthropology, Pennsylvania State
        University, University Park, Pennsylvania.

Aoyama, Kazuo, Toshiharu Tashiro, and Michael Glascock
1999   A pre–Columbian obsidian source in San Luis,
        Honduras: Implications for the relationship between
        Late Classic Maya political boundaries and the
        boundaries of obsidian exchange networks. *Ancient
        Mesoamerica* 10:237–249.

Arnold, Philip
1977   Conversation, Veracruz, Mexico, June.

Arnold, Philip, Christopher Pool, Robert Kneebone, and Robert
Santley
1993   Intensive ceramic production and Classic period political
        economy in the Sierra de los Tuxtlas, Veracruz, Mexico.
        Ancient Mesoamerica 4:175–191.

Arnold, Philip, V.J. McCormack, E.O. Juarez V., S.A. Wails, R.
Herrera B., G. de Jesus Fernandez S., and C. A. Skidmore
1996   El proyecto arqueológico La Joya: Informe final de
        campo–1995. Report submitted to the Consejo de
        Arqueología, Instituto Nacional de Anthropolgía e
        Historia, Mexico City.

Ascher, Robert
1961   Experimental archaeology. *American Anthropologist*
        63:793–816.

Athie, Ivonne
2001   La obsidiana del Templo Mayor de Tenochtitlan.
        Unpublished Licenciatura thesis, Escuela Nacional de
        Antropología e Historia, Mexico City.

Balkansky, Andrews, Gary Feinman, and Linda Nicholas
1997   Pottery kilns of ancient Ejutla, Oaxaca, Mexico. *Journal of Field Archaeology* 24:139–160.

Barrett, Thomas
ND   The obsidian production–distribution system in the Tuxtla mountains, southern Veracruz, Mexico. Unpublished manuscript.

Beekman, Christopher
1996   Political boundaries and political structure: The limits of the Teuchitlan tradition. *Ancient Mesoamerica* 7:135–147.
2000   The correspondence of regional patterns and local strategies in Formative to Classic period West Mexico. *Journal of Anthropological Archaeology* 19:385–412.

Benfer, Alice N.
1974   A preliminary analysis of the obsidian artifacts from Tula, Mexico. In *Studies of ancient Tollan*, edited by R. Diehl, 56–87. University of Missouri Monographs in Anthropology, No. 1, Columbia.

Berdan, Fances
1982   *The Aztecs of Central Mexico: An imperial society.* New York: Holt, Rinehart, and Winston.

Blanton, Richard, Stephen Kowalewski, Gary Feinman, and Jill Appel
1982   *Monte Alban's hinterland, part 1: The prehispanic settlement patterns of the central and southern parts of the Valley of Oaxaca, Mexico.* Memoirs of the Museum of Anthropology, No. 15. University of Michigan, Ann Arbor.

Bradley, Bruce and Yevgeny Giria
1996   Concepts of the technological analysis of flaked stone: a case study from the high Arctic. *Lithic Technology* 21:23–39.

Breton, Adela
1902   Some obsidian workings in Mexico. *Proceedings: XIII International Congress of Americanists* 1:265–268.

Brokaw, Nicholas, and Elizabeth P. Mallory
1993   *Vegetation of the Rio Bravo conservation and management area, Belize.* Manomet, Massachusetts and Belize City: Manomet Bird Observatory and the Programme for Belize.

Brown, Mary Kathryn
1995   1994 interim report on investigations of the Preclassic at Dos Hombres, Belize. In *The programme for Belize archaeological project: 1994 interim report*, edited by R.E.W. Adams and Fred Valdez, 95–101. The Center for Archaeology and Tropical Studies and The University of Texas at San Antonio.

Brumfiel, Elizabeth
1987   Elite and utilitarian crafts in the Aztec state. In *Specialization, exchange, and complex societies*, edited by E. Brumfiel and T. Earle, 102–118. Cambridge: Cambridge University Press.

Brumfield, Elizabeth, and Timothy Earle
1987   Specialization, exchange, and complex societies: an introduction. In *Specialization, exchange, and complex societies*, edited by E. Brumfiel and T. Earle, 1–9. Cambridge: Cambridge University Press.

Burleson, R.L.
1999   *Lithic analysis of the Postclassic Maya site Isla Cilvituk: Utilizing microwear and experimental approaches to evaluate Anthropological problems at a regional scale.* Master's thesis, New Mexico State University, Las Cruces.

Burton, John
1989   Repeng and the salt–makers: 'ecological trade' and stone axe production in the Papua New Guinea highlands. *Man* 24:255–272.

Burton, Susan
1987   Obsidian blade manufacturing debris on Terrace 37. In *Ancient Chalcatzingo*, edited by D. Grove ed., 321–328. Austin: University of Texas Press.

Cárdenas García, Efraín
1992   Avance y perspectivas de la investigación de las fuentes de abastecimiento de obsidiana. In *Origen y desarrollo de la civilización en el occidente de México*, edited by B. Boehm de Lameiras and P. Weigand, 41–68. El Colegio de Michoacán, Zamora.

Carr, Philip
1994   The organization of technology: impact and potential. In *The organization of North American prehistoric chipped stone technologies*, 1–8. Ann Arbor: International Monographs in Prehistory.

Carrasco, Pedro
1974   Introduction–La Matrícula de Huexotzingo como fuente sociológico. In *Matrícula de Huexotzingo* edited by H. Prem, 19–36. Instituto Nacional de Anthropología e Historia, Mexico City.

Cassiano, Gianfranco
1991   La tecnología de navajillas prismáticas. *Arqueología* 5:107–118.

Charlton, Thomas
1978   Teotihuacan, Tepeapulco, and obsidian exploitation. *Science* 200:1227–1236.
1984   Production and exchange: Variables in the evolution of a civilization. In *Trade and exchange in early Mesoamerica*, edited by K. Hirth, 7–42. University of New Mexico Press, Albuquerque.
1990   Operations 9 and 10, fields 33 and 34, the nucleated core of the site, In *Early state formation processes: The Aztec*

city–state of Otumba, Mexico, part 1, edited by T. Charlton and D. Nichols, 149–176. Research Report 3. Mesoamerican Research Colloquium, Department of Anthropology, University of Iowa, Iowa City.

Charlton, Thomas H., Deborah L. Nichols, and Cynthia Otis Charlton

1991   Aztec craft production and specialization: Archaeological evidence from the city–state of Otumba, Mexico. *World Archaeology* 23:98–114.

1993   Craft production units at Otumba. In *Household, compound, and residence*, edited by R. Santley and K. Hirth, 147–171. CRC Press, Boca Raton.

Charlton, Thomas, David Grove, and Philip Hopke

1978   The Paredón, Mexico, obsidian source and Early Formative exchange. *Science* 201:807–809.

Charlton, Thomas H., and Cynthia Otis Charlton

1994   Aztec craft production in Otumba, 1470–1570: Reflections of a changing world. In *Chipping away on earth*, edited by E. Quinones Keber, 241–251. Lancaster, California: Labyrinthos.

Charlton, Thomas, and Michael Spence

1982   Obsidian exploitation and civilization in the Basin of Mexico. *Anthropology* 6:7–86.

Clark, John

1982   Manufacture of Mesoamerican prismatic blades: An alternative technique. *American Antiquity* 47:355–376.

1983   Mesoamerican blade workshops and craft specialization. Paper Presented at the 48th Annual Meeting, Society for American Archaeology, Pittsburgh.

1985   Platforms, bits, punches and vises: A potpourri of Mesoamerican blade technology. *Lithic Technology* 14:1-15.

1986   From mountains to molehills: A critical review of Teotihuacan's obsidian industry. In *Research in economic anthropology, supplement No. 2. Economic aspects of prehispanic highland Mexico*, edited by B. Isaac, 23–74. JAI Press, Greenwich, Connecticut.

1987   Politics, prismatic blades, and Mesoamerican civilization. In *The organization of core technology*, edited by J. Johnson and C. Morrow, 259–285. Westview Press, Boulder.

1988   *The lithic artifacts of La Libertad, Chiapas, Mexico. An economic perspective*. Papers of the New World Archaeological Foundation, No. 52. Provo, Utah: Brigham Young University.

1989a   Hacia una definición de talleres. In *La obsidiana en Mesoamérica*, edited by M. Gaxiola and J. Clark, 213–217. Colección Científica, No. 176, Instituto Nacional de Antropología e Historia, Mexico City.

1989b   La fabricación de navajas prismáticas. In *La obsidiana en Mesoamérica*, edited by M. Gaxiola and J. Clark, 147–156. Colección Científica, No. 176, Instituto Nacional de Antropología e Historia, Mexico City.

1989c   Obsidian: The primary Mesoamerican sources. In *La obsidiana en Mesoamérica*, edited by M. Gaxiola and J. Clark, 299–318. Colección Científica, No. 176. Instituto

Nacional de Antropología e Historia, Mexico City.

1990a   Enfoque experimental en el análisis de talleres de obsidiana Mesoamericanos: un ejemplo: Ojo de Agua, Chiapas, México. In *Nuevos enfoques en el estudio de la lítica*, edited by M. de los Dolores Soto de Arechavaleta, 83–133. Universidad Nacional Autonóma de México, Mexico City.

1990b   Fifteen falacies in lithic workshop interpretation: an experimental and ethnoarchaeological perspective. In *Etnoarqueología: primer coloquio Bosch–Gimpera*, edited by Y. Sugiyama and M. Serra, 497–512. Universidad Nacional Autonóma de México, Mexico City.

1991   Flintknapping and debitage disposal among the Lacandon Maya of Chiapas, Mexico. In *Ethnoarchaeology of refuse disposal*, edited by E. Staski and L. Sutro, 63–78. Anthropological Research Papers No. 42. Arizona State University, Tempe.

1997   Prismatic blade making, craftsmanship, and production:An analysis of obsidian refuse from Ojo de Agua, Chiapas, Mexico. *Ancient Mesoamerica* 8:137–159.

ND   Craftsmanship and craft specialization. In *Experimentation and interpretation in Mesoamerican lithic technology*, edited by K. Hirth, J. Flenniken, P. Kelterborn, and J. Pelegrin et al. Manuscript on file, Department of Anthropology, Penn State University, University Park, Pennsylvania.

Clark, John, and Douglas Bryant

1997   A technological typology of prismatic blades and debitage from Ojo de Agua, Chiapas, Mexico. *Ancient Mesoamerica* 8:111–136.

Clark, John, and Thomas A. Lee

1979   A behavioral model for the obsidian industry of Chiapa de Corzo. *Estudios de Cultura Maya* 12:33–50.

1984   Formative obsidian exchange and the emergence of public economies in Chiapas, Mexico. In *Trade and exchange in early Mesoamerica*, edited by K. Hirth, 235–274. Albuquerque: University of New Mexico Press.

Clark, John, and William Parry

1990   Craft specialization and cultural complexity. In *Research in Economic Anthropology*, edited by B. Isaac, 12:289–346. Greenwich, Connecticut: JAI Press.

Clow, Barbara, and Gerry Clow

1976   *Stained glass: A basic manual*. Boston: Little, Brown and Company.

Cobean, Robert

1991   Principales yacimientos de obsidiana en el Altiplano central. *Arqueología*, 5:9–32.

Cobean, Robert, Michael Coe, Edward Perry, Karl Turekian, and Dinkar Kharkar

1971   Obsidian trade at San Lorenzo Tenochtitlan, Mexico. *Science* 174: 666–671.

Cobean, Robert, James Vogt, Michael Glascock, and Terrance Stocker

1991   High precision trace element characterization of major obsidian sources and further analyses of artifacts from

San Lorenzo Tenochtitlan, Mexico. *Latin American Antiquity* 2: 69–91.

Coe, Michael
1966   *The Maya.* New York: Praeger.

Coe, Michael and Richard Diehl
1980   *In the land of the Olmec, vol. I, the archaeology of San Lorenzo Tenochtitlan.* Austin: University of Texas Press.

Coe, William R.
1965   Tikal: ten years of study of a Maya ruin in the lowlands of Guatemala. *Expedition* 8:5–56.

Collins, Michael B.
1975   Lithic technology as a means of processual inference. In *Lithic technology: Making and using stone tools,* edited by E. Swanson, 15–34. The Hague: Mouton.

Corona Nuñez, José
1955   Tumba de El Arenal, Etzatlán, Jal. In *Dirección de Monumentos Pre–Hispánicos Informe* 3. Mexico City: Instituto Nacional de Anthropología e Historia.
1968   *Matrícula de tributos.* Mexico City: Secretaría de Hacienda y Crédito Público.

Costin, Cathy
1991   Craft specialization: Issues in defining, documenting, and explaining the organization of production. In *Archaeological method and theory,* edited by M. Schiffer, 1–56. University of Arizona Press, Tucson.

Crabtree, Donald
1966   A stoneworkers approach to analysing and replicating the Lindenmeier Folsom. *Tebiwa* 9:3–39.
1968   Mesoamerican polyhedral cores and prismatic blades. *American Antiquity* 33:446–478.
1972   *An introduction to flintworking.* Occassional Papers of the Idaho State University Museum No. 28, Pocatello, Utah.

Crabtree, Don and B. R. Butler
1964   Notes on experiments in flint knapping: 1–heat treatment of silica materials. *Tebiwa* 7:1–6.

Cruz Antillón, Rafael
1994   *Análisis arqueológico del yacimiento de obsidiana de Sierra de las Navajas, Hidalgo.* Colección Científica No. 74. Instituto Nacional de Anthropología e Historia, Mexico City.

Cyphers, Ann
2000   Cultural identity and interregional interaction during the Gobernador phase: A ceramic perspective. In *The Xochicalco mapping project. Archaeological research at Xochicalco Vol 2,* edited by K. Hirth, 11–16. Salt Lake City: University of Utah Press.

Dalton, George
1977   Aboriginal economies in stateless societies. In *Exchange systems in prehistory,* edited by T. Earle and J. Ericson, 191–212. Academic Press, New York.

Darling, Andrew
1993   Notes on obsidian sources of the southern Sierra Madre Occidental. *Ancient Mesoamerica* 4:245–253.

Darling, Andrew, and Michael Glascock
1998   Acquisition and distribution of obsidian in the north–central frontier of Mesoamerica. In *Rutas de intercambio en Mesoamérica: III Coloquio Bosch–Gimpera,* edited by E. Rattray, 345–364. Universidad Nacional Autonóma de México, Mexico City.

Darras, Veronique
ND   Economía y poder: La obsidiana entre los Tarascos del Malpais de Zacapu. Unpublished manuscript.

Domanski, M., J. Webb, and J. Boland
1993   Mechanical properties of stone artefact materials and the effect of heat treatment. *Archaeometry* 36:177–208.

Dreiss, Meredith L.
1988   Obsidian at Colha, Belize: A technological analysis and distributional study based on trace element data. In *Papers of the Colha project, vol. 4.* The Texas Archeological Research Laboratory and The Center for Archaeological Research, University of Texas, Austin and San Antonio.

Dreiss, Meredith L., and David O. Brown
1989   Obsidian exchange patterns in Belize. In *Research in economic Anthropology. Prehistoric Maya economies of Belize,* edited by P. McAnany and B. Issac, 57–90. Greenwich, Connecticut: JAI Press.

Drennan, Robert
1984a   Long distance movement of goods in the Mesoamerican Formative and Classic. *American Antiquity* 49:27–43.
1984b   Long–distance transport costs in pre–hispanic Mesoamerica. *American Anthropologist* 86:105–112.

Dumond, Donald E., and Florencia Muller
1972   Classic to Postclassic in highland central Mexico. *Science* 175:1208–1215.

Duncan, Alastair
1975   *Leaded glass: A handbook of techniques.* New York: Watson–Guptill Publications.

Durst, Jeffrey J.
1998   Investigations in the B–4 group, Dos Hombres, northwestern Belize: The 1997 field season. Manuscript on file, Department of Anthropology, University of Texas, Austin.

Ericson, Jonathon
1984   Toward the analysis of lithic production systems. In *Prehistoric quarries and lithic production,* edited by J. Ericson and B. Purdy, 1–9. Cambridge: Cambridge University Press.

Ericson, Jonathon, and Rainer Berger
1976   Physics and chemistry of the hydration process in

obsidians II: Experiments and measurements. In *Advances in obsidian glass studies: Archaeological and geochemical perspectives*, edited by R. Taylor, 46–62. Park Ridge: Noyes Press.

Ericson, Jonathon, and Jerome Kimberlin
1977   Obsidian sources, chemical characterization and hydration rates in west Mexico. *Archaeometry* 19:157–166.

Esparsa López, Juan Rodrigo
1999   Aplicación de las técnicas nucleares PIXE y NAA para el estudio de las redes de comercio de la obsidiana en tierra caliente, Michoacan. Unpublished Licenciatura thesis, ENAH, Mexico City.

Feinman, Gary
1999   Rethinking our assumptions: Economic specialization at the household scale in ancient Ejutla, Oaxaca, Mexico. In *Pottery and people*, edited by J. Skibo and G. Feinman, 81–98. Salt Lake City: University of Utah Press.

Feinman, Gary, Richard Blanton, and Stephen Kowalewski
1984   Market system development in prehispanic Valley of Oaxaca, Mexico. In *Trade and exchange in early Mesoamerica*, edited by K. Hirth, 157–178. University of New Mexico Press, Albuquerque.

Feldman, Lawrence H.
1971   Of the stone called iztli. *American Antiquity* 36:213–214.

Flenniken, J. Jeffrey
1981   *Replicative systems analysis: A model applied to the vein quartz artifacts from the Hoko river site*. Washington State University, Laboratory of Anthropology, Reports of Investigations, No. 59, Pullman.
1988   The Paleolithic Dyuktai pressure blade technique of Siberia. *Arctic Anthropology* 24:117–132.
1989   Replicative systems analysis: a model for the analysis of flaked stone artifacts, In *La obsidiana en Mesoamerica*, edited by M. Gaxiola and J. Clark, 175–176. Coleccion Cientifica No. 176. Instituto Nacional de Anthropolgía e Historia, Mexico City.

Flenniken, J. Jeffrey, and E.G. Garrison
1975   Thermally altered novaculite and stone tool manufacturing techniques. *Journal of Field Archaeology* 2:125–131.

Flenniken, J. Jeffrey, and Kenneth Hirth
1997   Reconstructing prehispanic production processes: An examination of Xochicalco's lithic technology. Paper presented at the 62nd Annual Meeting of the Society for American Archaeology, Nashville, Tennessee.
ND   Hand–held prismatic blade manufacture in Mesoamerica. In Experimentation and interpretation in Mesoamerican lithic technology, edited by K. Hirth, J. Flenniken, P. Kelterborn, and J. Pelegrin et al. Manuscript on file, Department of Anthropology, Penn State University, University Park, Pennsylvania.

Flenniken, J. Jeffrey, and Gene Titmus
1999   Conversation, Chicago, Illinois.

Flenniken, J. Jeffrey, and J.P. White
1983   Heat treatment of siliceous rock and its implications for Australian prehistory. *Australian aboriginal studies* 1:43–48.

Fletcher, Charles S.
1970   Escapable errors in employing ethnohistory in archaeology. *American Antiquity* 35: 209–213.

Foster, Michael
2000   The archaeology of Durango. In *Greater Mesoamerica: The archaeology of west and northwest Mexico*, edited by M. Foster and S. Gorenstein, 197–219. University of Utah Press, Salt Lake City.

Fowler, Melvin
1991   Mound 72 and early Mississippian at Cahokia. In *New perspectives on Cahokia: Views from the periphery*, edited by J. Stoltman, 1–28. Monographs in World Archaeology, No. 2. Prehistory Press, Madison.

García Bárcena, Juan
1975   Las minas de obsidiana de la Sierra de las Navajas Hgo., México. In *Proceedings of the XLI International Congress of the Americanists, Mexico 1974* 1:369–377.

García Chavez, Raul, Michael D. Glascock, J. Michael Elam and Harry B. Iceland
1990   Instituto Nacional de Anthropolgía e Historia, salvage archaeology excavations at Azcapotzalco, Mexico: an analysis of the lithic assemblage. *Ancient Mesoamerica* 1:225–232.

García Cook, Angel, and Raúl Arana
1978   *Rescate arqueológico del monolito Coyolxauhqui*. Mexico City: Instituto Nacional de Anthropología e Historia.

García Velázquez, Jorge, and Gianfranco Cassiano
1990   La producción de navajillas prismáticas en el Postclásico tardío: El caso de la plaza de la Banca Nacionalizada. In *Etnoarqueología: Primer Coloquio Bosch–Gimpera*, edited by Y. Sugiura and M. Carmen Serra, 513–526. Universidad Nacional Autonóma de México, Mexico City.

Garza Tarazona, Silvia, and Norberto González Crespo
1995   Xochicalco. In *La acrópolis de Xochicalco*, edited by B. de la Fuente, S. Garza, N. González, M. León, and J. Wimer, 89–143. Instituto de Cultura de Morelos, Cuernavaca, Mexico.

Gibson, Eric
1982   Excavation of a Late Classic Maya lithic workshop near Maskall, Belize. In *Archaeology at Colha, Belize: the 1981 interim report*, edited by T. Hester, H. Shafer, and J. Eaton, 182–186. San Antonio and Venezia: Center for Archaeological Research and the Centro Studi e Ricerche Ligabue.

Glascock, Michael, J. Elam, and Robert Cobean
1994   La obsidiana 'meca' del centro de México, análisis químico y petrográfico. In *Trace* 25:747–765. Centre d'Études exicaines et Centraméricaines, Mexico City.

Greene, Charles H.
1984   Secondary, or finishing, operations. In *Glass engineering handbook*, edited by G. McLellan and E. Shand, 1–8. McGraw–Hill, New York.

Grove, David
1974   *San Pablo, Nexpa, and the Early Formative archaeology of Morelos, Mexico.* Vanderbilt University Publications in Anthropology, No. 12, Nashville.
1987   Raw material and sources. In *Ancient Chalcatzingo*, edited by D. Grove, 376–386. University of Texas Press, Austin.

Guderjan, Thomas H., and W. David Driver
1995   Introduction to the 1994 season at Blue Creek. In *Archaeological research at Blue Creek, Belize. Progress report of the third (1994) field season*, edited by T. Guderjan and W. D. Driver, 1–12. Maya Research Program and Department of Sociology, St. Mary's University, San Antonio.

Hall, Grant D.
1986   Results of tomb investigations at Rio Azul, season of 1984. In *Rio Azul reports number 2, the 1984 season*, edited by R.E.W. Adams, 69–110. University of Texas, San Antonio: Center for Archaeological Research.

Hammond, Norman, and Gair Tourtellot, III
1993   Survey and excavations at La Milpa, Belize, 1993. *Mexicon* 15:71–75.

Harbottle, Garman, and Phil C. Weigand
1992   Turquoise in pre–Columbian America. *Scientific American* 266:78–85.

Hasbach Lugo, Barbara
1982   Restauración de 33 cuchillos ceremoniales policromados. In *El Templo Mayor: Excavaciones y estudios*, edited by E. Matos Moctezuma, 357–368. Instituto Nacional de Antropología e Historia, Mexico City.

Hassig, Ross
1985   *Trade, tribute, and transportation.* Norman: University of Oklahoma Press.

Hay, Conrad
1978   *Kaminaljuyu obsidian: Lithic analysis and the economic organization of a prehistoric Maya chiefdom.* Ph.D. dissertation, Department of Anthropology, Pennsylvania State University, University Park, Pennsylvania.

Hayden, Brian, and Margaret Nelson
1981   The use of chipped lithic material in the contemporary Maya highlands. *American Antiquity* 46:885–898.

Healan, Dan
1986   Technological and nontechnological aspects of an obsidian workshop excavated at Tula, Hidalgo, In *Research in economic anthropology, supplement No. 2. Economic aspects of prehispanic highland Mexico*, edited by B. Isaac, 133–152. Greenwich, Connecticut: JAI Press.
1989   *Tula of the Toltecs: Excavations and survey.* Iowa City: University of Iowa Press.
1993   Local versus non–local obsidian exchange at Tula and its implications for post–Formative Mesoamerica. *World Archaeology* 24: 449–466.
1997   Prehispanic quarrying in the Ucareo–Zinapecuaro obsidian source area. *Ancient Mesoamerica* 8:77–100.

Healan, Dan M., Thomas H. Charlton, and Deborah L. Nichols
1990   Operations 2 and 3, field 46, obsidian core–blade workshop. In *Early state formation processes: The Aztec city–state of Otumba, Mexico, part 1*, edited by T. Charlton and D. Nichols, 123–137. Research Report 3. Mesoamerican Research Colloquium, Department of Anthropology, University of Iowa, Iowa City.

Healan, Dan, Janet Kerley, and George Bey
1983   Excavations and preliminary analysis of an obsidian workshop in Tula, Hidalgo, Mexico. *Journal of Field Archaeology* 10:127–147.

Heizer, Robert, and Thomas Hester
1978   Great Basin, In *Chronologies in New World archaeology*, edited by R. Taylor and C. Meighan, 147–199. New York: Academic Press.

Helms, Mary
1979   *Ancient Panama.* Austin: University of Texas Press.
1993   *Craft and the kingly ideal: Art, trade, and power.* Austin: University of Texas Press.

Hernández, Francisco
1959   *Historia natural de Nueva España, volume 2.* , Mexico City: Universidad Nacional Autonóma de México.

Hester, Thomas Roy
1972   Notes on large blade cores and core–blade technology in Mesoamerica. *Contributions of the University of California Archaeological Research Facility* 14:95–105.
1975   The obsidian industry of Beleh (Chinautla Viejo), Guatemala. *Actas del XLI Congreso Internacional de Americanistas* 1:473–488.
1978a   *Archaeological studies of Mesoamerican obsidian.* Studies in Mesoamerican Art, Archaeology and Ethnohistory No. 3. Socorro: Ballena Press.
1978b   Preliminary notes on the technological analysis of obsidian artifacts from Villa Morelos, Michoacan, Mexico. In *Archaeological studies of Mesoamerican obsidian*, edited by T. Hester, 131–158. Socorro: Ballena Press.

Hester, Thomas, Robert Heizer, and Robert Jack
1971   Technology and geological sources of obsidian from

Cerro de las Mesas, Veracruz, Mexico, with observations on Olmec trade. *Contributions of the University of California Archaeological Research Facility* 13:133–142.

Hester, Thomas, Robert Jack, and Robert Heizer
1971   The Obsidian of Tres Zapotes. *Contributions of the University of California Archaeological Research Facility* 13:65–132.

Hirth, Kenneth
1978   Interregional trade and the formation of prehistoric gateway communities. *American Antiquity* 43:35–45.
1984   Trade and society in Late Formative Morelos. In *Trade and exchange in early Mesoamerica*, edited by K. Hirth, 125–146. Albuquerque: University of New Mexico Press.
1988   Beyond the Maya frontier: Cultural interaction and syncretism along the Central Honduran Corridor. In *The Classic Maya collapse*, edited by G. Willey, 297–334. Washington, D.C.: Dumbarton Oaks Research Library and Collection.
1989   Militarism and social organization at Xochicalco, Morelos. In *Mesoamerica after the collapse of Teotihuacan A.D. 700–900*, edited by R. Diehl and J. Berlo, 69–81, Washington, D.C.: Dumbarton Oaks Research Library and Collection.
1995a   Urbanism, militarism, and architectural design: An analysis of Epiclassic sociopolitical structure at Xochicalco. *Ancient Mesoamerica* 6:223–250.
1995b   The investigation of obsidian producton at Xochicalco, Morelos. *Ancient Mesoamerica* 6:251–258.
2000   *Ancient urbanism at Xochicalco. Archaeological research at Xochicalco Vol 1.* Salt Lake City: University of Utah Press.
ND   The Kaminaljuyu production sequence for obsidian prismatic blades: Technological characteristics and research questions. In Experimentation and interpretation in Mesoamerican lithic technology, edited by K. Hirth, J. Flenniken, P. Kelterborn, and J. Pelegrin et al. Manuscript on file, Department of Anthropology, Penn State University, University Park, Pennsylvania.

Hirth, Kenneth, and Jorge Angulo
1981   Early state expansion in Central Mexico: Teothuacan in Morelos. *Journal of Field Archaeology* 8:135–150.

Hirth, Kenneth, Jeffrey Flenniken, and Bradford Andrews
2000   Flaked–stone obsidian tools and their behavioral implications, In *The Xochicalco Mapping Project. Archaeological research at Xochicalco Vol 1,* edited by K. Hirth, 136–150. Salt Lake City: University of Utah Press.

Houk, Brett A.
1995   1994 Excavations of Late Classic atructures at Dos Hombres (RB–2). In *The programme for Belize archaeological project, 1994 interim report*, edited by R.E.W. Adams, and F. Valdez, 83–95. University of Texas, San Antonio: Center for Archaeology and Tropical Studies.
1996   *The archaeology of site planning: An example from the Maya site of Dos Hombres, Belize*. Ph.D. dissertation, Department of Anthropology, University of Texas, Austin.
1998   *The 1997 season of the Chan Chich archaeological project.* Papers of the Chan Chich Archaeological Project No. 3. San Antonio: Center for Maya Studies.

Inizan, Marie–Louise and Monique Lechevallier
1990   A techno–economic approach to lithics: some examples of blade pressure debitage in the Indo–Pakistani sub–continent. In *South Asian Archaeology* edited by M. Taddei, 43–59, Venice.
1994   L'adoption du débitage laminaire par pression au Proche–Orient. In *Neolithic stone industries of the fertile crescent*, edited by H. Gebel and S. Kozlowski, 23–32. Studies in Early Near Eastern Production, Subsistence, and Environment, Berlin.

Inizan, Marie–Louise, Michèle Reduron–Ballinger, Hélèn Roche, and Jacques Tixier
1999   *Technology and terminology of kanpped stone.* Préhistoire de la Pierre Taillée, Volume 5. Cercle de Recherches et d´ Etudes Préhistoriques.

Isenberg, Anita, and Seymour Isenberg
1972   *How to work in stained glass.* Chilton Book Company, Radnor, Pennsylvania.

Justice, Noel
1987   *Stone age spear and arrow points*, Indiana University Press, Bloomington and Indianapolis.

Katz, Friedrich
1966   *Situación social y económica de los aztecas durante los siglos XV y XVI.* Instituto de Investigaciones Históricas, , Mexico City: Universidad Nacional Autonóma de México.

Kelley, J. Charles
1986   The mobile merchants of Molino. In *Ripples in the Chichimec sea: New considerations of southwestern–Mesoamerican interactions*, edited by F. nces Mathien and R. McGuire, 81–104. Carbondale: Southern Illinois University Press.
2000   The Aztatlan mercantile system: Mobile traders and the northwestward expansion of Mesoamerican civilization. In *Greater Mesoamerica: The archaeology of west and northwest Mexico*, edited by M. Foster and S. Gorenstein, 137–154. Salt Lake City: University of Utah Press.

Kerley, Janet M.
1989   Preliminary report on a technological analysis of obsidian artifacts from an early Postclassic workshop in Tula, Hgo. In *La Obsidiana en Mesoamérica*, edited by M. Gaxiola and John Clark, 165–174. Colección Científica, No. 176. Mexico City: Instituto Nacional de Anthropología e Historia.

King, E., and D. Potter
1994   Small sites in prehistoric Maya socioeconomic organization: A perspective from Colha, Belize. In *Archaeological views from the countryside: Village communities in early complex societies*, edited by G. Schwartz and S. Falconer, 64–90. Washington, D.C.: Smithsonian Institution Press.

Knight, Charles L.F.
1999   *The Late Formative to Classic Period obsidian economy at Palo Errado, Veracruz, Mexico.* Ph.D. Dissertation, Department of Anthropology, University of Pittsburgh, Pittsburgh, Pennsylvania.

Kobayashi, T.
1970   Microblade industries in the Japanese archipelago. *Arctic Anthropology* 7:38–58.

Lewenstein, S.M.
1987   *Stone tool use at Cerros.* Austin: University of Texas Press.

Lips, Claude
1973   *Art and stained glass.* Garden City, New Jersey: Doubleday.

Lohse, Jon C.
1995   Results of survey and mapping during the 1994 Season at Gran Cacao. In *The programme For Belize archaeological project 1994 interim report*, edited by R.E.W. Adams and F. Valdez, 106–114. , University of Texas, San Antonio: Center for Archaeology and Tropical Studies.
1997   Results of 1996 season of mapping investigations: An interim view at residential organization at Dos Hombres, Belize. Manuscript on file, Department of Anthropology, University of Texas, Austin.
1998   Interim results from the 1997 season of household and community investigations at Dos Hombres. Manuscript on file, Department of Anthropology, University of Texas, Austin.
1999   Results of 1997 excavations at RB–1 (Op12) and 1998 mapping in the Dos Hombres site core. Manuscript on file, Department of Anthropology, University of Texas, Austin.

Luedtke, Barbara
1992   *An archaeologist's guide to chert and flint.* Archaeological Research Tools 7, Los Angeles: Institute of Archaeology, University of California.

MacNeish, Richard, Antoinette Nelken–Terner, and Irmgard Johnson
1967   *The Prehistory of the Tehuacan Valley, volume 2. The non-ceramic artifacts.*, Austin: University of Texas Press.

Marcus, Jane and Kent Flannery
1996   *Zapotec civilization.* London: Thames and Hudson Ltd.

McKeever, W.F.
2000   A new family handedness sample with findings consistent with X–liked transmission. *British Journal of Psychology* 91:21–39.

Meighan, Clement
1978   Application of obsidian dating to west Mexican archaeological problems. In *Across the Chichimec sea: Papers in honor of J. Charles Kelley*, edited by C. Riley and B. Hedrick, 127–133. Carbondale: Southern Illinois University Press.

Meighan, Clement, Frank Findlow, and Suzanne de Atley
1974   *Obsidian dates I: A compendium of the obsidian determinations made at the UCLA obsidian hydration laboratory.* Los Angeles: Institute of Archaeology, University of California Monograph 3.

Meighan, Clement and Glenn Russell
1979   Personal communication (letter)

Meighan, Clement, and P.I. Vanderhoeven
1978   *Obsidian dates II: A compendium of the obsidian determinations made at the UCLA obsidian hydration laboratory.* Los Angeles: Institute of Archaeology, University of California Monograph 6.

Mendieta, fray Gerónimo de
1870   *Historia eclesiástica indiana.* Mexico City: Antigua Libreria.

Michels, Joseph
1975   El Chayal, Guatemala: A chronological and behavioral reassessment. *American Antiquity* 40: 103–107.

Millon, Rene, Bruce Drewitt, and James Bennyhoff
1965   *The Pryamid of the Sun at Teotihuacan: 1959 investigations.* Transactions of the American Philosophical Society, Volume 55, Philadelphia.

Millon, Rene, Bruce Drewitt, and George Cowgill
1973   *Urbanization at Teotihuacan, Mexico. vol. 1, The Teotihuacan map, part 2, maps.* Austin: University of Texas Press.

Milner, George
1998   *The Cahokia chiefdom: The archaeology of a Mississippian society.* Washington D.C.: Smithsonian Institution Press.

Moholy–Nagy, Hattula
1979   Spatial distribution of flint and obsidian artifacts at Tikal, Guatemala. In In *Maya lithic studies: Papers from the 1976 Belize field symposium*, edited by T. Hester and N. Hammond, 91–108. San Antonio: Center for Archaeological Research, University of Texas.
1991   The flaked chert industry of Tikal, Guatemala. In *Maya stone tools, selected papers from the second Maya lithic conference*, edited by T. Hester and H. Shafer, 189–202. Madison, Wisconsin: Prehistory Press.

1997   Middens, construction fill, and offerings: Evidence for the organization of Classic period craft production at Tikal, Guatemala. *Journal of Field Archaeology* 24:293–313.

Motolinía, fray Toribio de Benavente
1950   *Motolinía's History of the Indians of New Spain.* Translated by E. Andros Foster, Berkeley: The Cortés Society.

Mountjoy, Joseph
1978   Prehispanic cultural contact on the south-central coast of Nayarit, Mexico. In *Mesoamerican Communication Routes and Cultural Contacts*, edited by Lee and C. Navarette, 127-139. Papers of the New World Archaeological Foundation 40.
1998   Personal communication, Chicago, Illinois.

Neivens, Mary, and David Libbey
1976   An obsidian workshop at El Pozito, northern Belize. In *Maya lithic studies: Papers from the 1976 Belize field symposium*, edited by T. Hester and N. Hammond, 137–149. , San Antonio: Center for Archaeological Research, University of Texas.

Nelson, M.C.
1991   The study of technological organization. In *Archaeological method and theory*, edited by M. Schiffer, 3:57–100. Tucson: University of Arizona Press.

Ohnersorgen, Michael, and Mark Varien
1996   Formal architecture and settlement organization in ancient west Mexico. *Ancient Mesoamerica* 7:103–120.

Olson, Kirsten A.
1994   *Inclusive and exclusive mechanisms of power: Obsidian blade production and distribution among the ancient Maya of the Belize River area.* Master's thesis, Department of Anthropology, University of California, Los Angeles.

Otis Charlton, Cynthia
1993   Obsidian as jewelry: Lapidary production in Aztec Otumba, Mexico. *Ancient Mesoamerica* 4: 231–243.

Otis Charlton, Cynthia, Thomas Charlton, and Deborah Nichols
1993   Aztec household–based craft production: Archaeological evidence from the city–state of Otumba, Mexico. In *Prehispanic domestic units in western Mesoamerica*, edited by R. Santley and K. Hirth, 147–171. Boca Raton: CRC Press.

Owen, Linda R.
1988   *Blade and microblade technology: Selected assemblages from the North American Arctic and the Upper Paleolithic of southwest Germany.* BAR International Series No. 441, Oxford: British Archaeological Reports

Parry, William J.
1990   Analysis of chipped stone artifacts from Otumba (TA–80) and neighboring rural sites in the eastern Teotihuacan Valley of Mexico. In *Early state formation processes: The Aztec city–state of Otumba, Mexico, part 1*, edited by T. Charlton and D. Nichols, 73–88. Research Report 3. Mesoamerican Research Colloquium, Department of Anthropology, University of Iowa, Iowa City.
1994   Prismatic blade technologies in North America. In *The organization of North American prehistoric chipped stone tool technologies*, edited by P. Carr, 87–98. Ann Arbor: International Monographs in Prehistory.
1998   Spatial structure of obsidian working in the Aztec city–state of Otumba, Mexico. Paper presented at the 63rd Annual Meeting of the Society for American Archaeology, Seattle.
2001   Production and exchange of obsidian tools in late Aztec city–states. Ancient Mesoamerica 12:101-111.

Parry, William J., and R.L. Kelly
1987   Expedient core technology and sedentism. In *The organization of core technology*, edited by J. Johnson and C. Morrow, 285–304. Boulder: Westview Press.

Pastrana Cruz, Alejandro
1987a   El proceso de trabajo de la obsidiana de las minas de Pico de Orizaba. *Boletín de Antropología Americana* 13:132–145.
1987b   Análisis microscópico de la obsidiana. *Revista Mexicana de Estudios Antropológicos* 23:5–26.
1991   Itzepec, Itzteyoca, e Itztla: Distribución mexicana de obsidiana. *Arqueología* 6:85–100.
1993   La obsidiana, los Mexicas y el imperio. *Arqueología Mexicana* 1:58–61.
1994   Yacimientos de obsidiana y técnicas de extracción. In *Cristales y obsidiana Prehispánicos,* edited by M. Carmen Serra and F. Solís Olguín, 18–39. Mexico City: Siglo Veintiuno.
1998   *La explotación azteca de la obsidiana en la Sierra de las Navajas.* Colección Científica, No. 383. , Mexico: Instituto Nacional de Anthropolgía e Historia.
2000   Personal communication, email.

Pelegrin, Jacques
1997   Débitage au Chalcolithique de grandes lames de silex par pression au levier. In *Annuel des sciences et techniques, La science au présent,* Paris: Encyclopedia Universalis.

Pendergast, David
1990   *Excavations at Altun Ha, Belize, 1994–1970.* Vol 3. Toronto: Royal Ontario Museum.

Pires–Ferreira, Jane W.
1971   Personal communication (letter).
1975   *Formative Mesoamerican exchange networks with special reference to the Valley of Oaxaca.* Memoirs of the Museum of Anthropology No. 7, University of Michigan, Ann Arbor.

Pollard, Helen
2000   Tarascan external relationships. In *Greater Mesoamerica: The archaeology of west and northwest Mexico*, edited by

M. Foster and G. Gorenstein, 71-80. Salt Lake City:
University of Utah Press.

Pollard, Helen, Christine Stephenson, and Thomas A. Vogel
1990   The political and economic implications of obsidian
        trade within the Tarascan state. Paper prepared for the
        annual meeting of the American Anthropological
        Association, New Orleans, Louisiana.

Pollard, Helen, and Thomas Vogel
1991   Late Postclassic imperial expansion and economic
        exchange within the Tarascan domain. Paper presented
        to the International Congress of Americanists, 1991.

Pool, Christopher
1990   *Ceramic production, resource procurement, and exchange
        in southern Veracruz: A view from Matacapan.* Ph.D.
        Dissertation, Department of Anthropology, Tulane
        University, New Orleans.
1997   The spatial structure of Formative houselots at
        Bezuapan. In *Olmec to Aztec: settlement patterns in the
        ancient Gulf lowlands*, edited by B. Stark and P. Arnold,
        40–67. Tucson: University of Arizona Press.

Prem, Hanns
1974   *Matrícula de Huexotzinco.* Graz: Akademische Druck–u,
        Verlagsanstalt.

Prentiss, William
1998   The reliability and validity of a lithic debitage typology:
        Implications for archaeological interpretation. *American
        Antiquity* 63:635–650.

Raisz, Erwin
1959   Landforms of Mexico. Report prepared for the
        geography branch of the Office of Naval Research.
        Cambridge, Massachusetts.

Ramos, Jorge and Lorena López
1998   Personal communication, Guadalajara, Mexico.

Rawson, Harold
1980   *Properties and applications of glass.* Glass Science and
        Technology, Vol. 3. Oxford: Elsevier Scientific
        Publishing.

Renfrew, Colin
1975   Trade as action at a distance. In *Ancient civilizations and
        trade*, edited by J. Sabloff and C.C. Lamberg–Karlovsky,
        3–59. Albuquerque: University of New Mexico Press.

Rice, Prudence
1987   Economic change in the lowland Maya Late Classic
        period. In *Specialization, exchange, and complex societies*,
        edited by E. Brumfiel and T. Earle, 76–85. Cambridge:
        Cambridge University Press.

Ritzenthaler, Robert
1971   *Wisconsin indian projectile point types.* Popular Science
        Series 11, Milwaukee Public Museum, Milwaukee.

Ruiz Aguilar, María Elena
1981   *Análisis tipológico y cronológico de la lítica tallada del
        Clásico Teotihuacano.* Unpublished Licenciatura. Escuela
        Nacional de Antropología e Historia, Mexico City.

Sackett, James
1990   Style and ethnicity in archaeology: The case for
        isochrestism. In *The uses of style in archaeology*, edited
        by M. Conkey and C. Hastorf, 32–43. Cambridge:
        Cambridge University Press.

Sahagún, fray Bernardino de
1959   *Florentine Codex: General history of the things of New
        Spain, book 9: The merchants.* Translated by A. Anderson
        and C. Dibble. Monographs No. 14, Part 10. Santa Fe:
        School of American Research.
1961   *Florentine Codex: General history of the things of New
        Spain, book 10: The people.* Translated by A. Anderson
        and C. Dibble. Monographs No. 14, Part 11. Santa Fe:
        School of American Research.
1963   *Florentine Codex: General history of the things of New
        Spain, book 11: Earthly things.* Translated by A.
        Anderson and C. Dibble. Monographs No. 14, Part 12.
        Santa Fe: School of American Research.
1977   *Historia general de las Cosas de Nueva España.* Edited by
        A. Maria Garibay K. Mexico City: Editorial Porrua.

Sanders, William
1977   Ethnographic analogy and the Teotihuacan horizon
        style. In *Teotihuacan and Kaminaljuyu*, edited by W.
        Sanders and J. Michels, 397–410. University Park,
        Pennsylvania: Pennsylvania State University Press.

Sanders, William, Jeffrey Parsons, and Robert Santley
1979   *The Basin of Mexico: Ecological processes in the evolution
        of a civilization.* New York: Academic Press.

Sanders, William, and Robert Santley
1983   A tale of three cities: Energetics and urbanization in
        pre–hispanic central Mexico. In *Prehistoric settlement
        patterns*, edited by E. Vogt and R. Leventhal, 243–291.
        Albuquerque and Cambridge: University of New Mexico
        Press and the Peabody Museum of Archaeology and
        Ethnology.

Sanders, William, and David Webster
1988   The Mesoamerican urban tradition. *American
        Anthropologist* 90:521–546.

Santley, Robert
1983   Obsidian trade and Teotihuacan influence in
        Mesoamerica, In *Highland–lowland interaction in
        Mesoamerica*, edited by A. Miller, 69–124. Washington,
        D.C.: Dumbarton Oaks Research Library and Collection.
1984   Obsidian exchange, economic stratification, and the
        evolution of complex society in the Basin of Mexico, In
        Trade and exchange in early Mesoamerica, edited by K.
        Hirth, 43–86. Albuquerque: University of New Mexico.
1989   Obsidian working, long–distance exchange, and the
        Teotihuacan presence on the South Gulf Coast. In

Mesoamerica after the decline of Teotihuacan A.D. 700–900, edited by R. Diehl and J. Berlo, 131–151. Washington, D.C.: Dumbarton Oaks Research Library and Collection.

1998   Chipped stone from the 1998 Hueyapan archaeological survey. Manuscript on file, Department of Anthropology, University of New Mexico.

Santley, Robert, and Rani Alexander
1992   The political economy of core–periphery systems. In *Resources, power, and interregional interaction*, edited by E. Schortman and P. Urban, 23–59. Plenum, New York.

Santley, Robert, and Philip Arnold
1996   Prehispanic settlement patterns in the Tuxtla mountains, southern Veracruz, Mexico. *Journal of Field Archaeology* 23: 225–249.

Santley, Robert, Philip Arnold, and Thomas Barrett
1997   Formative period settlement patterns in the Tuxtla mountains. In *Olmec to Aztec: Settlement patterns in the ancient Gulf lowlands*, edited by B. Stark and P. Arnold, 174–205. Tucson: University of Arizona Press.

Santley, Robert, Philip Arnold, and Christopher Pool
1989   The ceramics production system at Matacapan, Veracruz, Mexico. *Journal of Field Archaeology* 16:107–132.

Santley, Robert, Thomas Barrett, Michael Glascock, and Hector Neff
ND   Prehispanic obsidian procurement in the Tuxtla mountains, southern Veracruz, Mexico. Manuscript on file, Department of Anthropology, University of New Mexico

Santley, Robert, Janet Kerley, and Thomas Barrett
1995   Teotihuacan period lithic assemblages from the Teotihuacan Valley, Mexico. In *The Teotihuacan Valley project final report – volume 3, The Teotihuacan period occupation of the valley, part 2. Artifact analyses*, edited by W. Sanders, 466–497. Occasional Papers in Anthropology No. 20. University Park: Matson Museum of Anthropology, The Pennsylvania State University.

Santley, Robert, Janet Kerley, and Ronald Kneebone
1986   Obsidian working, long–distance exchange, and the politico–economic organization of early states in Central Mexico, In *Research in economic Anthropology, supplement 2. Economic aspects of prehispanic highland Mexico*, edited by B. Isaac, 101–132. Greenwich, Connecticut: JAI Press.

Santley, Robert, Ronald Kneebone, and Janet Kerley
1985   Rates of obsidian utilization in Central Mexico and on the south Gulf Coast. *Lithic Technology* 14:107–119.

Santley, Robert, Ponciano Ortiz, Thomas W. Killion, Philip J. Arnold, and Janet M. Kerley
1984   *Final field report of the Matacapan archaeological project:*

The 1982 season. Latin American Institute Research Paper Series, No. 15. Albuquerque: University of New Mexico.

Santley, Robert, Ponciano Ortiz, and Christopher Pool
1987   Recent archaeological research at Matacapan, Veracruz: A summary of the results of the 1982 to 1986 field seasons. *Mexicon* 9:41–48.

Santley, Robert, S. A. Nelson, B. K. Reinhardt, Christopher Pool, and Philip Arnold
ND   When day turned to night: Volcanism and the archaeological record from the Tuxtla mountains, southern Veracruz, Mexico. In *Human responses to disaster in prehistory*, edited by G. Bawden and R. Reycraft. Albuquerque: University of New Mexico Press.

Santley, Robert, and Christopher Pool
1993   Prehispanic exchange relationships between Central Mexico, the Valley of Oaxaca, and the Gulf Coast of Mexico. In *The American Southwest and Mesoamerica: Systems of prehistoric exchange*, edited by J. Ericson and T. Baugh, 179–211. New York: Plenum.

Schiffer, Michael
1972   Archaeological context and systemic context. *American Antiquity* 37:156–165.

Schmidt, Peter, Mercedes de la Garza, and Enrique Nalda
1998   *Maya*. New York: Rizzoli.

Shafer, Harry J.
1969   *Archaeological investigations in the Robert Lee Reservoir Basin*. Texas Archaeological Salvage Project Papers, Austin: University of Texas.
1982a   Maya lithic craft specialization in northern Belize. In *Archaeology at Colha, Belize: the 1981 interim report*, edited by T. Hester, H. Shafer, and J. Eaton, 31–38. San Antonio and Venezia: Center for Archaeological Research and the Centro Studi e Ricerche Ligabue.
1982b   A preliminary report on the lithic technology at Kichpanha, northern Belize. In *Archaeology at Colha, Belize: the 1981 interim report*, edited by T. Hester, H. Shafer, and J. Eaton, 167–181. San Antonio and Venezia: Center for Archaeological Research and the Centro Studi e Ricerche Ligabue.

Shafer, Harry, and Thomas Hester
1991   Lithic craft specialization and product distribution at the Maya site of Colha, Belize. *World Archaeology* 23:74–97.

Shaw, Leslie C., and Eleanor M. King
1997   Research in high places: The hilltop center of Ma'ax Na, Belize. Paper presented at the 62nd Annual Meeting of the Society for American Archaeology, Nashville.

Shaw, Leslie C., Eleanor M. King, and Bruce K. Moses
1999   Constructed landscape as ideology: Archaeology and

mapping at Ma'ax Na in the Three Rivers region of Belize. Paper presented at the 64th Annual Meeting of the Society for American Archaeology, Chicago.

Sheets, Payson

1972   A model of Mesoamerican obsidian technology based on Preclassic workshop debris in El Salvador. In *Ceramica de Cultura Maya* 8:17–33.

1975   Behavioral analysis and the structure of a prehistoric industry. *Current Anthropology* 16:369–391.

1978a   Artifacts. In *The prehistory of Chalchuapa, El Salvador*, edited by R. Sharer, 2:2–107. University of Pennsylvania Press, Philadelphia.

1978b   From craftsman to cog: Quantitative views of Mesomerican lithic technology. In Papers on the economy and architecture of the ancient Maya, edited by R. Sidrys, 40-71. Monograph VIII, Institute of Archaeology. Los Angeles: University of California.

1983a   Chipped stone from the Zapotitlan Valley. In *Archaeology and volcanism in Central America*, edited by P. Sheets, 195–223. University of Texas Press, Austin.

1983b   Paper No. 10: Guatemalan obsidian: A preliminary study of sources and Quirigua artifacts. In *Quirigua reports, vol. 2*, edited by E. Shortman and P. Urban, 87–101. Philadelphia: The University Museum, University of Pennsylvania.

Sheets, Payson, and Guy Muto

1972   Pressure blades and total cutting edge: An experiment in lithic technology. *Science* 175:632–634.

Shott, Michael

1989   Bipolar industries: Ethnographic evidence and archaeological implication. *North American Archaeologist* 10:1–24.

Sinopoli, Carla

1988   The organization of craft production at Vijayanagara, South India. *American Anthropologist* 90:580–597.

Smith, A. Ledyard

1972   *Excavations at Altar de Sacrificios: Architecture, settlement, burials and caches*. Papers of the Peabody Museum of Archaeology and Ethnology, Vol. 62, No. 2. Cambridge: Harvard University.

Smith, Michael, and Mary Hodge

1994   An introduction to Late Postclassic economies and polities. In *Economies and polities in the Aztec realm*, edited by M. Hodge and M. Smith, 1–42. Albany: Institute for Mesoamerican Studies, State University of New York.

Smith, Virginia

2000a   The art and iconography of the Xochicalco stelae. In *The Xochicalco mapping project. Archaeological research at Xochicalco Vol 2*, edited by K. Hirth, 83–101. University of Utah Press, Salt Lake City.

2000b   The iconography of power at Xochicalco: The pyramid of the plumed serpents, In *The Xochicalco mapping project. Archaeological research at Xochicalco Vol 2*, edited by K. Hirth, 57–82. Salt Lake City: University of Utah Press.

Solis, Felipe

1993   Conversation, Instituto Nacional de Antropología e Historia, Mexico City.

Sollberger, J.B., and L.W. Patterson

1976   Prismatic blade replication. *American Antiquity* 41:517–531.

Soto de Arechavaleta, Maria de los Dolores

1982   *Análisis de la tecnología de producción del taller de obsidiana de Guachimontón, Teuchitlán, Jalisco*. Unpublished Licenciatura, Mexico City: Universidad Nacional Autonóma de México.

1990   Areas de actividad en un taller de manufactura de implementos de piedra tallada. In *Nuevos enfoques en el estudio de la lítica*, edited by M. de los Dolores Soto de Arechavaleta, 215–242. Universidad Nacional Autonóma de México, Mexico City.

Spence, Michael W.

1967   The obsidian industry at Teotihuacan. *American Antiquity* 32:507–514.

1971   *Some lithic assemblages of western Zacatecas and Durango*. Carbondale: Southern Illinois University Museum Mesoamerican Studies 8.

1974   Comments. In *Obsidian dates I: A compendium of the obsidian determinations made at the UCLA obsidian hydration laboratory*, edited by C. Meighan, F. Findlow and S. de Atley, 181–182. Los Angeles: Institute of Archaeology, University of California Monograph 3.

1978   Comments on Zacatecas, Durango and Jalisco obsidian hydration dates. In *Obsidian dates II: A compendium of the obsidian determinations made at the UCLA obsidian hydration laboratory*, edited by C. Meighan and P.I. Vanderhoeven, 165–169. Los Angeles: Institute of Archaeology, University of California Monograph 6.

1981   Obsidian production and the state in Teotihuacan. *American Antiquity* 46:769–788.

1984   Craft production and polity in early Teotihuacan. In *Trade and exchange in early Mesoamerica*, edited by K. Hirth, 87–114. Albuquerque: University of New Mexico Press.

1985   Specialized production in rural Aztec society: Obsidian workshops of the Teotihuacan Valley. In *Contributions to the archaeology and ethnohistory of greater Mesoamerica*, edited by W. Folan, 76–125. Carbondale: Southern Illinois University Press.

1986   The San Martin complex: An obsidian workshop area in Teotihuacan, Mexico. Unpublished manuscript.

1987   The scale and structure of obsidian production in Teotihuacan, In *Teotihuacan. Nuevos datos, nuevas sintesis, nuevos problemas*, edited by E. McClung de Tapia and E. Rattray, 429–450. Mexico City: Universidad Nacional Autonóma de México.

1996   Commodity or gift: Teotihuacan obsidian in the Maya region. *Latin American Antiquity* 7:21–39.

Spence, Michael W., and Jerome Kimberlin
1979   Obsidian procurement in Teotihuacan, Mexico. Paper Presented at the 44th Annual Meeting, Society for American Archaeology, Vancouver.

Spence, Michael, Jerome Kimberlin, and Garmon Harbottle
1984   State–controlled procurement at the obsidian workshops of Teotihuacan, Mexico. In *Prehistoric quarries and lithic production*, edited by J. Ericson and B. Purdy, 97–105. Cambridge: Cambridge University Press.

Spence, Michael, and Jeffrey Parsons
1972   Prehispanic obsidian exploitation in Central Mexico: A preliminary synthesis, In *Miscellaneous studies in Mexican prehistory*, edited by M. Spence, J. Parsons, and M. Parsons, 1–44. Ann Arbor: Museum of Anthropology Anthropological Papers, No. 45.

Spence, Michael W., Phil C. Weigand and Maria de los Dolores Soto de Arechavaleta
1980   Obsidian exchange in west Mexico. In *Rutas de intercambio en Mesoamérica y el norte de México, XVI mesa redonda* 1:357–361. Mexico City: Sociedad Mexicana de Antropología e Historia.

Stanworth, J. E.
1950   *Physical properties of glass.* Oxford: Clarendon Press.

Stark, Barbara, Lynette Heller, Michael Glascock, and Hector Neff
1992   Obsidian artifact source analysis for the Mixtequilla region, south–central Veracruz, Mexico. *Latin American Antiquity* 3: 221–239.

Stiver, Laura R.
1994   Obsidian assemblages of the Petexbatun region, Guatemala: Interim report on analysis from 1991–1993. Manuscript on file, Department of Anthropology, Vanderbilt University, Nashville.

Storey, Glenn
1985   *The obsidian assemblage of Tlajinga 33, Teotihuacan, Mexico.* Unpublished Master's paper, Department of Anthropology, Pennsylvania State University, University Park, Pennsylvania.

Stross, Fred and Frank Asaro
1976   Personal communication (letter).
Stross, Fred, Thomas Hester, Robert Heizer, and Robert Jack
1976   Chemical and archaeological studies of Mesoamerican obsidians. In *Advances in obsidian glass studies: Archaeological and geochemical perspectives*, edited by R. Taylor, 240–258. Park Ridge: Noyes Press.

Suhm, Dee Ann and Edward Jelks
1962   *Handbook of Texas archaeology: Type descriptions.* The Texas Archaeological Society, Special Publication Number One and the Texas Memorial Museum, Bulletin Number Four, Austin, Texas.

Sullivan, Lauren A.
1997   *Classic Maya social organization: A perspective from Las Abejas.* Ph.D. dissertation, Department of Anthropology, Austin: University of Texas.

Sugiyama, Saburo
1991   El entierro central de la Pirámide de la Serpiente Emplumada. *Arqueología* 6:33–40.

Taube, Karl
1990   Obsidian polyhedral cores and prismatic blades in the writing and art of ancient Mexico. *Ancient Mesoamerica* 2:61–70.

Thomas, David Hurst
1981   How to classify the projectile points from Monitor Valley, Nevada. *Journal of California and Great Basin Anthropology* 3:7–43.

Titmus, Gene
1996   Conversation, Washington State University, Pullman, Washington.

Titmus, Gene, and Peter Kelterborn
2000   Personal communication, May, Penn State Conference on Mesoamerican Obsidian Blades, University Park, Pennsylvania

Tixier, Jacques
1976   L'industrie lithique capsienne de l'Aïn Dokkara, région de Tébessa, Algérie. *Libyca* 24:21–53.

Tolstoy, Paul, Suzanne Fish, Martin Boksenbaum, and Kathryn Blair Vaughn
1977   Early sedentary communities of the Basin of Mexico. *Journal of Field Archaeology* 4:91–106.

Torrence, Robin
1986   *Production and exchange of stone tools.* Cambridge: Cambridge University Press.

Tosi, Maurizio
1984   The notion of craft specialization and its representations in the archaeological record. In *Marxist perspectives in archaeology*, edited by M. Spriggs, 22–52. Cambridge: Cambridge University Press.

Trachman, Rissa M.
1998   *Trade/exchange, technology and ritual: An analysis of obsidian artifacts from an early Classic tomb at the site of Dos Hombres, Belize.* Undergraduate Honor's thesis, Department of Anthropology, University of Texas, Austin.
1999a   An additional technological perspective on obsidian polyhedral core platform rejuvenation. *Lithic Technology* 24:199-125.
1999b   Trade/exchange, technology and ritual: An analysis of obsidian artifacts from an early Classic tomb at the site of Dos Hombres, Belize. Paper presented at the 64th

Annual Meeting of the Society for American Archaeology, Chicago.

Trombold, Charles, J. Luhr, T. Hasenaka, and Michael Glascock
1993   Chemical characteristics of obsidian from archaeological sites in western Mexico and the Tequila source area: Implication for regional and pan–regional interaction within the northern Mesoamerican periphery. *Ancient Mesoamerica* 4:255–270.

Valdez, Fred
1986   The Santa Leticia obsidian assemblage: Form, technology, and use wear. In *The archaeology of Santa Leticia and the rise of Maya civilization*, edited by A. Demarest, 210–216. Middle American Research Institute, Publication No. 52. New Orleans: Tulane University.
1994   Chipped stone (obsidian). In *Ceramics and artifacts from excavations in the Copan residential zone*, edited by G. Willey, R. Leventhal, A. Demarest, and W. Fash, 273–290. Papers of the Peabody Museum of Archaeology and Ethnology, Vol. 40. Cambridge: Harvard University.
1998   Conversation, The R.E.W. Adams Archaeological Research Facility, Northwestern Belize.

Valdez, Fred, and Richard E.W. Adams
1995   The programme for Belize archaeological project: An overview of research goals. Manuscript on file, Texas Archaeological Research Laboratory, Austin.

Weigand, Phil C.
1974   The Ahualulco site and the shaft–tomb complex of the Etzatlan area. In *The archaeology of west Mexico*, edited by B. Bell, 120–131. Ajijic: Sociedad de Estudios Avanzados del Occidente de México.
1976   Circular ceremonial structure complexes in the highlands of western Mexico. In *Archaeological frontiers: Papers on New World high cultures in honor of J. Charles Kelley*, edited by R. Pickering, 183–227. Carbondale: Southern Illinois University Museum Studies No. 4.
1977   Rio Grande glaze sherds in western Mexico. *Pottery Southwest* 4:3–6.
1979   Largo Glaze polychromes in western Mexico. *Pottery Southwest* 6:2–3.
1985   Evidence for complex societies during the western Mesoamerican Classic period. In *The archaeology of west and northwest Mesoamerica*, edited by M. Foster and P. Weigand, 47–91. Boulder: Westview Press.
1989   Architecture and settlement patterns within the western Mesoamerican Formative tradition. In *El Preclásico o Formativo: Avances y perspectivas*, edited by M. Carmona Macías, 39–64. Mexico City: Instituto Nacional de Anthropología e Historia.
1990a   The Teuchitlan tradition of western Mesoamerica. In *La epoca Clásica: Nuevos hallazgos, nuevas ideas*, edited by A. Cardós, 25–54. Mexico City: Instituto Nacional de Anthropología e Historia.
1990b   Discontinuity: The collapse of the Teuchitlan tradition and the Early Postclassic cultures of western Mesoamerica. In *Mesoamérica y el norte de México, siglo IX–XII*, edited by F. Sodi Miranda, 215–222. Mexico

City: Instituto Nacional de Antropología e Historia.
1992   Central Mexico's influences in Jalisco and Nayarit during the Classic period. In *Resources, power and interregional interaction*, edited by E. Schortman and P. Urban, 221–232. New York: Plenum Press.
1993a   *Evolución de una civilización prehispánica*. El Colegio de Michoacán, Zamora.
1993b   The political organization of the trans–Tarascan zone of western Mesoamerica on the eve of Spanish conquest. In *Culture and contact: Charles C. Di Peso's Gran Chichimeca*, edited by A. Woosley and J. Ravesloot, 191–217. Albuquerque: University of New Mexico Press.
1996   The architecture of the Teuchitlan tradition of the occidente of Mesoamerica. *Ancient Mesoamerica* 7:91–101.
2000   The evolution and decline of a core of civilization: The Teuchitlan tradition and the archaeology of Jalisco. In *Greater Mesoamerica: The archaeology of west and northwest Mexico*, edited by M. Foster and S. Gorenstein, 43–58. Salt Lake City: University of Utah Press.

Weigand, Phil C. and Arcelia García de Weigand
1994   Minería prehispánica en Jalisco. *Estudios Jaliscienses* 17:5–21.

Weigand, Phil C., Arcelia García de Weigand, and Andrew Darling
1999   El sitio arqueológico 'Cerro de Tepecuarzo' (Jalpa, Zacatecas), y sus relaciones con la tradición Teuchitlán (Jalisco). In *Los altos de Jalisco a fin de siglo*, edited by C. González, 241–274. Guadalajara: Universidad de Guadalajara.

Weigand, Phil C., and Michael W. Spence
1982   The obsidian mining complex at La Joya, Jalisco. *Anthropology* 6:175–188.

Whittaker, John
1994   *Flintknapping, making and understanding stone tools*. Austin: University of Texas Press.

Widmer, Randolph
ND   Late Classic Maya craft workshops at patio H9N–8, Copan. Manuscript, Department of Anthropology, University of Houston.

Wilke, Philip, Jeffrey Flenniken, and Terry Ozbun
1991   Clovis technology at the Anzick site, Montana. In *Case studies in lithic technology of western North America*, edited by J. Flenniken, T. Ozbun, and J. Markos, *Journal of California and Great Basin Anthropology* 13:242–272.

Zeitlin, Robert, and Ray Heimbuch
1978   Trace element analysis and the archaeological study of obsidian procurement in precolumbian Mesoamerica. In *Lithics and subsistence: The analysis of stone tool use in prehistoric economies*, edited by D. Davis, 117–159. Nashville: Vanderbilt University Publications in Anthropology, No. 20.

Contributors

Bradford Andrews
Pennsylvania State University

Thomas P. Barrett
University of New Mexico

Maria de los Dolores Soto de Arechavaleta
Universidad Nacional Autónoma de México

J. Jeffrey Flenniken
Lithic Analysts Inc.

Dan M. Healan
Tulane University

Kenneth Hirth
Pennsylvania State University

William J. Parry
Hunter College, City University of New York

Alejandro Pastrana
DICPA-INAH, Mexico City

Robert S. Santley
University of New Mexico

Michael W. Spence
University of Western Ontario

Rissa M. Trachman
University of Texas

Phil C. Weigand
El Colegio de Michoacán